SHARE the Music

MACMILLAN/McGRAW-HILL

AUTHORS

Judy Bond,
Coordinating Author

René Boyer-Alexander

Margaret Campbelle-Holman

Marilyn Copeland Davidson,
Coordinating Author

Robert de Frece

Mary Goetze,
Coordinating Author

Doug Goodkin

Betsy M. Henderson

Michael Jothen

Carol King

Vincent P. Lawrence,
Coordinating Author

Nancy L.T. Miller

Ivy Rawlins

Susan Snyder,
Coordinating Author

McGraw Hill Macmillan McGraw-Hill

New York   Farmington

HAL•LEONARD®

Acknowledgments

Grateful acknowledgment is given to the following authors, composers, and publishers. Every effort has been made to trace the ownership of all copyrighted material and to secure the necessary permissions to reprint these selections. In the case of some selections for which acknowledgment is not given, extensive research has failed to locate the copyright holders.

Shalom Altman for *Vine and Fig Tree*. © 1948 by Shalom Altman. English version by Leah Jaffa and Fran Minkoff. Used by permission of Jerry Altman.

Boosey & Hawkes, Inc for *A New Year Carol*. Music by Benjamin Britten, Words Anonymous. © 1971 by Boosey & Hawkes Ltd. Reprinted by permission of Boosey & Hawkes, Inc. For *Autumn Canon* by L. Bardos. © Copyright 1933 by Magyar Korus, Budapest; Copyright Renewed. Copyright & Renewal assigned 1950 to Editio Musica Budapest. Reprinted by permission of Boosey & Hawkes, Inc. English translation © Sean Deibler. For *Fanfare for the Common Man* by Aaron Copland. © Copyright 1947 by Aaron Copland; Copyright Renewed. Used by permission of The Aaron Copland Fund for Music, Inc., Copyright Owner, and Boosey & Hawkes, Inc., Sole Licensee. For *To Music* by Betty Bertaux. © 1987, 1989 by Boosey & Hawkes, Inc. Reprinted by permission.

Curtis Brown, Ltd. for *The Swallow* (in the Teacher's Edition) by Ogden Nash from THE NEW NUTCRACKER SUITE AND OTHER INNOCENT VERSES. Copyright © 1962 by Ogden Nash. Reprinted by permission of Curtis Brown, Ltd.

Carnes D. Burson for *Go, My Son* by Arliene Nofchissey Williams and Carnes D. Burson, arrangement copyright © 1993, Carnes Burson. All rights reserved.

Warren Casey & Jim Jacobs for *We Go Together* from GREASE. Words and Music by Jim Jacobs and Warren Casey. © 1971, 1972 by Warren Casey and Jim Jacobs. All rights throughout the world controlled by Edwin H. Morris & Company, a division of MPL Communications, Inc. International copyright secured. All rights reserved. Used by permission.

Cherry Lane Music Publishing Company, Inc. for *Feliz Navidad* by José Feliciano. © Copyright 1970 J & H Publishing Company. Administered by Cherry Lane Music Publishing Company, Inc. This Arrangement © Copyright 1994 J & H Publishing Company. For *The Music Is You* by John Denver. © Copyright 1974 (renewed 1981) Cherry Lane Music Publishing Co., Inc. International Copyright Secured. All Rights Reserved.

Clara Music for *Turn the World Around (We Come from the Fire)*. Music by Robert M. Freedman. Words by Harry Belafonte. Used by permission of Clara Music Publishing Corp. Rights Administered by Next Decade Entertainment, Inc. (ASCAP).

Frances Collin Literary Agency for *The Yesterdays and the Tomorrows* by Hal Borland. From SUNDIAL OF THE SEASONS. Reprinted by permission of Frances Collin, Literary Agent. Copyright © 1952, 1964 by Hal Borland. Copyright © renewed 1992 by Donal Borland.

CPP/Belwin, Inc. for *On the Trail* by Ferde Grofé. Copyright © 1931, 1932 (Renewed 1959, 1960) c/o EMI ROBBINS CATALOG INC. World Print Rights Controlled and Administered by CPP/ Belwin, Inc., Miami, FL. All Rights Reserved. For *San Francisco*, music by Bronislaw Kaper and Walter Jurmann, lyrics by Gus Kahn. Copyright © 1936 (Renewed 1964) ROBBINS MUSIC CORPORATION. Rights Assigned to EMI CATALOGUE PARTNERSHIP. All Rights Controlled and Administered by EMI Robbins Catalog, Inc. All Rights Reserved. For *Shabat Shalom* by N. Frankel. Copyright © 1956 by Mills Music, Inc. International Copyright Secured. All Rights Reserved. For *Silver Bells* by R. Evans & J. Livingston. © 1950 by Paramount Music Corporation. Copyright Renewed 1977 by Paramount Music Corporation, 1 Gulf + Western Plaza, New York, NY 10023. International Copyright Secured. Made in USA. All Rights Reserved. For *Theme from New York, New York* by Fred Ebb and John Kander. Copyright © 1977 United Artists Corporation. All Rights Controlled by Unart Music Corporation. All Rights of Unart Music Corporation Assigned to EMI Catalogue Partnership. All Rights Administered by EMI Unart Catalog Inc. International Copyright Secured. Made in USA. All Rights Reserved. For *Tzena, Tzena*, folk song from Israel, words by Mitchell Parish, music by Issachar Miron and Julius Grossman. Copyright © 1950 by Mills Music Inc. Copyright Renewed. Used With Permission. All Rights Reserved.

Marilyn C. Davidson for *Gau Shan Ching*. English lyrics by Marilyn Davidson. Translation printed by permission. For *The Horseman*. Words by The Literary Trustees of Walter de la Mare and The Society of Authors as their representative. Music by permission of Marilyn C. Davidson © 1987.

Sean Deibler for *Autumn Canon* by L. Bardos. © Copyright 1933 by Magyar Korus, Budapest; Copyright Renewed. Copyright & Renewal assigned 1950 to Editio Musica Budapest. Reprinted by permission of Boosey & Hawkes, Inc. English translation © Sean Deibler.

Doubleday for *Celebration* by Alonzo Lopez, from WHISPERING WIND by Terry Allen. Copyright © 1972 by the Institute of American Indian Arts. Used by permission of Doubleday, a division of Bantam Doubleday Dell Publishing Group, Inc.

Duane Music, Inc. for *I Wish I Knew How It Would Feel to Be Free, Music* by Billy Taylor, Lyrics by Billy Taylor and Dick Dallas, Copyright 1964 and 1968 by Duane Music, Inc. All rights reserved.

EMI Blackwood Music Inc. for *We Shall Be Free*. Words and Music by Stephanie David and Garth Brooks. Copyright © 1992 by EMI Blackwood Music Inc./Beartooth Music (BMI)/Major Bob Music Co., Inc. (ASCAP)/No Fences Music (ASCAP). Administered by Major Bob Music Co. (ASCAP). International copyright secured. Made in U.S.A. All rights reserved.

continued on page 433

Macmillan/McGraw-Hill
A Division of The McGraw-Hill Companies

Published by Macmillan/McGraw-Hill, of McGraw-Hill Education, a division of The McGraw-Hill Companies, Inc., Two Penn Plaza, New York, New York 10121.

Macmillan/McGraw-Hill
Two Penn Plaza
New York, New York 10121

Printed in the United States of America
ISBN 0-02-295567-4 / 5
4 5 6 7 8 9 058 07 06 05 04 03

SPECIAL CONTRIBUTORS

Contributing Writer

Janet McMillion

Consultant Writers

Teri Burdette, Signing
Brian Burnett, Movement
Robert Duke, Assessment
Joan Gregoryk, Vocal Development/
  Choral
Judith Jellison, Special Learners/
  Assessment
Jacque Schrader, Movement
Kathy B. Sorensen, International Phonetic
  Alphabet
Mollie Tower, Listening

Consultants

Lisa DeLorenzo, Critical Thinking
Nancy Ferguson, Jazz/Improvisation
Judith Nayer, Poetry
Marta Sanchez, Dalcroze
Mollie Tower, Reviewer
Robyn Turner, Fine Arts

Multicultural Consultants

Judith Cook Tucker
JaFran Jones
Oscar Muñoz
Marta Sanchez
Edwin J. Schupman, Jr., of ORBIS
  Associates
Mary Shamrock
Kathy B. Sorensen

Multicultural Advisors

Shailaja Akkapeddi (Hindi), Edna Alba
(Ladino), Gregory Amobi (Ibu), Thomas
Appiah (Ga, Twi, Fanti), Deven Asay
(Russian), Vera Auman (Russian, Ukrainian),
David Azman (Hebrew), Lissa Bangeter
(Portuguese), Britt Marie Barnes (Swedish),
Dr. Mark Bell (French), Brad Ahawanrathe
Bonaparte (Mohawk), Chhanda Chakroborti
(Hindi), Ninthalangsonk Chanthasen
(Laotian), Julius Chavez (Navajo), Lin-Rong
Chen (Mandarin), Anna Cheng (Mandarin),
Rushen Chi (Mandarin), T. L. Chi (Mandarin),
Michelle Chingwa (Ottowa), Hoon Choi
(Korean), James Comarell (Greek), Lynn
DePaula (Portuguese), Ketan Dholakia
(Gujarati), Richard O. Effiong (Nigerian),
Nayereh Fallahi (Persian), Angela Fields
(Hopi, Chemehuevi), Gary Fields (Lakota,

Cree), Siri Veslemoy Fluge (Norwegian),
Katalin Forrai (Hungarian), Renee Galagos
(Swedish), Linda Goodman, Judith A. Gray,
Savyasachi Gupta (Marati), Elizabeth Haile
(Shinnecock), Mary Harouny (Persian),
Charlotte Heth (Cherokee), Tim Hunt
(Vietnamese), Marcela Janko (Czech), Raili
Jeffrey (Finnish), Rita Jensen (Danish), Teddy
Kaiahura (Swahili), Gueen Kalaw (Tagalog),
Merehau Kamai (Tahitian), Richard Keeling,
Masanori Kimura (Japanese), Chikahide
Komura (Japanese), Saul Korewa (Hebrew),
Jagadishwar Kota (Tamil), Sokun Koy
(Cambodian), Craig Kurumada (Balkan),
Cindy Trong Le (Vietnamese), Dongchoon Lee
(Korean), Young-Jing Lee (Korean), Nomi Lob
(Hebrew), Sam Loeng (Mandarin, Malay),
Georgia Magpie (Comanche), Mladen Marič
(Croatian), Kuinise Matagi (Samoan), Hiromi
Matsushita (Japanese), Jackie Maynard
(Hawaiian), David McAllester, Mike
Kanathohare McDonald (Mohawk),
Khumbulani Mdlefshe (Zulu), Martin Mkize
(Xhosa), David Montgomery (Turkish), Kazadi
Big Musungayi (Swahili), Professor Akiya
Nakamara (Japanese), Edwin Napia (Maori),
Hang Nguyen (Vietnamese), Richard Nielsen
(Danish), Wil Numkena (Hopi), Eva Ochoa
(Spanish), Drora Oren (Hebrew), Jackie
Osherow (Yiddish), Mavis Oswald (Russian),
Dr. Dil Parkinson (Arabic), Kenny Tahawisoren
Perkins (Mohawk), Alvin Petersen (Sotho),
Phay Phan (Cambodian), Charlie Phim
(Cambodian), Aroha Price (Maori), Marg Puiri
(Samoan), John Rainer (Taos Pueblo, Creek),
Lillian Rainer (Taos Pueblo, Creek, Apache),
Winton Ria (Maori), Arnold Richardson
(Haliwa-Saponi), Thea Roscher (German),
Dr. Wayne Sabey (Japanese), Regine Saintil
(Bamboula Creole), Luci Scherzer (German),
Ken Sekaquaptewa (Hopi), Samouen Seng
(Cambodian), Pei Shin (Mandarin), Dr. Larry
Shumway (Japanese), Gwen Shunatona
(Pawnee, Otoe, Potawatomi), Ernest Siva
(Cahuilla, Serrano [Maringa´]), Ben Snowball
(Inuit), Dr. Michelle Stott (German), Keiko
Tanefuji (Japanese), James Taylor
(Portuguese), Shiu-wai Tong (Mandarin),
Tom Toronto (Lao, Thai), Lynn Tran
(Vietnamese), Gulavadee Vaz (Thai), Chen
Ying Wang (Taiwanese), Masakazu Watabe
(Japanese), Freddy Wheeler (Navajo), Keith
Yackeyonny (Comanche), Liming Yang
(Mandarin), Edgar Zurita (Andean)

CONTENTS

Time for Singing!. viii

Time for Singing!

Most people enjoy singing a familiar song. Think of a song you like, and remember an occasion that makes this song special. Blend your voices with those of friends, neighbors, and family to sing a new song that expresses a desire to make the world a better place.

EXPRESS excitement and joy as you sing "We Want to Sing."

We Want to Sing

Words and Music by
Roger Emerson and the
Shasta Music Camp Staff

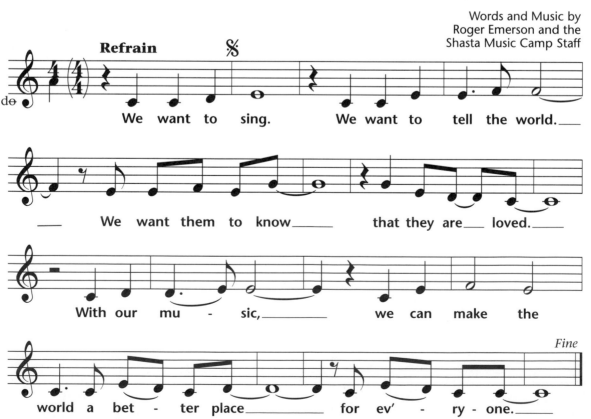

We want to sing. We want to tell the world.___

___ We want them to know___ that they are___ loved.___

With our mu - sic,___ we can make the

world a bet - ter place___ for ev' - ry - one.___

Verse

The songs that we sing___ have a spe - cial ring;___ the

peo - ple we meet___ can't be beat.___ The

days that we spend___ we hope will nev - er___ end,___ so

D.S. al Fine

join in now, my friend.___ We want to

"Laugh, Ha, Ha!" is easy and fun to sing as a round. Add body percussion and it's even more fun!

CREATE a body-percussion part for the song.

Traditional Round

Laugh, ha, ha! Here's a mer - ry jest;

But if you will laugh last, You will laugh best.

"Rock-a-My Soul" is an African American spiritual that people throughout the United States have grown to love. It's a great song to sing in the car or around a campfire.

LISTEN for words that repeat, and feel the constant rhythmic drive.

SING the melody and the two other parts. Then sing them together.

ROCK-A MY SOUL

Spiritual
Arranged by René Boyer-Alexander

Part 1

Rock - a my soul in the bo - som of A - bra- ham,

Rock - a my soul in the bo - som of A - bra - ham,

Rock - a my soul in the bo - som of A - bra - ham,

Oh, Rock - a my soul.

The rhythms of the West Indies are exciting! When you listen to the music from these islands, you may want to move, or sing, or play!

REPEAT the word *Ja-mai-ca* as you pat this rhythm.

Ja - mai - ca

PAT this rhythm or play it on a cowbell as you sing "Mary Ann."

West Indian Calypso

All day, all night, Miss Ma - ry Ann,_____

Down by the sea - shore sift - ing sand._____

1. E - ven lit - tle chil - dren join in the band_____
2. Young and old, all come now, join in the band_____
3. Ev' - ry - bod - y, come now, join in the band_____

Down by the sea - shore sift - ing sand._____

The melody of "The Water Is Wide" is smooth and flowing like a gentle river. It is one of the most beautiful melodies in all folk music. The melody has inspired people to write different sets of words for it. When you know the song well, try making up your own words.

LISTEN for the long notes in this flowing melody.

English Folk Song

1. The wa-ter is wide,_____ I can-not get o'er,
2. There is_____ a ship_____ sail-ing on the sea,
3. Oh, love____ is sweet,_____ and____ love is fair,

And nei-ther have_____ I wings to____ fly,
She's load-ed deep_____ as deep can____ be,
Fresh as the dew____ when it is____ new,

Give me a boat_____ that can car - ry two,
But not so deep_____ as the love I'm in;
But love grows old,_____ and____ it grows cold,

And both shall row,_____ my love and I._____
I care not if_____ I sink or swim._____
And fades a - way_____ like morn-ing dew._____

Hundreds of folk songs are part of your rich American musical heritage. Some of the folk songs reflect the hard work and sweat that went into making the United States the great country that it is today. "I've Been Working on the Railroad" is one of these songs.

IMAGINE the movement of a railroad worker pounding the spikes with a sledgehammer as you sing "I've Been Working on the Railroad."

Traditional American Folk Song

I've been work-ing on the rail-road, all the live-long day.

I've been work-ing on the rail-road, just to pass the time a-way.

Can't you hear the whis-tle blow-in'? Rise up so ear-ly in the morn.

Can't you hear the cap-tain shout-in', "Di-nah, blow your horn"?

6

UNIT 1

united

8

CHORUS OF THE WORLD

If you look around
You can hear a sound
Of a great big chorus's song.
It is not of sadness,
It is not of badness,
It's of love, and it's never wrong.

Every mouth sings it loud,
Everyone is very proud.
We are singing
　in the chorus of the world.
All the nations sing together,
All the people now are gathered
To sing the song
　about a nation of the world.

—Anat Blum, Israeli Student

by music

WE GO TOGETHER

Words and Music
by Jim Jacobs and Warren Casey

1. We go to-geth-er, like ra-ma la-ma la-ma ka
2. We're one of a kind____ like dip__ da dip__ da dip

ding - a da ding - a dong, Re-mem - bered for
doo wop - a doo-bee doo, our names are

ev - er as shoo-bop - sha - wad - da wad - da
signed____ boog-e -dy boog -e - dy boog-e -dy boog -e - dy

yip - pi - ty boom____ de - boom Chang chang
shoo - by doo wop____ she - bop Chang chang

chang-it - ty chang__ shoo - bop, that's the way it____ should
chang-it - ty chang__ shoo - bop, we'll al - ways be____ like

be._____ Wha oooh, yeah! one._____

Wa - wa - wa - waah._____ When we go

out at night,____ and stars are shin-ing bright____

up in the skies a-bove._____ Or at the

cresc.

high school dance__ where you can find ro-mance,___

f

may-be it might be love._____

Vocal ad lib. **26** *mp*

We're for each oth - er____ like-a

wop ba-ba lu-mop and wop bam boom.___ Just like my

broth-er____ is sha-na-na-na-na-na-na, yip-pi-ty-dip-de doom

mf

Chang chang chang-it-ty chang____ shoo-bop,

f *cresc.*

We'll al-ways be_____ to-geth-er._____

Moving Together

Have you ever been at a musical or sports event where the crowd started clapping the beat together? Did you join in? Showing the beat together is a way people can be united by music.

EXPLORE ways to show the beat with "Get Up!"

GET UP!

Words and Music by Teresa Jennings

Get up!   Get on your feet!   Ev'-ry-bod-y up! Gon-na

move to the beat! Get up!   Get on your feet!   Ev'-ry-bod-y up! Gon-na

Second time to Coda

move to the beat! Here it is!   Do you

feel it?   O, yeah! Stomp your feet!   Clap your hands!

Raise up your knees like a march-ing band!   Lean to the left,

In "Get Up!" there are two beats in each measure. This is shown by the $\frac{2}{4}$ meter signature.

PAT-CLAP with the beat as you listen again. Each pat will be on a strong, stressed beat, and each clap will be on a weak, unstressed beat. This will show the meter.

PROCESSIONALS FROM AROUND THE WORLD

All over the world, people have processions and parades for special occasions. Music for one of these occasions is called a **processional.** What processions can you name?

Music for processions and parades usually has a steady **beat** that helps people to march or walk together. Although a musical beat is steady, like a heartbeat, the speed of the beat can change. The speed of the beat, or **tempo,** can become faster or slower. *Tempo* is an Italian word meaning "time."

LISTENING

Montage of Processionals

LISTENING MAP *Follow the map as you hear processionals from around the world. Listen to the rhythms, feel the beat, and notice the changes in tempo. Also listen to the different* **rhythms,** *or combinations of longer and shorter sounds and silences.*

1 United States 2 Italy 3 Bolivia 4 New Orleans, U.S.A. 5 Northern Plains, U.S.A. 6 Philippines 7 Western Africa 8 England

5 Northern Plains, U.S.A.

8 England

7 Western Africa

3 Bolivia

1 United States

4 New Orleans, U.S.A.

6 Philippines

2 Italy

THINK IT THROUGH
What effect does music have on the way people move in a group? How is this different from moving in a group without music?

Here's a song about how people can be united by music.

FEEL the beat as you listen to the song.

DECIDE whether the tempo is slow, medium, or fast.

Words and Music by Garry Smith

Chil - dren, sing all o - ver the place.

Mu - sic brings us to - geth - er!

A hap - py song brings a smile to your face.

Refrain

Mu - sic brings us to - geth - er! Sing a song

loud and clear, for ev' - ry - one to

MELODIES THAT MOVE

Some songs seem to draw people together. "This Land Is Your Land" is one of them. It was written by Woody Guthrie, a folk singer and composer. Guthrie traveled all over the United States and wrote more than a thousand songs about the land and its people. Some of his songs helped people lift their spirits during times of hardship.

LISTEN and watch for upward and downward movement in this famous song.

Woody Guthrie

This Land Is Your Land

Words and Music
by Woody Guthrie

Refrain

This land is your land,___ this land is my land,___

From Cal - i - for - nia___ to the New York is - land,___

From the red-wood for - est___ to the Gulf Stream wa - ters;___

This land was made for you and me.

18

Verse

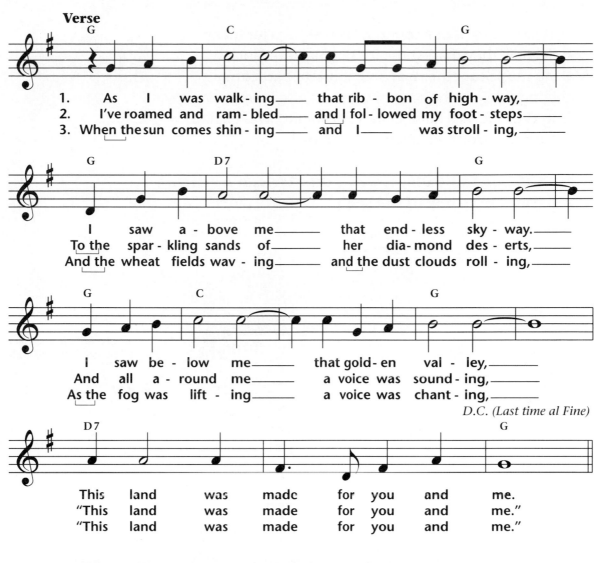

1. As I was walk-ing —— that rib-bon of high-way, ——
2. I've roamed and ram-bled —— and I fol-lowed my foot-steps ——
3. When the sun comes shin-ing —— and I —— was stroll-ing, ——

I saw a-bove me—— that end-less sky-way. ——
To the spar-kling sands of —— her dia-mond des-erts, ——
And the wheat fields wav-ing—— and the dust clouds roll-ing, ——

I saw be-low me—— that gold-en val-ley, ——
And all a-round me—— a voice was sound-ing, ——
As the fog was lift-ing—— a voice was chant-ing, ——

D.C. (Last time al Fine)

This land was made for you and me.
"This land was made for you and me."
"This land was made for you and me."

The highness or lowness of a sound is its **pitch**. When you sing a **melody**, you are singing a pattern of pitches that move upward or downward, or stay the same.

You can help yourself learn to read music by noticing **melodic direction**, the way that a melody moves.

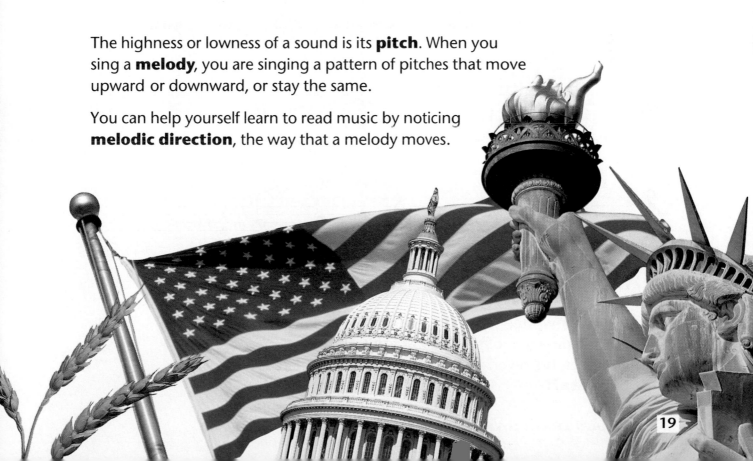

19

In the early days of our country, life was hard for many people. Still, they made time for singing and dancing. Making music together was an important part of many gatherings. Before the days of compact discs and television, a song like "We Will Raise a Ruckus Tonight" was passed along from person to person by singing.

TRACE the melodic direction of this African American jubilee as you listen to the song.

We Will Raise a Ruckus Tonight

African American Jubilee
Adapted By René Boyer-White

With Jubilation

Come a - long, you chil - dren, come a - long

While the moon is shin - ing bright to - night.

Come a - long, you chil - dren, come a - long.

We will raise a ruck - us to - night.

In the **score**, or written music, for "We Will Raise a Ruckus Tonight," the direction of the melody is tinted. To read the specific pitches, however, you must know the letter names on the five-line **staff**.

The **G clef**, or **treble clef**, shows that a note placed on the second line of the staff is G. Other lines and spaces follow the musical alphabet: A B C D E F G.

FIND G A B on the staff below.

By remembering the position of these three notes, you will be able to figure out the other lines and spaces.

SING "We Will Raise a Ruckus Tonight" with letter names. It should be easy!

Another way to read music is with pitch syllables. "We Will Raise a Ruckus Tonight" uses only the first three steps of the scale: *do re* and *mi.*

SING "We Will Raise a Ruckus Tonight" with pitch syllables.

Your Voice

A Personal Musical Instrument

When you hear a new recording by your favorite singer, why can you recognize his or her voice immediately? It's because that singer's voice is a unique musical instrument. Like all instruments, it has its own special sound, called **tone color**. Can your family and friends recognize the tone color of your voice?

LISTENING

Don't Worry, Be Happy (excerpt)
by Bobby McFerrin

Bobby McFerrin surprises audiences with the variety of vocal sounds in his performances. His style is unique and shows how a great imagination can expand our ideas about how the voice can be used.

LISTEN to the different vocal sounds in this recording by Bobby McFerrin. How do you think these sounds were created?

The distance from the highest to the lowest pitch you can sing is your vocal **range**. Your voice also has qualities that result from the way you produce the sound. The terms **heavier register** and **lighter register** describe these qualities. Singers usually find it more comfortable to sing the lowest pitches in the heavier register and the highest pitches in the lighter register. By understanding your voice, you will learn how to sing easily over your full range.

Everyone shared music in Bobby McFerrin's family. Both his parents were professional classical singers. Music surrounded Bobby and his sister from the time they were born. It's not surprising that they both became musicians. After studying music in college, Bobby worked as a keyboard player. He has become a popular concert vocalist, and his recordings are big hits all over the world.

LISTEN as Bobby McFerrin tells you about his unique vocal performance style.

Meet Bobby McFerrin

23

EXPLORING VOCAL REGISTERS

Any time you speak, shout, or sing, you use your heavier or lighter vocal register or a combination of the two.

SPEAK "Over My Head" in your lower, heavier register, then in your higher, lighter register.

SING "Over My Head" in these registers.

OVER MY HEAD

African American Spiritual

"Over My Head" is an African American spiritual. This melody is full of expression even though it uses only three pitches.

NAME the pitches at the end of each phrase.

SING "Over My Head" in your lighter register.

OVER MY HEAD

African American Spiritual

O - ver my head, I hear mu - sic in the air.

O - ver my head, I hear mu - sic in the air.

O - ver my head, I hear mu - sic in the air.

There must be a God some - where.

THINK IT THROUGH

How can you show expression as you sing "Over My Head"?

Peace for all people. . . . Is this one of your hopes for the world?
People from many times and places have shared this hope. Folk
singer Jean Ritchie has combined an ancient saying with an old
melody to create a new song about peace.

Old English Canon
Words by Jean Ritchie
Adapted from Psalm 133:1

What a good-ly thing if the chil-dren of the world

could dwell to-geth-er in_____ peace.

COMPARE the range of "Peace Round" to the pitches
below. Which part of the song would be easier to sing in
the lighter register?

NAME the pitches that are
included in both registers.

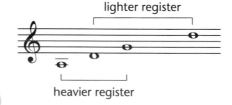

lighter register

heavier register

THINK IT THROUGH
When you sing, what differences
do you hear between your
lighter and heavier registers?

Hirshhorn Museum and Sculpture Garden, Smithsonian Institution,
Gift of Joseph H. Hirshhorn, 1966

HOLY MOUNTAIN III

American artist Horace Pippin created this painting in 1945. Pippin began to paint after he was injured in World War I. At first, he painted war scenes, but later he used subjects from the Bible and scenes of African American family life. In this painting, the artist shows his idea of a perfect world in which people and both wild and tame animals live together in peace.

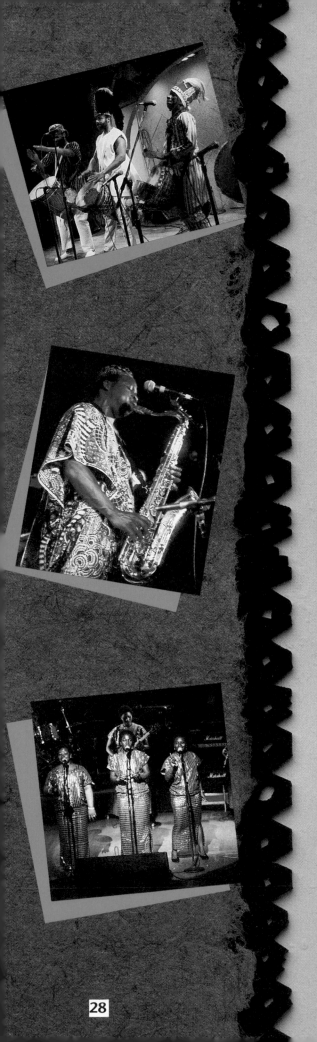

EVERYBODY LOVES A MELODY

"Ev'rybody Loves Saturday Night" was created at a time when many western African countries were under European rule. During that period, African people in some areas were forbidden to gather at night, except on Saturdays.

This song became popular with musical groups called "highlife bands" in cities throughout western Africa. Later, it became known in other parts of the world. People translated the words of the song into many different languages. Can you add a verse in another language?

Top to bottom:
Ladjii Camara and band, Senegal
O. J. Ekemode and the Nigerian
    Allstars, Nigeria
Les Amazones du Guinea, Guinea

EV'RY BODY LOVES SATURDAY NIGHT

Western African Song

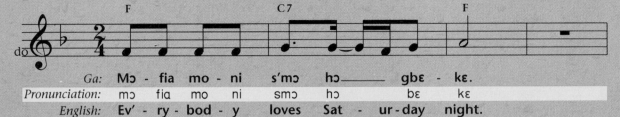

Ga: Mɔ - fia mo - ni s'mɔ hɔ——— gbɛ - kɛ.
Pronunciation: mɔ fia mo ni smɔ hɔ bɛ kɛ
English: Ev' - ry - bod - y   loves   Sat - ur - day   night.

Mɔ - fia mo - ni s'mɔ hɔ——— gbɛ - kɛ.
mɔ fia mo ni smɔ hɔ bɛ kɛ
Ev' - ry - bod - y   loves   Sat - ur - day   night.

Mɔ - fia mo - ni,   mɔ - fia mo - ni,   mɔ - fia mo - ni,   mɔ - fia mo - ni,
mɔ fia mo ni   mɔ fia mo ni   mɔ fia mo ni   mɔ fia mo ni
Ev' - ry - bod - y,   ev' - ry - bod - y,   ev' - ry - bod - y,   ev' - ry - bod - y,

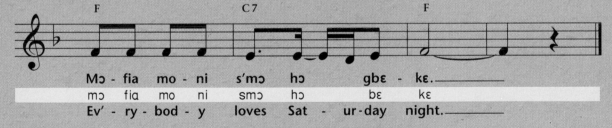

Mɔ - fia mo - ni s'mɔ hɔ gbɛ - kɛ.———
mɔ fia mo ni smɔ hɔ bɛ kɛ
Ev' - ry - bod - y   loves   Sat - ur - day   night.———

Highlife bands play western instruments such as drum sets, electric guitars, and Latin percussion, as well as African drums, rattles, and bells. Highlife started in Ghana and Sierra Leone. From there it spread to other African countries and to other parts of the world. The enjoyment of this music unites people from many cultures.

STEP-TOUCH to the beat as you sing "Ev'rybody Loves Saturday Night." When you get to the third line, stand and face your partner. Clap on each rest, and give your partner a "high five" on the third syllable of each *ev'rybody*. On the fourth line, move to a new partner with two side-close steps.

1

To do a step-touch, take a step with one foot. Then lightly touch the floor next to it with the other foot, without putting weight on it.

2

Face your partner and clap.

4 To do a side-close, take a step sideways and move the other foot next to it.

3 Give your partner a "high five."

ADD A NEW PART

When you learned "Ev'rybody Loves Saturday Night," everyone sang the melody. This is called singing in **unison.**

Two or more pitches sounding at the same time create **harmony.** At the bottom of the page is a harmony part to sing with the melody of "Ev'rybody Loves Saturday Night." This part includes the pitch F, written in the first space.

F G A B

TRACE the melodic direction of the harmony part as you listen to it.

IDENTIFY the pitch letter names.

SING the harmony part with pitch syllables. F is *do.*

Ev' - ry - bod - y,   ev' - ry - bod - y,

Ev' - ry - bod - y   loves   this   night.

Top design based on raffia mat pattern from Zaire. Bottom design based on a mud relief on wall of Nigerian house.

A line near the treble clef connects parts that are sung at the same time. These connected parts form a **system**.

SING this song from a two-part system.

Western African Song

Unison

Ga: Mɔ - fia mo - ni s'mɔ hɔ gbɛ kɛ.
Pronunciation: mɔ fia mo ni smɔ hɔ bɛ kɛ
English: Ev' - ry - bod - y loves Sat - ur - day night.

Mɔ - fia mo - ni s'mɔ hɔ gbɛ kɛ.
mɔ fia mo ni smɔ hɔ bɛ kɛ
Ev' - ry - bod - y loves Sat - ur - day night.

Melody

Mɔ - fia mo - ni, mɔ - fia mo - ni, mɔ - fia mo - ni, mɔ - fia mo - ni,
mɔ fia mo ni mɔ fia mo ni mɔ fia mo ni mɔ fia mo ni
Ev' - ry - bod - y, ev' - ry - bod - y, ev' - ry - bod - y, ev' - ry - bod - y,

Harmony

Mɔ - fia mo - ni, mɔ - fia mo - ni,
mɔ fia mo ni mɔ fia mo ni
Ev' - ry - bod - y, ev' - ry - bod - y,

Mɔ - fia mo - ni s'mɔ hɔ gbɛ - kɛ.
mɔ fia mo ni smɔ hɔ bɛ kɛ
Ev' - ry - bod - y loves Sat - ur - day night.____

Mɔ - fia mo - ni s'mɔ hɔ gbɛ - kɛ.
mɔ fia mo ni smɔ hɔ bɛ kɛ
Ev' - ry - bod - y loves____ this night.

IT'S A MYSTERY TO ME!

The harmony part of "Ev'rybody Loves Saturday Night" uses the pitches F, G, and A. Here is another melody written with only those three pitches. It is a song you have already sung.

PLAY the "Mystery Tune" below. Do you recognize the song?

MYSTERY TUNE

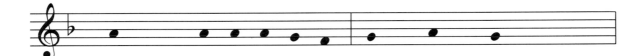

SING the melody with letter names and name the mystery tune.

Remember the clue that helped you solve this mystery: reading the notes!

The border designs are from a Benin bronze sculpture from Nigeria. The three wooden masks are from Nigeria (top left), the Congo (top right), and the Ivory Coast (bottom).

TIME FOR RHYTHM

Reading pitches helps you to sing a melody you have never heard before. However, to sing or play a melody correctly, you must also be able to read rhythmic notation. Rhythmic **notation** shows you how to perform the long and short sounds and silences that make up a piece of music.

ECHO rhythm patterns you hear as some of your classmates pat to the beat.

LISTEN and decide whether each beat contains one sound, two sounds, or no sound.

Here is rhythm notation for one sound, two sounds, and no sound in a beat.

quarter note (one sound)   eighth notes (two sounds)   quarter rest (no sound)

In music that you play and sing, the **meter,** which is a set of beats, organizes the rhythms. **Bar lines** separate the sets of beats into **measures.** The first beat of each measure is usually stressed more than the other beats.

number of beats
in measure

measure

meter
signature

quarter gets the beat   measure line   double bar

The **meter signature** tells you the number of beats in a measure and what rhythm value gets the beat. A **double bar** shows the end of the piece.

CLAP the patterns below, reading from notation.

Four times

Four times

A RHYTHM "GET-TOGETHER" IN THE PHILIPPINE ISLANDS

Percussion players all over the world enjoy combining instrumental sounds for exciting rhythmic effects. In the Mindanao Islands of the Philippines, there are musical groups called **kulintang**. The kulintang contains only **percussion** instruments, those played by striking or shaking. The kulintang is made up of gongs and drums. Pictures below and on the next page show the instruments in the kulintang.

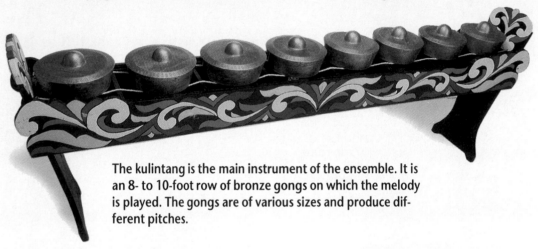

The kulintang is the main instrument of the ensemble. It is an 8- to 10-foot row of bronze gongs on which the melody is played. The gongs are of various sizes and produce different pitches.

Other large gongs, called agungs, provide the bass part. They are often played by two people. One person plays a pattern. The other person **improvises**, or makes up on the spot, another pattern to play. The improvised pattern is played during the rests of the first person's pattern.

The dabakan, a drum, is struck with two pieces of split bamboo. The dabakan plays a rhythmic accompaniment of faster notes.

Some groups use hanging gongs called gandingan. These gongs play a melodic ostinato that supports the main melody. The frame stands about five feet high.

The babandir, a small, hand-held gong, often plays a short, repeated pattern, or **ostinato.** Its sharp tone color adds rhythmic "spice" to the ensemble.

LISTENING

Adongko Dongko a Gakit

Philippine Kulintang
Wedding Processional

*Like the instruments in a rock band or orchestra, each set of instruments in the kulintang plays a special role in creating the **ensemble**, or group, sound.*

LISTEN for the following patterns, played by an agung, as you listen to the kulintang ensemble. Where have you heard these patterns before?

Four times

Four times

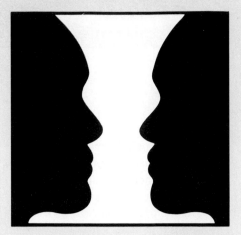

CAN YOU BELIEVE YOUR EYES?

What do you see in the drawing? Close your eyes and look again. Did you see the same thing? This drawing is an optical illusion. You might see it as a vase one time you look, and as two faces when you look again. Can you see both at the same time?

SKY AND WATER I, JUNE 1938

The woodcut *Sky and Water I, June 1938* by M.C. Escher uses positive and negative shapes. The first shape that you see is called a figure, or *positive*, shape. The surrounding area is called the ground, or *negative*, shape. You can shift your eyes between the positive and negative shapes. What do you see?

CAN YOU BELIEVE YOUR EARS?

When you listened to the kulintang music, you may have noticed a second rhythm blending in with the pattern you were clapping. The second agung, which has a slightly higher sound than the first one, played this rhythm. The second instrument fills in all the rests in the first instrument's pattern.

THINK IT THROUGH

How are the agung parts of the kulintang music like the art above?

THE POSITIVE-NEGATIVE GAME

Here is a rhythm echo game to help you learn to play music in the style of the Philippine kulintang ensemble.

READ the first line below. Say *gong* for each note in the first line. This line is the same as the rhythm patterns you have been practicing.

PRACTICE clapping each note in the second line. Form two groups. Have each group do one of the lines.

READ both lines yourself. Be your own echo! This time, you will speak the first line and clap the second line. This is the first half of the song.

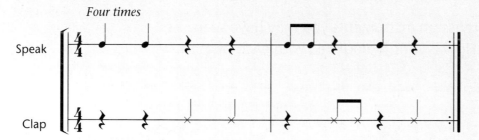

PLAY the other pattern you have practiced. Use the same echo style. This is the second half of the song.

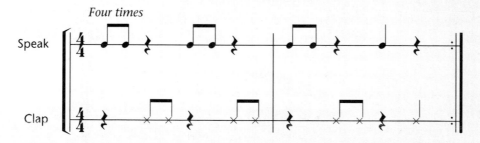

PERFORM the patterns with "Adongko Dongko a Gakit."

PERCUSSION

The instruments that you heard in the Philippine kulintang ensemble are all part of the percussion family. The sound of percussion instruments is made by two objects striking one another. The objects may be struck directly together, or one object may be scraped, shaken, rubbed, plucked, or struck with the hand or a mallet.

Here are some percussion instruments you may have seen, heard, or played. How is sound produced with each of them?

1. bongo drums

2. triangle

3. tambourine

4. claves

5. güiro

6. cymbals

7. snare drum

40

INSTRUMENTS

SOURCES FOR MUSICAL SOUNDS

Most percussion instruments began from simple sound sources. At first, people used natural materials and objects that they found around them. The first maracas were made from dried gourds filled with seeds or other small objects that rattle.

maracas

It's easy to see where the log drum came from!

log drum

Percussion instruments can be created from many everyday objects. Where might instruments such as the cowbell, the claves, and the güiro have come from?

LOOK for objects in your classroom that might be used as percussion instruments.

THINK IT THROUGH

When are sounds musical and when are they noise? Think of a noise. How can you change it to make it more musical?

MAKING PERCUSSION MUSIC TOGETHER

You have already practiced the rhythms you need to play along with the kulintang ensemble.

PLAY the drum and cowbell with "Adongko Dongko a Gakit" using the patterns below.

Drum (timpani, lower agung or similar sound)
Four times

Four times

Cowbell (babandir or similar sound)
Eight times

CHINA

MYANMAR

VIETNAM

LAOS

THAILAND

CAMBODIA

BRUNEI

MALAYSIA

INDONESIA

kulintang ensemble

42

IT'S MORE THAN RHYTHM

The kulintang ensemble plays more than rhythm. The gongs play melodies as well. You can play the melody of "Adongko Dongko a Gakit." Some of the sounds in the melody are two beats long. In $\frac{4}{4}$ meter, a sound that lasts for two beats is shown with a **half note** (♩). A **half rest** (▬) shows a silence for the same length as a half note.

FIND the half notes and half rests in the score below.

PRACTICE clapping the rhythm of the melody. Use a clap-slide for the half notes.

TAIWAN

PHILIPPINES

● Mindanao

ADONGKO DONGKO
A GAKIT

Philippine Kulintang
Wedding Processional

Resonator bells

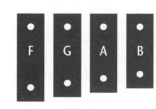

PRACTICE singing this melody with letter names, and then practice playing the melody.

COMBINE the drum, cowbell, and resonator-bell parts to form a *percussion ensemble.*

Find That Phrase

A piece of music is a bit like a story or a mosaic. All are made up of small ideas that combine to make larger ones. In a story, the small idea is the sentence. In music, a complete thought or idea is called a **phrase.** Phrases are combined to form a longer piece of music. In "Over My Head," the first phrase is this:

O - ver my head,_____ I hear mu- sic in the air._____

SING the entire song. How many phrases do you hear?

You can figure out how a piece of music is put together by noticing if the phrases are the same, almost the same, or different. Small letters can be used to label phrases.

The first phrase is called a . If any other phrase is exactly

the same as the first, it is also called a . If the next phrase is

almost the same, it is called a' (*a* prime). If the next phrase is

really different, it is called b .

44

FIND THAT FORM

The sentences in a story must be put together in an orderly form for the story to make sense. This is also true of music—phrases must be put together in an orderly way. Here are some ways phrases can be put together to make a musical form.

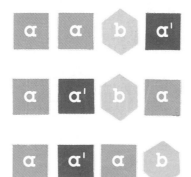

Do these forms match any songs you know?
Which one matches the form of "Over My Head"?

FIND THAT SECTION

Musical phrases can be combined into larger **sections** that have more than one musical idea. Each section is identified by a capital letter. "Side by Side" has four sections. Its form is A A B A. Many other popular songs have this form.

THINK about how the B section is different from the A sections as you learn "Side by Side."

A A B A

Words and Music by Harry Woods

A With A Swing
mf

C   F   C

Oh, we ain't got a bar-rel of mon-ey,

C   F   C

May-be we're rag-ged and fun-ny, but we'll

F   C   A7   D7 G7   C

trav-el a-long sing-in' a song, side by side.

TEXTURE IN MUSIC

If you could touch these pieces of cloth, you might say that the example on the bottom felt rough or thick, while the example on the top felt smooth or thin. These words describe the texture of the fabric.

Art also has texture. Notice the textures of the two oil paintings, *Abstract No. 2* by Lee Krasner and *Winter Road I* by Georgia O'Keeffe. Which has a thin texture? Which has a thick texture?

DESCRIBE other art you have seen with a thick or a thin texture.

The words *thick* and *thin* can also be used to describe texture in music. Musical **texture** is the sound created by different pitches, rhythms, and tone colors played or sung together. Just as there are many kinds of form in music, there are many kinds of texture.

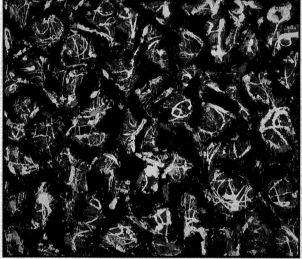

Lee Krasner, ABSTRACT NO. 2 1946–1948
Robert Miller Gallery, NY

Winter Road I by Georgia O'Keeffe © The Georgia O'Keeffe Foundation/ARS, New York;
Photo by Malcom Varon, NYC © 1987

48

When a single melody is played or sung, the texture is thin.

When many parts are heard at the same time, the texture is thicker. Adding a musical background, or **accompaniment**, to a melody makes the texture thicker.

Listening to the Nightingale

Listening to the nightingale singing
among the flowers
or to the cry of the frog which dwells
in the water,
we recognize the truth
that of all living things
there is not one
which does not utter song.

—Ki Tsurayuki

Accompaniments can be created from both instrumental and vocal sounds.

SELECT percussion sounds to play as an accompaniment. Play the percussion sounds while a classmate speaks.

CREATE a background of vocal sounds. Include the sounds of birds and animals mentioned in the poem.

THINK IT THROUGH
How did each accompaniment add to the meaning of the poem? How would the texture change if both accompaniments were heard at the same time?

Change the musical texture to enrich a song you already know. How does the texture change in the refrain?

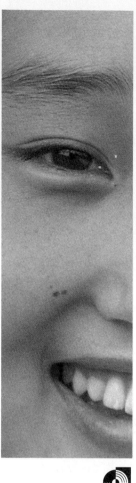

Music Brings Us Together

Words and Music by Garry Smith

F   *mf*   C   B♭   F

do

1. Chil - dren, sing   all   o - ver the place.____
2. Sing a song   to   bright - en your day.____

B♭   Am

Mu - sic brings us to - geth - er!
Mu - sic brings us to - geth - er!

F   C   B♭   F

A hap - py song brings a   smile to your face.____
Sing it at work or____   sing it at play.____

A **canon,** or round, has a melody that is imitated in one or more parts. Each time a new part is added, the texture becomes thicker.

Peace Round

Old English Canon
Words by Jean Ritchie
Adapted from Psalm 133:1

do | What a good-ly thing if the chil-dren

do | What a

of the world could dwell to-geth-er

good-ly thing if the chil-dren of the world

in_____ peace.

could dwell to-geth-er in_____ peace.

MUSIC THAT UNITES

When friends get together, there's often music in the air. Sing "Get Up!" and think about the title of this unit, "United by Music." What kept you together when you all were singing and moving? It was the music—most noticeably, the beat and the rhythm of the music.

The ideas expressed in the words of a song can also unite people. The message of "This Land Is Your Land" has united people all over the country since it was first sung by Woody Guthrie. As you sing this song, notice the upward movement of the melody at the beginning of most phrases.

Singing with a group, whether it is in unison or in harmony, unites people through a shared experience. Sing "We Will Raise a Ruckus Tonight" in unison or "Ev'rybody Loves Saturday Night" in unison or with the harmony part.

Watching television or a movie, attending a baseball game or a party, listening to the radio, participating in religious services— think about all of the things you do, and then think about them without music. It's almost impossible to imagine. Music is with us everywhere. Sing "Music Brings Us Together!"

1. Which rhythm do you hear?

    a.

    b.

    c.

    d.

2. Choose the melodic direction that you hear.

    a. ↗   b. ↘   c. ↘ ↗   d. →

3. Choose the melodic direction that you hear.

    a. ↗   b. ↘   c. ↘ ↗   d. →

4. Choose the melodic direction that you hear.

    a. ↗   b. ↘   c. ↘ ↗   d. →

5. Which example shows the pitches you hear?

    a.    c.

    b.    d.

6. Which example shows the pitches you hear?

    a.    c.

    b.    d.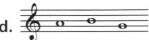

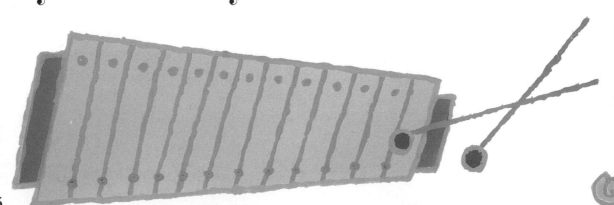

CREATE

Make a Melody

Choose ♩, ♫ , and 𝄽 to fill four measures
in 4/4 meter. The last beat should be a quarter rest.

Play the first two measures on a percussion instrument
or found sound, and the last two measures on a contrasting percussion instrument or found sound. For example,
you could use a hand drum and woodblocks or a
desk and radiator.

**CREATE a melody by choosing pitches for your rhythms.
Use the pitches F G A or G A B. If you use F G A, end on F.
If you use G A B, end on G.**

**PLAY your melody on resonator bells or other
pitched instruments.**

Write

In your family or community, when is music
performed? Write a brief description of an
event you have attended that included music
or an experience you had performing music.
In what way did the music help to bring
people together?

Reach Out and Touch
(Somebody's Hand)

Words and Music by
Nickolas Ashford and Valerie Simpson

Freely
Refrain

Reach out and touch some - bod - y's hand,

make this world a bet - ter place if you can.

Reach out and touch some - bod - y's hand,

make this world a bet - ter place if you can.

Verse

(Just try)
1. Take a lit - tle time out of your bus - y day, To
2. If you see an old friend on the street, and he's

give en - cour - age - ment to some - one who's lost the way.
down, re - mem - ber, his shoes could fit your feet.

(*Just try*) Or would I be talk-ing to a stone
Just try a lit-tle kind-ness and you'll see

if I asked you to share a prob-lem that's not your own
it's some-thing that comes ver-y nat-u-ral-ly.

We can change things if we start

1.
giv-ing. Why don't you

2.
Why don't you (*Why don't you*)

reach out and touch some-bod-y's hand.

OUR HANDS, OUR HEARTS

A traditional Native American worldview is that the earth is like a caring mother. The earth provides everything needed to survive. It provides food, water, medicine, and materials to make beautiful and useful housing, clothing, and tools. The elements and the living things of the earth also teach important lessons about life. Native Americans believe that people should respect and care for the earth because of all that it gives and teaches us. This respect for the earth is shown in many Native American songs and dances.

The photographs of the Zuni family, pueblo, and jar all date from the early 1900s. The pieces of jewelry pictured are modern Zuni designs.

READ "Song of the Skyloom."
How does this poem explain
the relationship between
people and nature?

SONG of the SKYLOOM

Oh our Mother the Earth, oh our Father the Sky,

Your children are we, and with tired backs

We bring you the gifts that you love.

Then weave for us a garment of brightness;

May the weft be the red light of evening,

May the fringes be the falling rain,

May the border be the standing rainbow.

Thus weave for us a garment of brightness

That we may walk fittingly where birds sing,

That we may walk fittingly where grass is green,

Oh our Mother the Earth, oh our Father the Sky!

—from *Songs of the Tewa*

How the Fawn Got its Spots

The following Lakota legend tells how some animals are protected from their natural enemies. As you read the legend, think of instrumental sounds that might represent the animals mentioned.

Long ago, when the world was new, Wakan Tanka, The Great Mystery, was walking around. As he walked, he spoke to himself of the many things he had done to help the four-legged ones and the birds survive.

"It is good," Wakan Tanka said. "I have given Mountain Lion sharp claws and Grizzly Bear great strength. It is much easier now for them to survive. I have given Wolf sharp teeth and I have given his little brother, Coyote, quick wits. It is much easier now for them to survive. I have given Beaver a flat tail and webbed feet to swim beneath the water and teeth which can cut down the trees and I have given slow-moving Porcupine quills to protect itself. Now it is easier for them to survive. I have given the birds their feathers and the ability to fly so that they may escape their enemies. I have given speed to the deer and the rabbit so that it will be hard for their enemies to catch them. Truly it is now much easier for them to survive."

However, as Wakan Tanka spoke, a mother deer came up to him. Behind her was her small fawn, wobbling on weak legs.

"Great One," she said. "It is true that you have given many gifts to the four-leggeds and the winged ones to help them survive. It is true that you gave me great speed and now my enemies find it hard to catch me. My speed is a great protection, indeed. But what of my little one here? She does not yet have speed. It is easy for our enemies, with their sharp teeth and their claws, to catch her. If my children do not survive, how can my people live?"

"Wica yaka pelo!" said Wakan Tanka. "You have spoken truly; you are right. Have your little one come here and I will help."

Then Wakan Tanka made paint from the earth and the plants. He painted spots upon the fawn's body so that, when she lay still, her color blended in with the earth and she could not be seen. Then Wakan Tanka breathed upon her, taking away her scent.

"Now," Wakan Tanka said, "your little ones will always be safe if they only remain still when they are away from your side. None of your enemies will see your little ones or be able to catch their scent."

So it has been from that day on. When a young deer is too small and weak to run swiftly, it is covered with spots that blend in with the earth. It has no scent and it remains very still and close to the earth when its mother is not by its side. And when it has grown enough to have the speed Wakan Tanka gave its people, then it loses those spots it once needed to survive.

LISTENING

Zuni Sunrise Song

"Zuni Sunrise Song" is a morning greeting song. It expresses respect for nature.

This musical greeting occurs several times in the song.

Ha - yoo

The singer also addresses the Zuni people, calling them *Shiwona*.

Shee-wa - yoo - wa - o - na

from
African Dance

The low beating of the tom-toms,
The slow beating of the tom-toms,
    Low…slow
    Slow…low
Stirs your blood.

—*Langston Hughes*

POWER IN RHYTHM

All Join In

by Aden G. Lewis
Adapted

1. Ev'-ry-bod-y clap your hands, ev'-ry-bod-y clap, ev'-ry-
(2.) tap your foot, ev'-ry-bod-y tap, ev'-ry-
(3.) nod your head, ev'-ry-bod-y nod, ev'-ry-

bod-y clap, ev'-ry-bod-y clap, ev'-ry-bod-y clap, ev'-ry-bod-y clap, ev'-ry-
bod-y tap, ev'-ry-bod-y tap, ev'-ry-bod-y tap, ev'-ry-bod-y tap, ev'-ry-
bod-y nod, ev'-ry-bod-y nod, ev'-ry-bod-y nod, ev'-ry-bod-y nod, ev'-ry-

1.

bod-y clap, ev'-ry-bod-y clap!_____ Ev'-ry-bod-y
bod-y tap, ev'-ry-bod-y tap!_____ Ev'-ry-bod-y
bod-y nod, ev'-ry-bod-y nod!_____ Ev'-ry-bod-y

2. vs 1 to B; vs 2 to B; vs 3 to C

bod-y clap, ev'-ry-bod-y clap!
bod-y tap, ev'-ry-bod-y tap!
bod-y nod, ev'-ry-bod-y nod!

B

Ev'-ry-one sway,_____ ev'-ry-one sway,

ev'-ry-one sway,_____ ev'-ry-one sway,

66

ev' - ry - one   sway, _____   ev' - ry - one   sway, _____

D.S.

___   ev' - ry - one   sway, _____   ev' - ry - one   sway, _____   2. Ev' - ry - bod - y
                                                                              3. Ev' - ry - bod - y

C

Ev' - ry - bod - y   tap, _____   ev' - ry - bod - y

nod, _____   ev' - ry - bod - y   clap,   ev' - ry - bod - y

clap,   ev' - ry - bod - y   clap,   ev' - ry - bod - y   clap,   ev' - ry - bod - y

tap,   and   tap,   and   tap,   and   tap,   and
clap,   and   clap,   and   clap,   and   clap,   and

1.

nod,   nod,   nod,   nod,   nod,   nod,   nod,   nod,
tap,   tap,   tap,   tap,   tap,   tap,

2.

tap,   ev' - ry - bod - y   nod, _____

ev' - ry - bod - y   stop!

DRUMS!

You've had the experience: someone turns on the radio and you find yourself "drumming" on your chair. It's not anything you learn. You just do it. It's the power of rhythm at work!

LISTENING

Drum Montage

LISTEN to drumming from many parts of the world in "Drum Montage."

MOVE in a different way each time you hear a new drum sound and style begin.

2 Bata drum from Nigeria

1
Drum set from the United States

Tabla from North India
4

Taiko drums from Japan 3

5
Conga drum from South America

"Funga Alafia" is a greeting song from western Africa. If you were to hear it performed by African musicians, you most certainly would hear drums.

PLAY drums on the beat as you sing this song.

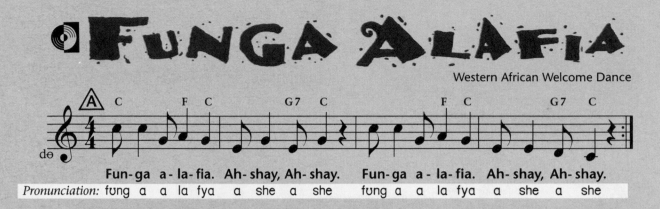

FUNGA ALAFIA

Western African Welcome Dance

Fun- ga a - la- fia. Ah- shay, Ah- shay. Fun- ga a - la- fia. Ah- shay, Ah- shay.

Pronunciation: fung a a la fya a she a she fung a a la fya a she a she

B *Spoken freely*
With my thoughts, I welcome you.
With my words, I welcome you.
With my heart, I welcome you.
See? I have nothing up my sleeve.

How many times do you see this rhythm ♪♩ ♪ ?

EXPRESS the B section of the song with gestures and speech.

1. With my thoughts,

3. With my words,

5. With my heart,

7. See? I have nothing up my sleeve.

2. I welcome you.

4. I welcome you.

6. I welcome you.

In Jamaica, where this calypso song was created, old oil barrels are made into pitched **steel drums.** They play both rhythm and melody.

Mango Walk

Jamaican Calypso

My moth - er deed - a tell me that you go man - go walk,

you go man - go walk, you go man - go walk.

My moth - er deed - a tell me that you go man - go walk

and eat all the num - ber 'lev - en.

COMPARE the rhythm of the tinted measures with the rhythm of *ahshay, ahshay* **in "Funga Alafia."**

DRUMMING RIGHT ALONG

Drums are everywhere. Look around. What drums do you see—floor, desk, radiator, chair, book, your lap? Some famous drummers started out playing on the streets using the bottoms of plastic buckets!

A rhythm pattern consists of long and short sounds and silences, usually with an underlying steady beat. **Syncopation** is a type of rhythm in which some stressed notes come between beats instead of on beats.

PLAY these patterns on a drum and tell which has syncopation. If you don't have an actual drum, use something else.

Go man - go walk

Moth - er deed - a tell me that you

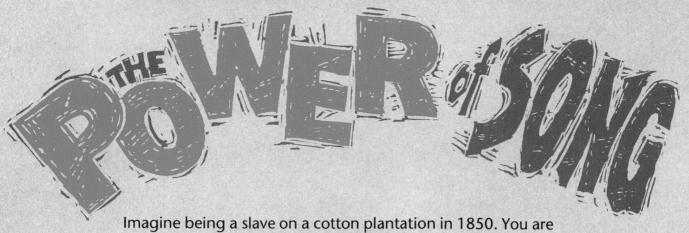

Imagine being a slave on a cotton plantation in 1850. You are working in the fields when you hear soft voices singing "This train is bound for glory. . . ." You add your voice to the song, and that night, under cover of darkness, you and several others begin your escape to freedom. This song was a code song, one of many that pointed the way to freedom in the North.

This Train

African American Spiritual

1. This train is bound for glo-ry, this train,——
2. This train don't car-ry no gam-blers, this train,——
3. This train is bound for glo-ry, this train,——

This train is bound for glo-ry, this train,——
This train don't car-ry no gam-blers, this train,——
This train is bound for glo-ry, this train,——

This train is bound for glo-ry, If you ride it, you
This train don't car-ry no gam-blers, No hy-po-crites,—— no
This train is bound for glo-ry, Don't car-ry noth-ing but the

must be ho-ly, This train is bound for glo-ry, this train.——
mid-night ram-blers, This train is bound for glo-ry, this train.——
right-teous and the ho-ly, This train is bound for glo-ry, this train.——

72

PENTATONIC: A FIVE-TONE SCALE

The folk song "This Train" uses the pitches *do re mi so la.* A folk song usually ends on its **tonal center**, or resting place. For "This Train," the tonal center is *do.*

The pitches of "This Train" are based on a **scale**, which is an ordered series of pitches. You can form a scale by placing the pitches from any song in order from lowest to highest or highest to lowest. A common **pentatonic scale** includes the five pitches *do re mi so la.* The pentatonic scale may include higher or lower pitches, and it may start on any pitch, letter name, or syllable.

CHOOSE the example that matches the pitches in "This Train," and you'll see how this works.

PLAY and sing these pentatonic scales.

VIEWING MOUNTAINS IN YÜ-HANG (*detail*)

Landscapes are important subjects in Chinese painting. This landscape was painted by Shih-t'au, who lived from 1642 to 1707.

GAU SHAN CHING

ALI MOUNTAIN

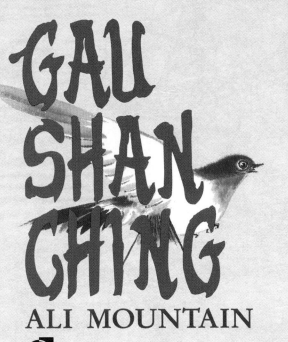

The view is breathtaking: mountain peaks rising from the mist, lush green trees, the rush of a mountain stream, and the scent of jasmine in the air. A swallow swoops above as you watch the changing clouds. Do you have a place like this to visit? In Taiwan, people enjoy the peace of Ali Mountain.

Taiwanese Folk Song
English Words by Marilyn Davidson
and Judy Bond

Mandarin: 高　　　山　　　青

Pronunciation: ga　u　sha　n　ching

English: A - li　moun - tain's so green.

澗　　　水　　　藍

jyɛ　n　shwe　lan

Near a stream so blue.

阿 里 山 的 姑 娘 美 如 水

a li shan da gu niang me ru shwe

A - li moun - tain peo - ple, love - ly to see.

阿　里　山　的　少　年　壮　　　如　山
a　li　shan　da　shau　niɛn　tjuang　　ru　shan
A - li moun - tain dan - cers, grace - ful and strong.

啊
a
Ah! _____

啊
a
Ah! _____

This song includes these pitches. The D and E are used at both high and low pitch levels.

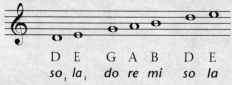

D E   G A B   D E
so₁ la₁   do re mi   so la

COMPARE the notes in "Gau Shan Ching" with these pitches. What pitches are used in each phrase? How are the phrases alike and different?

RHYTHM
IT'S CLEARLY POPULAR

Popular music is what you're likely to hear wherever you go. Back in the 1920s and 1930s, some of the most popular songs came from the pens of George Gershwin and his brother, Ira. They wrote many of these songs for musicals.

A **musical** features a story told with singing, drama, and dancing. *Oklahoma, The Wiz, The Sound of Music, West Side Story, Phantom of the Opera,* and *Grease* are all famous musicals that have played on Broadway. Many musicals have been made into movies. The Gershwin brothers wrote "I Got Rhythm" in the 1930s for their musical *Girl Crazy*. Ethel Merman, a famous singer of that time, made the song a hit.

I GOT RHYTHM

Music by George Gershwin
Words by Ira Gershwin

FORM: IT HOLDS THOSE SONGS TOGETHER

Have you ever listened to songs that were popular when your grandparents were your age? Why are some of these songs still appealing? It might be great rhythm or a singable melody, or it might be something else that can make a song easy to learn—an easy-to-follow form.

"I Got Rhythm" and "Side by Side," along with many other songs, have the same form. It's A A B A—the form most often used in American popular music.

Ⓐ The first A section is a melody with one set of words.

Ⓐ The second A section is the same melody with different words.

Ⓑ The B section has a different melody and words.

Ⓐ The last A section is like the first, with different words. The ending is sometimes changed by adding extra measures, called the **tag.** "I Got Rhythm" has this kind of ending.

LISTENING

I Got Rhythm (xylophone version)
by George Gershwin

Jazz is a type of popular music. It began in the United States in the early 1900s and is enjoyed all over the world today. Jazz musicians often improvise around known songs and forms such as "I Got Rhythm" and A A B A form.

LISTEN for the A A B A form in this jazz version of "I Got Rhythm."

PAT to the beat with alternating hands during the A section.

Acrylic and fabric on canvas 90" × 96" Collection: Dr. and Mrs. Acinapura Courtesy Steinbaum Krauss Gallery, NYC

PAS DE DEUX

Pas de Deux means "Step by Two." The painting was created by Miriam Schapiro in 1986. It is made up of both acrylic and fabric. This painting shows energy through the use of color and objects in motion. Where might these dancers be?

"The Rhythm of Life" is a song from *Sweet Charity,* a musical written in 1966. The music has a bold, energetic style.

LISTEN to "The Rhythm of Life." Are there any syncopated patterns in this song?

COMPARE the sections. Is the song in A A B A form?

THE RHYTHM OF LIFE

Music by Cy Coleman
Words by Dorothy Fields (Adapted)

Moderately Fast

When I start-ed down the street last Sun-day,

Feel-in' might-y low and kind-a mean, Sud-den-ly a voice said,

"Go forth, neigh-bor! Spread the pic-ture on a wid-er screen!" And the

voice said, "Neigh-bor, there's a mil-lion rea-sons Why you should be glad in

all four sea-sons! Hit the road, neigh-bor, leave your wor-ries and strife!

Spread the re-li-gion of the rhy-thm of life." For the

get the beat

In many parts of the world, if there's music, there's movement. In this scene of Jamaican musicians, the steel drummer feels the rhythm throughout her body. The listeners are just as involved. They're dancing, caught up in the power of rhythm.

in your feet!

MOVE to "Mango Walk," a Jamaican folk song, using the steps listed. After some practice, you'll probably be able to move as you sing the song. Even though many of the song rhythms are syncopated, you will be stepping on the steady beat.

DANCE STEPS

1. four steps forward
2. side-close-side, touch (moving to one side)
3. side-close-side, touch (moving to the other side)
4. three steps circling in place, touch
5. four steps backward
6. side-close-side, touch
7. side-close-side, touch
8. stamp, three claps

KEY

touch

left   right

START

MOVE facing a partner to really get into the calypso spirit. Move in the same or opposite directions.

TIE IT ALL TOGETHER

A sound that lasts for one beat can be written in two ways: ♩ or ♫

A **tie** (⌣) is a musical sign that joins two notes of the same pitch. The tie combines the two notes into a single sound equal to their total **duration** (length).

LISTEN and echo-clap or play the patterns below.

hand drum

How do the ties make the patterns sound syncopated?

The syncopated pattern ♩ ♪‿♪ ♩ can also be written as ♪ ♩ ♪

LISTEN for the sound of ♪ ♩ ♪ as you clap or play these patterns.

COMPARE them to the tied patterns on page 84.

claves

CREATE your own composition with syncopation. Make up new patterns or choose two or three of the patterns above. Then decide how to combine them.

PLAY your rhythms on a drum while a classmate plays on the beat with another percussion instrument. Trade parts.

"Sweet Potatoes" and "Mango Walk" have the same form and meter, but their rhythm patterns are completely different.

LISTEN for ♩. ♪♪ ♩♩ | ♩ in "Sweet Potatoes."

Sweet Potatoes

Louisiana Creole Folk Song

1. Soon as we all cook sweet po-ta-toes,
2. Soon as sup-per's gone, Mam-ma calls us,
3. Soon's we touch our heads to the pil-low,
4. Soon's the roost-er crow in the morn-ing,

sweet po-ta-toes, sweet po-ta-toes.
Mam-ma calls us, Mam-ma calls us.
to the pil-low, to the pil-low.
in the morn-ing, in the morn-ing.

Soon as we all cook sweet po-ta-toes,
Soon as sup-per's gone, Mam-ma calls us,
Soon's we touch our heads to the pil-low,
Soon's the roost-er crow in the morn-ing,

Eat 'em while they're hot.
Get a-long to bed.
Go to sleep right smart!
Got-ta wash our face.

A **dotted quarter note** (♩.) is equal in length to one quarter note plus one eighth note.

PRACTICE clapping these patterns.

SING "Sweet Potatoes" and "Mango Walk" at the same time. Notice how the two tunes and their different rhythms fit together.

Folk songs such as "Mango Walk" and "Sweet Potatoes" are often accompanied with percussion instruments. Many of these instruments can be made from everyday objects such as gourds or discarded oil drums.

SAY the words as you practice the rhythms below.

PLAY the patterns on percussion instruments.

ACCOMPANY "Mango Walk" with instruments.

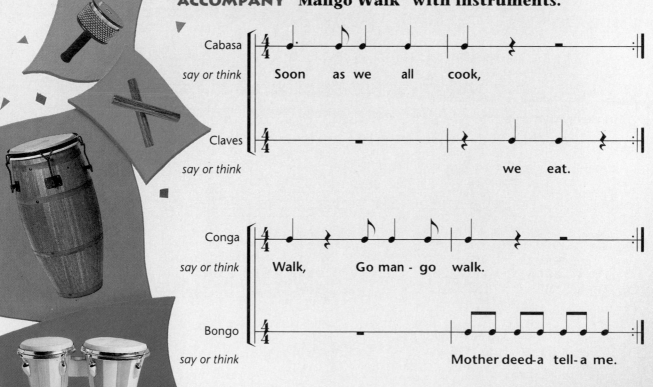

Cabasa
say or think: Soon as we all cook,

Claves
say or think: we eat.

Conga
say or think: Walk, Go man-go walk.

Bongo
say or think: Mother deed-a tell-a me.

PARTNERS

"Sweet Potatoes" and "Mango Walk" can be sung as **partner songs**. They are separate songs, but they sound good when sung at the same time. "Sweet Potatoes" also has a **countermelody**, a contrasting melody written to go with a song.

CLAP the rhythm pattern in the countermelody that is also found in "Sweet Potatoes."

The first pitch in the countermelody is C. The first pitch in the melody is high C (C'). What are the pitch letter names of the notes in both of these melodies? Are there notes in one song that are not sung in the other?

SING the countermelody together with "Sweet Potatoes," reading the notation below.

Sweet Potatoes

Countermelody *(Verses 2 and 4 only)*   Louisiana Creole Folk Song

do | Roo,   roo,   roo,   roo,   hoo,

Melody

do |
1. Soon   as   we   all   cook   sweet po - ta - toes,
2. Soon   as   sup - per's gone,   Mam - ma calls   us,
3. Soon's   we   touch our   heads   to   the   pil - low,
4. Soon's   the   roost - er   crow   in   the   morn - ing,

Louisiana Creole Folk Song
and Jamaican Calypso

Sweet Potatoes

Soon as we all cook sweet po - ta - toes,

Countermelody

Roo, roo, roo, roo, hoo,

Mango Walk

My moth - er deed - a tell me that you go man - go walk, you

sweet po - ta - toes, sweet po - ta - toes.

hoo, Sing ho - ke - dink - um!

go man - go walk, you go man - go walk. My

Soon as we all cook sweet po-ta-toes,

Roo, roo, roo, roo, hoo,

moth-er deed-a tell me that you go man-go walk and

Eat 'em while they're hot.

hoo, hoo, hoo!

eat all the num-ber 'lev-en.

THINK IT THROUGH

Why do you think these three melodies
sound good together?

THESE MELODIES REALLY GET AROUND!

Arthur Benjamin used the melody of "Mango Walk" and part of the countermelody of "Sweet Potatoes" in his composition "Jamaican Rumba."

LISTENING

Jamaican Rumba *by Arthur Benjamin*

LISTEN to a section of "Jamaican Rumba." Sing along with the orchestra when you hear a melody you know.

Theme 1

Theme 2

LISTENING MAP *Follow the listening map as you listen to "Jamaican Rumba."*

Introduction

Theme 1 Theme 1 Theme 2 Bridge

Theme 1 Bridge Theme 2 Theme 1 / Theme 2

Coda

MOVE with "Jamaican Rumba." Do the steps you know on "Mango Walk" or create movements on the countermelody.

WORK RHYTHMS

Working to the rhythm of a song can make almost any task easier. "Zum gali gali" is a work song from Israel. The phrase *Zum gali gali* imitates the sound of a stringed instrument.

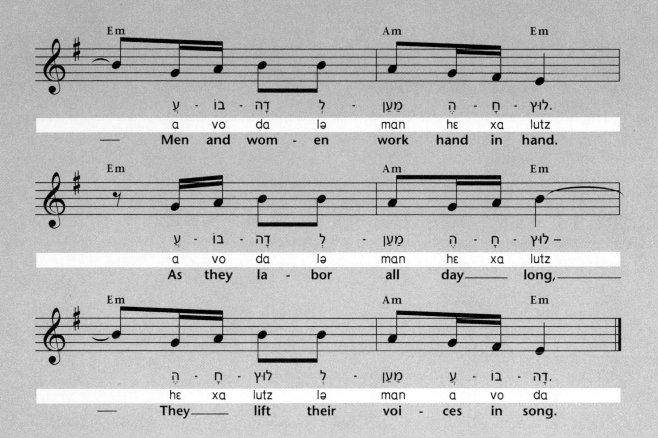

The sixteenth notes in "Zum gali gali" give it a driving rhythm. Since four **sixteenth notes** equal one quarter note (♬♬ = ♩), many of these notes can fit in each ²⁄₄ measure. Rhythm patterns such as ♬♪ or ♪♬ can be made by combining sixteenth notes and eighth notes. Which combination of notes is used in "Zum gali gali"?

Name the songs that have the rhythm patterns below.

PLAY AN ACCOMPANIMENT

"The Rhythm of Life" shares the same driving rhythmic energy as "Zum gali gali." You can add even more energy with a rhythmic accompaniment.

PLAY these patterns as an accompaniment to "The Rhythm of Life." Start by playing A once with its repeat, B once with its repeat, and C once with its repeat. Then play all three patterns at the same time until the end.

A Claves or Clap

B Drum or Desk top

C Tambourine or Speak

Brr   rum bum bum bum Brrr   rum bum bum bum

CREATE a new pattern to play with the A or B section. Choose a new percussion sound to perform the new pattern.

RHYTHM WORKOUT

Here's a chance to put what you've learned about rhythm into action.

READ the rhythms below silently.

IDENTIFY the song from which each rhythm comes and match each pattern with one of the pictures.

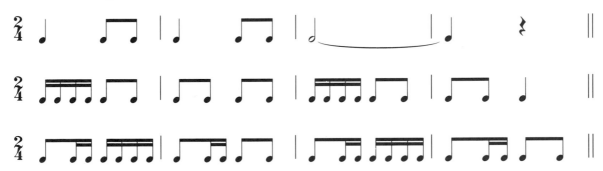

FASCINATING MELODIES

Look at the melody below. The pitches are here, but where is the rhythm? It's in your memory!

Read and sing these pitches to yourself. The order of the pitches will be so familiar that you'll probably fill in the missing rhythm as you sing and play.

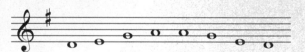

PLAY the melody on resonator bells.

Have you guessed the song yet?

MOVE with your hands to show each pitch.

FOLLOW the pictures to do a "hand dance" of the pitches in the melody.

Compose a different ending for the A section of "I Got Rhythm." Play or sing the pitches Gershwin used for the words *I got rhythm, I got music, I got my friends.* Create a new ending by choosing a different order for the pitches, still ending on G, the tonal center. Here are some possibilities.

PLAY or sing your new melody, and then trade melodies with a classmate. Do you think Gershwin might have experimented in this way?

Spotlight on the GERSHWIN BROTHERS

When the Gershwin brothers, George and Ira, started out in the songwriting business back in the 1920s, ragtime was the rage in St. Louis, and Dixieland jazz was taking over in New Orleans. George Gershwin understood how to shape an easy-to-remember melody with toe-tapping rhythms.

LISTENING

I Got Rhythm (piano version)
by George Gershwin

A **variation** in music occurs when a composer makes changes. Variations are enjoyable because you can recognize what you know and at the same time be surprised by something new.

LISTENING MAP Listen and follow the map as André Watts plays George Gershwin's piano variations on "I Got Rhythm." It should be easy because you are familiar with the form.

A
A
B
A'

INTERLUDE

A
A
B
A'

Both George and Ira grew up in New York City. Ira was quiet and shy and loved to read books. George, however, was mischievous and always looking for adventure. When the Gershwin family bought a secondhand piano, it was intended for the older son, Ira, but George was far more interested. He couldn't seem to get enough music. Ira became a writer, and often wrote lyrics for George's songs. "Fascinating Rhythm" is from Lady, Be Good, a musical that was a smash hit in both New York and London.

Fred Astaire with George and Ira Gershwin

LISTENING

Fascinating Rhythm *from Lady, Be Good*

by George Gershwin and Ira Gershwin

IDENTIFY the pitches by their letter names.

A **motive** *is a small building block of melody or rhythm. The first six notes of "Fascinating Rhythm" make up a motive. By starting the motive on a different beat each time, Gershwin changed where the stresses fall as the motive is repeated.*

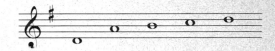

TAP lightly on the dashes as you listen to this section of "Fascinating Rhythm," and then repeat and sing as you tap.

A *Latin American* EXPERIENCE

Colombia
SOUTH AMERICA

Imagine the sound of a bass drum, then cowbells ringing out. As you run towards the plaza, the rhythm of the conga drum joins in. You see a blur of whiteness and light as dancers shuffle and swirl with candles held high.

On the Atlantic coast of Colombia, the *cumbia* dance is performed at night, with candles providing the only light. The woman dances with shuffling steps and the man moves in a zigzag pattern around her. The music for the *cumbia* is the most popular kind of folk song in that region.

LA CUMBIA

Popular Colombian Dance

A G   A   G   1. A   2. A

Spanish: **Ai - e tim-ba-le - ro, bai-le cum-bia del sol.___ Ai -___**
Pronunciation: ai e tim ba le ɾo bai le kum bya ðel sol ai

102

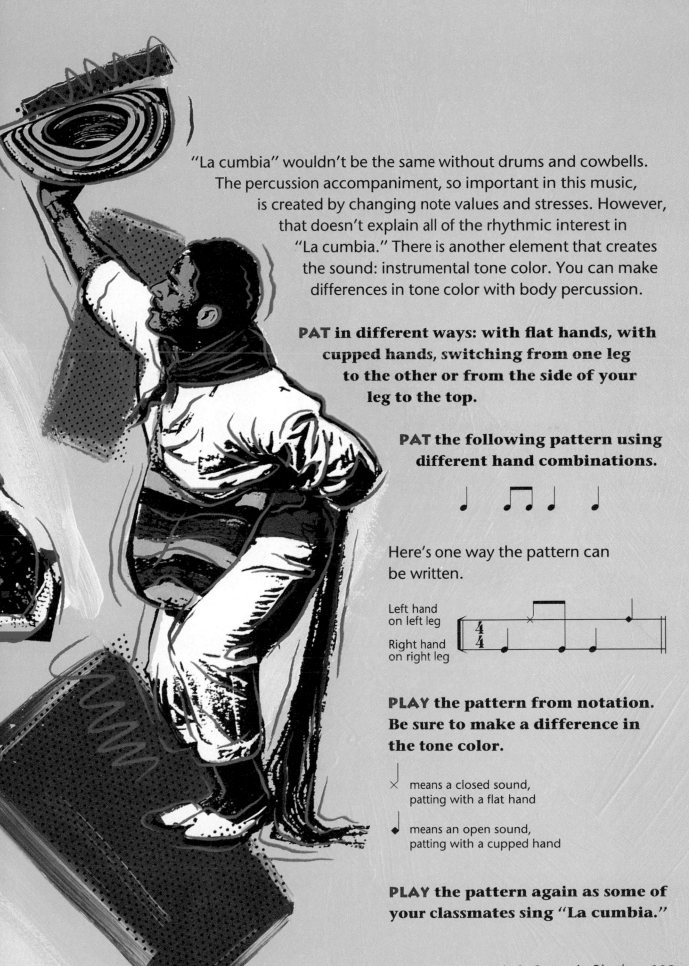

"La cumbia" wouldn't be the same without drums and cowbells. The percussion accompaniment, so important in this music, is created by changing note values and stresses. However, that doesn't explain all of the rhythmic interest in "La cumbia." There is another element that creates the sound: instrumental tone color. You can make differences in tone color with body percussion.

PAT in different ways: with flat hands, with cupped hands, switching from one leg to the other or from the side of your leg to the top.

PAT the following pattern using different hand combinations.

Here's one way the pattern can be written.

Left hand on left leg

Right hand on right leg

PLAY the pattern from notation. Be sure to make a difference in the tone color.

✕   means a closed sound, patting with a flat hand

♦   means an open sound, patting with a cupped hand

PLAY the pattern again as some of your classmates sing "La cumbia."

"La cumbia" has percussion parts for a conga drum, two cowbells, and bass drum. Each instrument makes more than one sound.

TRY these sounds. If you don't have an instrument, use substitute instruments or body percussion.

Conga drum—open (ringing) sound

Hit edge of drumhead with fingers. Let hand bounce.

Conga drum—closed (muffled) sound

Hit middle of drumhead with hand flat.

Strike side of drum with stick for a different sound.

Cowbell—open sound

Hold cowbell up. Keep index finger away from cowbell.

Hit side of cowbell with stick. Let it ring.

Cowbell—closed sound

Hit side of cowbell with stick while holding index finger against side of cowbell.

Bass drum—open sound

Strike drumhead with mallet. Let it ring.

Bass drum—closed sound

Hold free hand flat on drumhead and strike drumhead with mallet.

Play these parts with "La cumbia." In the score below, ♩ means to play with an open sound. ♩ means to play with a closed sound.

Play the top line of the conga part with the left hand. Play the bottom line of the conga part with a stick on the side of the drum.

For body percussion, use these sounds.

Cowbell 1:   ♩ = clap fingers of one hand on the palm of the other

             ♩ = clap palm of one hand on the other

Cowbell 2:   ♫ = straight clapping

Conga: ♩ = right hand pats right leg

             ♩ = pat left, flat hand (closed)

             ♩ = pat left, cupped hand (open)

Bass drum: ♩ = jump to side with both feet (second jump is in the opposite direction)

             ♩ = step

THINK IT THROUGH
Was there a good balance between playing and singing? Did you feel the power of rhythm as you performed?

RHYTHM IN THE AIR

Where there's music, there's rhythm. Rhythmic characteristics of music can vary widely, depending on where it was created.

Think about differences in the cultures of western Africa and Taiwan. Cultural differences as well as differences in subject matter can affect music and the way that rhythm is treated.

Sing "Funga Alafia" and "Gau Shan Ching" and compare their moods. Notice how the African welcome song is syncopated and the Taiwanese mountain song has a more flowing rhythm.

The rhythm pattern ♪♩ ♪ that gives "Funga Alafia" its syncopation appears in music all over the world. It is a rhythmic motive in the Jamaican song "Mango Walk" and "This Train," a spiritual from the southern United States. Sing "Mango Walk" and "This Train" and clap the syncopated patterns.

Singing two different melodies at the same time can create a new rhythm not present in either of the separate songs. Sing "Sweet Potatoes" with its countermelody and notice the rhythmic "jigsaw puzzle" that results as these two pieces fit together.

If two melodies sung together can create rhythmic interest, think of the even more interesting combination of triple partner songs: "Mango Walk," "Sweet Potatoes," and the countermelody. Sing the triple partner songs "Sing for Your Supper."

Arthur Benjamin based his composition "Jamaican Rumba" on themes from "Mango Walk" and the countermelody of "Sweet Potatoes."

DANCE to "Jamaican Rumba." Add the rhythm of your movement to the rhythms of the orchestra.

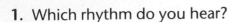HECK IT OUT

1. Which rhythm do you hear?

   a.

   b.

   c.

   d.

2. Which rhythm do you hear?

   a.

   b.

   c.

   d.

3. Which rhythm do you hear?

   a.

   b.

   c.

   d.

4. Choose the pitches that you hear.

   a.

   b.

   c.

   d.

CREATE

Create Percussion Music

Compose a piece of music with two contrasting sections. Work with a partner. Create two different four-measure patterns in ♩♩ meter. Use ♩. ♪ and ♪♩ ♪ in one or both patterns.

COMPOSE a melody for each pattern using C D E F G. Begin on C or G. End on C.

CHOOSE a pitched percussion instrument to play each section.

PERFORM your composition.

Write

Arthur Benjamin used "Mango Walk" as part of a composition for orchestra. If you were going to write a composition for orchestra based on a song, what song would you choose? Write a brief paragraph describing your planned composition.

Words and Music by Louis Prima
Adapted

Brightly

1. Sing, sing, sing, sing, Ev' - ry - bod - y start to sing___
2. Swing, swing, swing, swing, Ev' - ry - bod - y start to swing___

La - dle - la___ Whoa - ho - ho___ Now you're sing - ing with a swing.___
La - dle - la___ Whoa - ho - ho___ Now you're swing - in' while you sing.___

When the mu - sic goes a - round___ ev' - ry - bod - y goes to town,___
When the mu - sic goes a - round___ ev' - ry - bod - y goes to town,___

but here's some - thing you should know___ ho - ho ba - by ho - ho - ho.
just re - lax and take it slow___ ho - ho ba - by ho - ho - ho.

Sing, sing, sing, sing, Ev' - ry - bod - y start to sing___

La - dle - la___ Whoa - ho - ho___ Now you're sing - ing with a swing.___

110

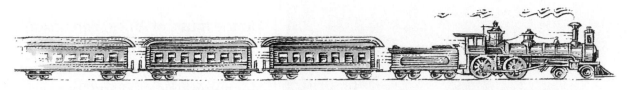

NINE HUNDRED MILES

American Traditional Song

1. Well, I'm walk-in' down this track, I've got tears in my eyes,
2. Well, this train that I ride on, it's one hun-dred coach-es long.

Tryin' to read a let-ter from my home.
You can hear the whis-tle sound for miles.

Refrain

And if this train runs me right, I'll be home to-mor-row night,

'Cause I'm nine hun-dred miles from my home.

Messages in SOUND

In the music of Africa, percussion instruments are widely used. Drumming is especially important for communication and for celebration. The master drummer holds an honored position in society.

LISTEN to William Amoaku, a master drummer, talk about his art.

Proverbs, wise sayings that are passed down from generation to generation, are important in many cultures. The proverbs below are from the western part of Africa.

Learn well! Learn well!

One falsehood spoils the truth.

Little is better than nothing.

A dog's bark is not might but fright.

Children are rewards, (yes I say) children are rewards.

The teeth are smiling, but is the heart?

William Amoaku, master drummer

PRACTICE the rhythm of these proverbs. Use body percussion.

Like the master drummer, the griot plays an important role in traditional African culture. The griot, an expert in music, poetry, and story telling, travels from place to place sharing information among various communities. Griots, with their extensive memories and skill in narration, are important in helping to transmit the cultural heritage of the African people.

AFRICA

West Africa

Kenya

Selina Akua Ahoklui, a griot from Ghana

PRACTICE the rhythm of the proverbs on percussion instruments. Then plan a performance with other class members that uses percussion instruments, movement, and speech.

THE FIERCE CREATURE

A FOLKTALE FROM KENYA

"The Fierce Creature" is a story told by the Masai people, who live in the high country of Kenya in eastern Africa. The story might be told by a griot at an outdoor gathering where the sounds of percussion and chirping insects can be heard.

The story tells of a tired caterpillar who, upon finding the empty home of a hare, sees a chance to take a nap. When the hare returns, he sees strange marks on the ground. He demands to know who is in his house. Afraid of being eaten, the cowardly caterpillar calls out in his fiercest voice. "I am the terrible warrior, deadlier than the leopard. I crush the rhinoceros to earth and trample the mighty elephant!" Hearing this, the hare hops up and down in fright.

A prowling leopard passes by, and the hare asks her for help. When the leopard calls out, asking who is there, the caterpillar repeats his warning. "I am the terrible warrior, deadlier than the leopard. I crush the rhinoceros to earth and trample the mighty

elephant!" This so frightens the leopard that she hides behind the hare.

A cranky rhinoceros comes next. Then a huge elephant thunders by. Each is asked for help. But after hearing the voice of the "warrior," they quake with fear and hide behind the others.

Finally, a frog hops by. He answers the caterpillar's cry with a ferocious shout of his own. "I, the hideous leaper, have come. I am slimy, green, and full of great warts!" This time, the frightened caterpillar makes a run for it. The others, catching sight of the little insect they had thought to be a fierce creature, enjoy a good laugh. The clever frog, however, makes off for a tasty meal.

DRAMATIZE the folk tale. Set the scene using the percussion sounds from the proverbs on page 112. Then choose instruments to represent each character. Play the instruments to accompany different parts of the folk tale.

EXPRESSIONS OF FREED

The Sidewalk Racer

or On the Skateboard

Skimming
an asphalt sea
I swerve, I curve, I
sway; I speed to whirring
sound an inch above the
ground; I'm the sailor
and the sail, I'm the
driver and the wheel
I'm the one and only
single engine
human auto
mobile.

—Lillian Morrison

We Shall Be Free

Words and Music by
Stephanie Davis and Garth Brooks

Freely

do

When the last child cries___ for a crust of bread,___ when the

last___ man dies___ for just words that he said,___ when there's

shel - ter o - ver the poor - est head,_____

we shall___ be free._____ 1. When the

Verse

last thing we no - tice is the col - or of skin,___ and the
(2.) free to love_____ an - y - thing___ we choose,_ when this

first thing we look for is the beau - ty with - in___ when the
world's big e - nough___ for all dif - fer - ent views,_ when we

skies___ and the o - ceans___ are clean a - gain,_____
all___ can wor - ship from our own kind of pew,_____

then   we   shall____   be   free,____
then   we   shall____   be   free.____

𝄋 Refrain

1., 3., 4. We   shall____   be   free,____   we   shall__   be   free.____
2. We   shall____   be   free,____   we   shall__   be   free,____

Stand   straight,_____   walk   proud,__   'cause   we   shall__   be   free.__
Have   a   lit-tle   faith,__   hold   out,____   'cause   we   shall__   be   free.__

1. D   2. D   *to Bridge*   *repeat refrain ad lib and fade*
                                         3., 4. D

____   2. When we're   ____   And   when   ____

Bridge

mon - ey   talks____   for   the   ver - y   last   time,____   and

no - bod - y   walks____   a   step   be - hind,____   when there's

on - ly   one   race,____   and   that's   man - kind,____

D.S. al Fine

then   we   shall____   be   free.____

Sing Out For Freedom

In the musical *The Wiz,* Dorothy, the heroine, melts the Wicked Witch with a bucket of water. Then everyone sings "Everybody Rejoice."

LISTEN to "Everybody Rejoice," and describe the differences in the voices you hear.

EVERYBODY REJOICE

Words and Music by Luther Vandross

1. Ev'-ry-bod-y look a-round, 'cause there's a rea-son to__ re-joice,__
2. Ev'-ry-bod-y be glad,__ be-cause the sun is shin-ing just__

__ you see.__ Ev'-ry-bod-y come out, and let's com-
__ for us.__ Ev'-ry-bod-y wake up, in-to the

mence to sing-ing joy-ful-ly.__ Ev'-ry-bod-y look up
morn-ing in-to hap-pi-ness.__ Hel-lo, world!

120

THE CHANGING SINGING VOICE

As you grow into an adult, your voice will become richer in quality and different in range. Your **unchanged** voice will become a **changed** adult voice.

Adult singing voices, both male and female, develop over a period of several years. They are usually classified according to their tone color and ranges. Below are the ranges of the four basic changed voices: **soprano, alto, tenor,** and **bass.**

└ soprano ┘ └ alto ┘ └ tenor ┘ └ bass ┘

Unchanged voices share the same vocal range as the soprano and alto changed voices. The tenor and bass voices are lower. A singer with a tenor or bass voice often reads from the **bass clef** (𝄢).

Lift Every Voice and Sing

**by James Weldon Johnson and
J. Rosamond Johnson**

*"Lift Every Voice and Sing" was written by two
brothers. J. Rosamond Johnson composed the music
and James Weldon Johnson wrote the **lyrics** (words).
They wrote the song in 1900 to honor the late Abra-
ham Lincoln. Lincoln was President during the Civil
War and had ended slavery in the United States.*

*James Weldon Johnson later helped to found
the National Association for the Advancement of
Colored People (NAACP). "Lift Every Voice and
Sing" is the NAACP's official song.*

LISTEN to "Lift Every Voice and Sing."
Decide if you hear changed voices or
unchanged voices in this recording.

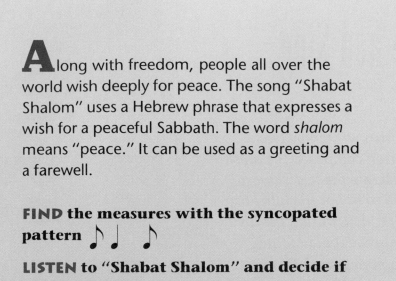

Along with freedom, people all over the world wish deeply for peace. The song "Shabat Shalom" uses a Hebrew phrase that expresses a wish for a peaceful Sabbath. The word *shalom* means "peace." It can be used as a greeting and a farewell.

FIND the measures with the syncopated pattern ♪ ♩ ♪

LISTEN to "Shabat Shalom" and decide if you hear changed or unchanged voices.

The modified grapevine step is part of a dance done with "Shabat Shalom."

Shabat Shalom

Words and Music
by N. Frankel

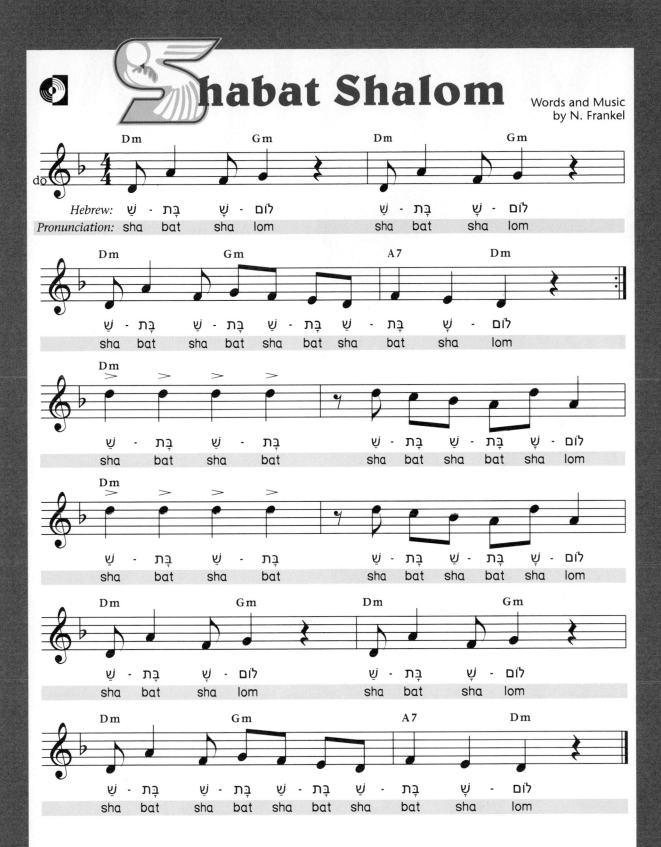

THINK IT THROUGH

You have been hearing and singing music that expresses
everyone's need for freedom. How do you think music can
express freedom in ways that words alone cannot?

MUSICAL

"When the Saints Go Marching In" was one of the first songs to be played in what was, in the early 1900s, a new and daring style of music called **Dixieland jazz.** Dixieland jazz started with small bands that played in New Orleans. These bands would begin with traditional spirituals and would freely experiment, or improvise, with the melodies to give them a completely new sound. Watch for the pitch between *mi* and *so* as you learn "When the Saints Go Marching In."

FREEDOM

When the Saints Go Marching In

African American Spiritual

1. Oh, when the saints_____ go march-ing in,_____
2. Oh, when the stars_____ re-fuse to shine,_____
3. Oh, when I hear_____ that trum-pet sound,_____

Oh, when the saints go march - ing in,
Oh, when the stars re - fuse to shine,
Oh, when I hear that trum - pet sound,

Oh, Lord, I want to be in that num - ber_____
Oh, Lord, I want to be in that num - ber_____
Oh, Lord, I want to be in that num - ber_____

When the saints go march - ing in.
When the stars re - fuse to shine.
When I hear that trum - pet sound.

BEYOND PENTATONIC—A NEW PITCH!

What are the letter names of the first four notes of "When the Saints Go Marching In"?

How many times do these pitches appear at the beginning of the song?

G is *do*. What are the pitch syllable names for B and D?

When G is *do*, the pitch syllable name for C is *fa*. You have sung and played this pitch many times. Now you can name it and read it on the staff.

G		B	C	D
do		*mi*	*fa*	*so*

The melody of "Joyful, Joyful, We Adore Thee" was composed by Ludwig van Beethoven, one of Europe's most famous composers of the early 1800s. Beethoven is admired not only because of his musical genius but also because he brought a new type of creative freedom to music.

Henry van Dyke, an American, wrote English words to be sung to Beethoven's melody. "Joyful, Joyful, We Adore Thee" is the best known of van Dyke's hymns. It was first published in 1911.

Beethoven's manuscript for Sonata No. 30 in E Major, Op. 109

Joyful, Joyful We Adore Thee

Music Arranged from Ludwig van Beethoven
Words by Henry van Dyke
Words Adapted by Judy Bond

1. Joy - ful, joy - ful, we a - dore Thee, God of glo - ry,
2. All Thy works with joy sur - round Thee; Earth and heaven re -
3. Mor - tals join the might - y chor - us, Which the morn - ing

God of love, Hearts un - fold like flowers be - fore Thee,
flect Thy rays, Stars and an - gels sing a - round Thee,
stars be - gan. All cre - a - tion joins to - geth - er,

Open - ing to the sun a - bove. Melt the clouds of
Cen - ter of un - bro - ken praise. Field and for - est,
Son and daugh - ter, wom - an, man. Ev - er sing - ing,

sin and sad - ness, Drive the dark of doubt a - way.
vale and moun - tain, Flow' - ring mead - ow, flash - ing sea.
march we on - ward, Vic - tors in the midst of strife.

Giv - er of im - mor - tal glad - ness, Fill us with the light of day.
Chant-ing bird and flow - ing foun - tain, Call us to re - joice in Thee.
Joy - ful mu - sic lifts us sun - ward, In the tri - umph song of life.

Ludwig van
BEETHOVEN

Ludwig van Beethoven was born in 1770 and lived until 1827. He began composing music when he was only 11. He was a skilled pianist and often performed his piano music in public.

Beethoven's career influenced the lives and music of future composers. Up to that time, most musicians were treated like servants. Wealthy people hired composers to write music for special occasions.

During Beethoven's lifetime, public concerts were performed more often. Music publishing was growing into a profit-making industry. These developments helped composers earn money from works they had written. Beethoven had a strong personality. He insisted on writing music for his own satisfaction. The changing times, his abilities, and his fame allowed him to work almost independently of the wealthy.

Beethoven wrote music of all types, including nine symphonies. When he was at the height of his fame, he began to lose his hearing. In spite of this, he continued to compose and perform. By the end of his life, he was unable to hear at all. When Symphony No. 9 was first performed, Beethoven conducted, but he could not hear the applause. One of the musicians had to turn him around so that he could see the outpouring of enthusiasm from the audience. Because of Beethoven's great creativity and his courage, he is considered both a great composer and an inspiration to all who have to work in the face of difficulties.

Leonard Bernstein

LISTENING

Symphony No. 9

in D Minor, Op. 125 ("Choral"),
Fourth Movement (excerpt)

by Ludwig van Beethoven

A **symphony** *is a musical work. It is usually composed for instruments. During Beethoven's lifetime, the symphony was a very popular form. Beethoven was always looking for ways to make his music more powerful. In his last symphony, he added voices to the sound of the orchestra. The chorus sings part of a poem by Friedrich Schiller called "Ode to Joy." The words and music combine to create an exciting feeling of rejoicing and celebration.*

This symphony was performed at a special concert in Germany in 1989. In that year, the Berlin Wall was taken apart. For nearly 30 years the wall had divided the city of Berlin into East and West zones. The destruction of the wall was a symbol of liberty and unity for the German people and the world. For this concert, American conductor Leonard Bernstein had the original word for "joy" in German changed to the word that means "freedom."

LISTEN for a melody you know in Symphony No. 9.

Brandenburg Gate and
the Berlin Wall

Unit 3 *Expressions of Freedom* **131**

TONE COLORS
of Orchestral Percussion

Percussion instruments play an important part in an orchestra. In the picture below are some of the percussion instruments Beethoven used in his Symphony No. 9. Can you name them?

MEET THE TIMPANI

There are two types of percussion instruments: unpitched and pitched. Snare drums and maracas are two examples of those that do not sound a definite pitch. Xylophones and timpani are examples of those that can sound exact pitches.

Timpani (also called **kettledrums**) are usually played in sets of two or more. The player strikes the drums with large padded mallets. Each drum is tuned to a different pitch. The drum consists of a bowl-shaped copper base, across which is stretched a skin or plastic drumhead. The drumhead is held in place by a metal ring.

drumhead

mallets

pedal

A player can change the pitch of each drum by adjusting the tension of the drumhead either by turning large screws around the rim of the drumhead or by raising or lowering a pedal attached to the drumhead by rods.

Timpani are known for their ability to produce loud rolls (rapidly repeating notes), which can be heard over the entire orchestra. Timpani also make the **bass line** (low notes) stronger by playing selected notes.

LISTEN again to Symphony No. 9 by Beethoven.
Decide whether the timpani are playing rolls
or playing selected notes.

Galerie Louis Carré et Cie., Paris

ORCHESTRE À LA PIANISTE, 1941
Raoul Dufy made many sketches and
paintings of orchestras. The figures are
general shapes, not finely detailed.
Where are the timpani in this painting?
What other orchestral instruments can
you identify?

LISTENING

Fanfare for the Common Man

by Aaron Copland

A **fanfare** is a short, showy tune for trumpets or brass, played to honor important people or to announce an important event. Aaron Copland wrote "Fanfare for the Common Man" to express his concern for each individual's right to live in freedom and dignity. This piece honors every man and woman.

LISTENING MAP *Listen for the brass and percussion instruments as you follow the listening map.*

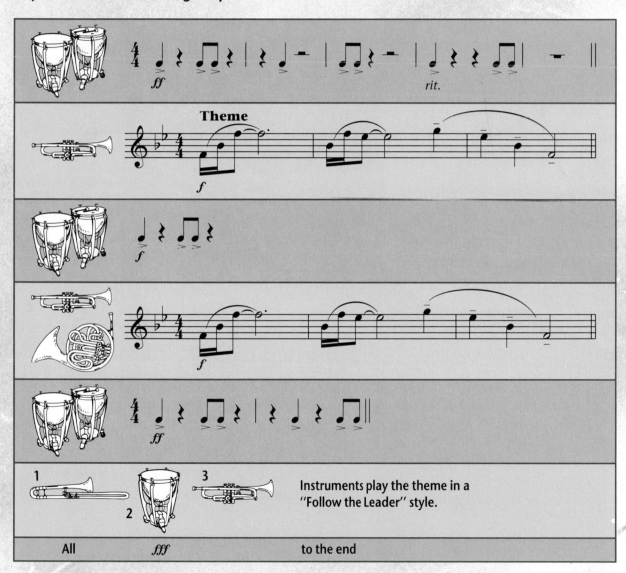

THINK IT THROUGH

If you were to write music to honor someone, whom would you choose? Why?

SEVEN

STEPS TO MELODY

The melody for "Song of Peace" was written in 1899 by Jean Sibelius, Finland's most famous composer. The words to "Song of Peace" were written by Lloyd Stone. They speak of the special love one has for a homeland and express a wish for world peace.

LISTEN to the recording of "Song of Peace." It is sung *a cappella,* or without instrumental accompaniment.

DECIDE if you hear changed or unchanged voices in "Song of Peace."

136

Song of PEACE

Music by Jean Sibelius
Words by Lloyd Stone
Words Adapted by Judy Bond

1. This is my song, a song for all the na-tions,
2. My coun-try's skies are blu-er than the o-cean,

A song of peace for lands a-far and mine.
And sun-light beams in clo-ver leaf and pine.

This is my home, the coun-try where my heart is,
But oth-er lands have sun-light, too, and clo-ver,

Here are my hopes, my dreams, my ho-ly shrine;
And skies are ev'-ry-where as blue as mine.

But oth-er hearts in oth-er lands are beat-ing
O hear my song, a song for all the na-tions,

With hopes and dreams as true and high as mine.
A song of peace for their land and for mine.

A JOKE BACKFIRES

There is a lot of mystery about when "Yankee Doodle" was written and who wrote it. The tune is very old and came from Europe. Many sets of words have been used with this melody.

One story of the song's origin tells that new words were written by a British officer in 1755 to make fun of the colonial soldiers in America. The colonial soldiers, instead of being offended by the words, liked them. The song became one of the most popular songs during the time of the American Revolution.

YANKEE DOODLE

Traditional Melody
Words by Dr. Richard Shuckburgh
Descant by Mary Goetze

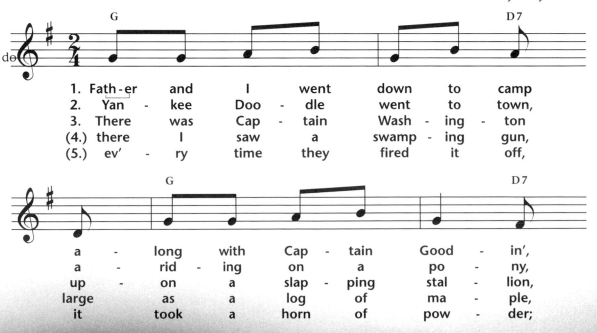

1. Fath-er	and	I	went	down	to	camp
2. Yan - kee	Doo - dle	went	to	town,
3. There	was	Cap - tain	Wash - ing - ton
(4.) there	I	saw	a	swamp - ing	gun,
(5.) ev' - ry	time	they	fired	it	off,

a - long	with	Cap - tain	Good - in',
a - rid - ing	on	a	po - ny,
up - on	a	slap - ping	stal - lion,
large	as	a	log	of	ma - ple,
it	took	a	horn	of	pow - der;

and   there   we   saw   the   men   and   boys
He   stuck   a   feath -   er   in   his   cap
a -   giv -   ing   or -   ders   to   his   men;
up -   on   a   might -   y   lit -   tle   cart;
it   made   a   noise   like   Fath -   er's   gun

as   thick   as   hast -   y   pud   -   din'.
and   called   it   mac -   a -   ron   -   i.
I   guess   there   were   a   mil   -   lion.
a   load   for   Fath -   er's   cat   -   tle.
on -   ly   a   na -   tion   loud   -   er.

Refrain

Descant

Step with   the   mu -   sic and   step with   the   band.

Melody

Yan - kee Doo - dle   keep it   up,   Yan - kee Doo - dle   dan - dy,

Step with   the   mu -   sic,   it's   Yan - kee Doo - dle   dan - dy.

Mind   the mu - sic   and the   step, and   with   the   girls   be   han - dy.

4. And
5. And

6. And there I saw a little keg,
   Its head all made of leather,
   They knocked upon't with little sticks
   To call the folks together.
   Refrain

7. I can't tell you half I saw,
   They kept up such a smother;
   I took my hat off, made a bow,
   And scampered home to Mother.
   Refrain

ONE LAST PITCH!

With one more pitch, you will know
all the tones of the major scale.

**LOOK at part of "Yankee Doodle" written below.
Figure out the syllables you know. Stop when you
come to a pitch that is a new one to you.**

The new pitch leads us "home" to *do*. This pitch is between
la and *do*. *Ti* is the name of this new pitch syllable.

THE DIATONIC SCALE

The pitches in a **diatonic scale** include all the pitches you have
learned: *do re mi fa so la ti do'*. A diatonic scale with *do* as the
tonal center is called a **major scale.** All of the songs in this lesson
use the major scale.

**NAME the syllables for "Ev'rybody Loves Saturday
Night" when G is *do*.**

EV'RYBODY LOVES SATURDAY NIGHT

Ev' - ry - bod - y   loves   Sat - ur - day   night.

Ev' - ry - bod - y   loves   Sat - ur - day   night.

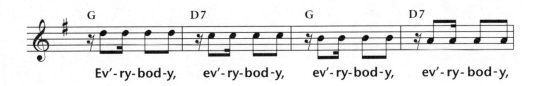

Ev'-ry-bod-y,   ev'-ry-bod-y,   ev'-ry-bod-y,   ev'-ry-bod-y,

Ev' - ry - bod - y   loves   Sat - ur - day   night._____

STEPS TO A NEW SOUND

Paris Opera House stairway

You have learned that a diatonic scale with *do* as its tonal center is a major scale. The word *scale* comes from the Italian word *scala,* which means "stairway."

G
do¹

F#
ti

E
la

D
so

C
fa

B
mi

A
re

G
do

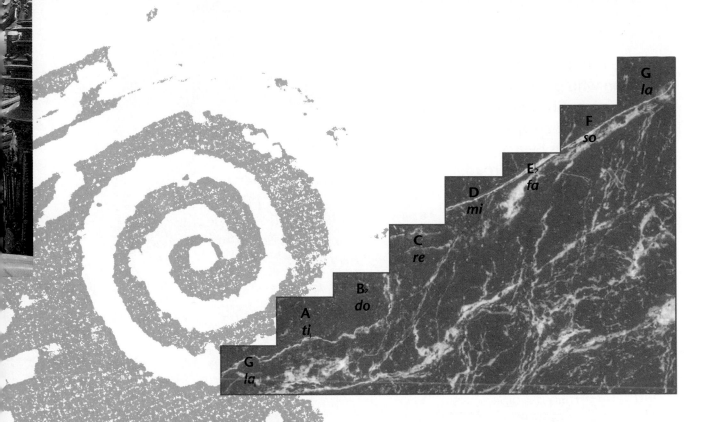

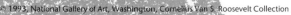

When the tonal center is changed to *la,* the scale sounds different and has a different name. A diatonic scale with *la* as its tonal center is called a **minor scale.**

RELATIVITY

Relativity is an optical illusion by M. C. Escher. Follow the flights of steps and notice what happens to them. Floors turn into walls and walls become floors.

"Harriet Tubman" is a song about an American who played an important role in history. She helped about 300 enslaved people escape to freedom in the mid-1800s by a route known as the Underground Railroad.

DECIDE if "Harriet Tubman" is in major or minor.

The Granger Collection

HARRIET TUBMAN

Moderate, With Rhythmic Drive

Words and Music by Walter Robinson

Gm

1. One night I dreamed— I was in slav - ery,
2. Hun - dreds of miles— we trav - elled on - ward,

'bout eigh - teen fif - ty was— the time;—
gath - er - ing slaves— from town— to town.—

Sor - row was the on - ly sign,—
Seek - ing ev' - ry lost— and found,—

noth - ing a - round— to ease— my mind.—
set - ting those free— that once— were bound.—

Out of the night— ap - peared a la - dy
Some - how my heart— was grow - ing weak - er,

Expressio

Music is a powerful way to express emotions and ideas. Movement can provide yet another way to express both words and music.

EXPRESS the drama of "Harriet Tubman" with gestures.

1. One night I dreamed

2. I was in slavery

5. nothing around to ease my mind.

6. Out of the night appeared a lady

3. 'bout eighteen fifty was the time;

4. Sorrow was the only sign,

7. leading a distant pilgrim band.

8. "First mate," she called, pointing her hand, "make room aboard for this young woman."

This song was written in the 1960s. What events or situations might have inspired Billy Taylor to write this song?

I Wish I Knew How It Would Feel To Be Free

Music by Billy Taylor
Words by Billy Taylor and Dick Dallas

Moderate Gospel Tempo

1. & 5. I wish I knew how—— it would feel—— to be free.—— I
2. I wish I could share—— all the love—— in my heart,—— Re-
3. I wish I could give—— all I'm long - ing to give.—— I
4. I wish I could be—— like a bird—— in the sky;—— How

wish I could break—— all these chains—— hold-ing me.—— I
move all the bars—— that still keep—— us a-part.—— I
wish I could live—— like I'm long - ing to live.—— I
sweet it would be—— if I found—— I could fly.—— I'd

wish I could say—— all the things—— I should say,—— Say 'em loud,-
wish you could know—— what it means—— to be me.—— Then you'd see-
wish I could do—— all the things—— I can do.—— Though I'm way-
soar to the sun—— and look down—— at the sea,—— then I'd sing,-

—— Say 'em clear,—— for the whole—— world to hear.——
—— and a - gree,—— ev' - ry - one—— should be free.——
—— o - ver - due,—— I'd be start - ing a - new.——
—— 'cause I'd know—— how it feels—— to be free.——

ASPIRATION

Aspiration, the title of Aaron Douglas's painting, means "a desire to reach a goal." What goals do you think the people in the painting are moving toward?

THINK IT THROUGH

If you wrote a song about freedom today, what freedoms would you write about?

Billy Taylor

FINLAND'S FREEDOM

SPOTLIGHT ON JEAN SIBELIUS

The melody for "Song of Peace" was written by Jean Sibelius (1865-1957), Finland's most famous composer. It wasn't until he was 15 that Sibelius began to take a serious interest in music. When he finally began his musical studies, he quickly became a very good violin player and even tried composing. When he was 20, he was sent to Helsinki to study law. Within the year, he decided that music was what he really wanted as his life's work.

Sibelius studied music in Berlin and Vienna for several years. When he returned to Finland in 1891, his love for his homeland led him to compose a piece for orchestra based on Finnish subjects. A work for orchestra that tells a story through music is called a **tone poem.**

Sibelius's music was so highly valued in Finland that when he was 32 years old, his government awarded him a yearly amount of money so that he could spend all of his time composing.

Finlandia
Op. 26, No. 7 (excerpt)
by Jean Sibelius

Finland is a small country, one of the farthest north in Europe. It has often been involved in struggles for its freedom. When Sibelius was growing up, Finland was ruled by Russia. Sibelius was one of many Finnish people who worked for independence from Russia.

Sibelius's music inspired the Finnish people. His famous tone poem Finlandia, *written in 1899, became the anthem for the Finnish independence movement. The Russian government would not allow it to be performed. In 1917, Finland finally gained its independence from Russia and* Finlandia *could be heard again.*

Ateneum, Helsinki/The Central Art Archives

THE FIGHTING CAPERCAILLIES

The Fighting Capercaillies by Ferdinand von Wright is a favorite painting in Finland. It shows a scene in a Finnish forest. It is early morning and the mist is rising above a lake and bog. Can you find the third bird?

LISTEN to *Finlandia.* **What qualities of this music might inspire you to love your country? Which parts of the music suggest a struggle? When do you hear the sound of hope for freedom?**

THEME

a a' b b'

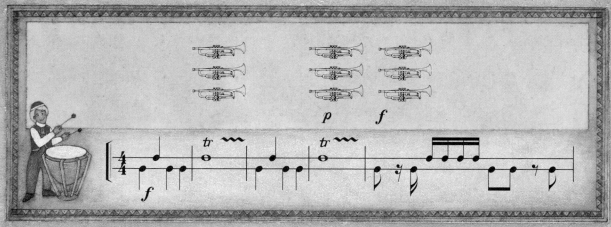

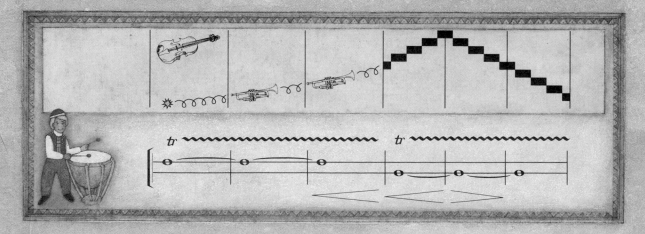

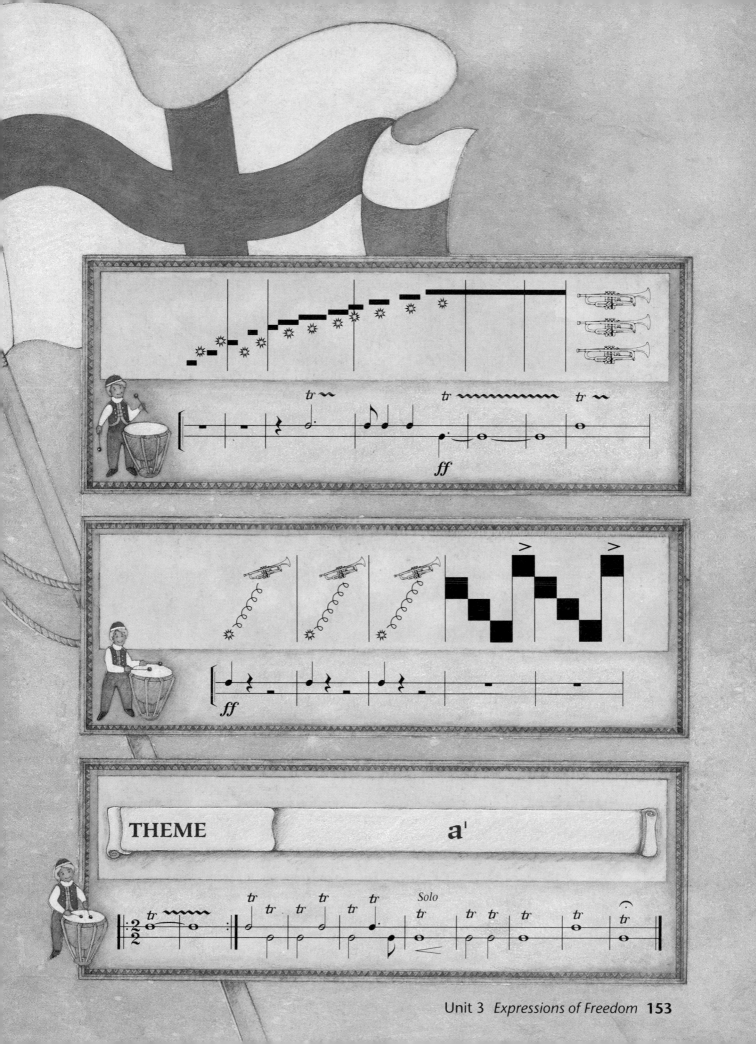

THEME a¹

LOOKING TOWARD FREEDOM

LISTENING

N'kosi Sikelel' i Afrika

by Enoch Sontonga (additional sections by SEK Mqhayi and others)

Africans brought by force to the United States by slave traders were not the only people who were not free. People from many parts of the world have suffered at the hands of other people. Black people in South Africa have lived under unfair authority of white people for many years.

In 1897, Enoch Sontonga composed "N'kosi Sikelel' i Afrika," also known as "Prayer for Africa." This song captured the hearts of black Africans. Soon schoolchildren and popular singing groups were singing this song in many parts of Africa.

The African National Congress adopted it as a closing anthem for its meetings. It is accepted today by many black Africans as their national anthem.

FOLLOW the words as you listen to "N'kosi Sikelel' i Afrika."

ZULU	ENGLISH
N'kosi sikelel' i Afrika,	Bless, oh Lord, our country Africa,
Maluphakanyisw' uphondo lwayo;	So that all may see her glory held high;
Yizwa imithandazo yethu.	Listen and protect us, be our guide.
N'kosi sikelela, N'kosi sikelela.	God bless, God bless.
(N'kosi sikelela, Thina lusapho lwayo.)	God bless, we her children.
Woza moya, Woza moya,	Spirit descend, Spirit descend,
Woza moya, oyingcwele.	Spirit descend, Spirit divine.
N'kosi sikelela, Thina lusapho lwayo.	God bless, we her children.

Think about how you treat others. How is the person in the poem being treated?

from Equality

You declare you see me dimly
through a glass which will not shine,
though I stand before you boldly,
trim in rank and marking time.

You do own to hear me faintly
as a whisper out of range,
while my drums beat out the message
and the rhythms never change.

Equality, and I will be free.
Equality, and I will be free.

—Maya Angelou

Above: Capetown, South Africa   *Right:* Masai women singing   *Borders:* Designs from Ndebele walls, Transvaal, South Africa

LISTENING

La golondrina *by Francisco Serradell*

In Mexico, a symbol of freedom is the swallow, la golondrina. This song often reminds people of their homeland. The singer feels like the homesick swallow but hasn't the freedom to fly back home as the bird does.

Think of your favorite memories of home as you listen to "La golondrina." What would you choose for a symbol of your hometown?

Many African American spirituals speak of going to heaven. For those who were enslaved, heaven was a symbol of a happy home where all would be free. "When the Saints Go Marching In" expresses this joyous view of heaven.

Moving On

When the Saints Go Marching In

African American Spirituals

SONGS OF FREEDOM

"Yankee Doodle" is more than just a silly song about a man with a feather in his cap. It was an important song in the American colonists' struggle to become free from England's rule. The British sang a version of it to make fun of the colonists' armies early in the Revolutionary War. The American patriots turned the song around and used it to unite themselves against the British. Sing this song and enjoy its catchy rhythms.

Freedom—could anyone doubt its importance to all of us? Enslaved people, torn from their homelands in Africa, knew how important freedom was. Many were willing to risk life itself to gain their freedom. Think about their journeys to freedom as you sing "Harriet Tubman." Listen to how the minor key helps to express the feeling of the words.

Joy can come with freedom. This joy is clearly expressed in the song "Everybody Rejoice." Sing "Everybody Rejoice" and notice that the major key supports the positive message of this song.

The hope of all is that peace will come with freedom. The melody of "Song of Peace" comes from the stirring tone poem *Finlandia* by Jean Sibelius, a work for orchestra that deals with love of country. Sing "Song of Peace" with the recording and listen to the soprano, alto, tenor, and bass voices as you sing.

People all over the world work in many ways for peace and freedom. Sing "Shabat Shalom," an Israeli song. The words mean "peaceful Sabbath."

CHECK IT OUT

1. What do you hear?

   a. changed   b. unchanged voices

2. What do you hear?

   a. changed   b. unchanged voices

3. What do you hear?

   a. changed   b. unchanged voices

4. Which of these is major?

   a. Example A   b. Example B   c. Example C

5. Which of these is minor?

   a. Example A   b. Example B   c. Example C

CREATE

Freedom Songs Interview

PLAN an interview on the topic of freedom songs. Work with a small group to develop questions for the interview and choose the person to be interviewed.

Tape the interview if possible. Record your subject's name, occupation, and national background. During the interview, ask your subject to sing a freedom song and tell something about the song.

PRESENT your findings to the class, using excerpts from the tape.

End your presentation by performing a freedom song selected by members of the group. Tell why the group chose the song.

Write

Which song or listening selection in this unit best agrees with your own idea of freedom? Write a letter to an imaginary friend sharing one of your ideas or opinions about freedom. Include a description of the music you chose and explain to your friend why this fits your idea of freedom.

FOLLOW THE DRINKIN' GOURD

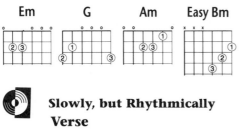

African American Spiritual
Adapted by Paul Campbell

Slowly, but Rhythmically
Verse

mp   Em

1. When the sun comes back and the first quail calls,_____
2. Now the riv-er bank-'ll make_____ a might-y good road;_____ The
3. Now the riv-er ends_____ be-tween two hills;_____

Am   Em

Fol-low_____   the Drink-in' Gourd._____ Then the
dead trees -   'll show you the way. And the
Fol-low_____   the Drink-in' Gourd._____ And_____

G   Em

Old Man is a-wait-in' for to car-ry you to
left_____ foot,_____ peg-foot,_____ trav-el-in'_____
there's an-oth-er riv-er on the oth-er_____

freedom,___ Follow the Drink - in' Gourd.
on; Just you fol - low the Drink - in' Gourd.
side, Just you fol - low the Drink - in' Gourd.

Refrain

Fol - low_____ the Drink - in' Gourd,___

Fol - low_____ the Drink - in' Gourd,___

For the Old Man is a - wait - in' for to

car - ry you to free - dom, Fol - low the Drink - in' Gourd.

ENCORE

HARRIET,
the Woman Called
MOSES

"This Train" and "Swing Low, Sweet Chariot" are African American spirituals that express the longing of enslaved Africans for freedom. One person who led many Africans to freedom was Harriet Tubman. Born in slavery in Maryland around 1820, she escaped to freedom in 1849. Soon afterwards, she worked with the Underground Railroad. This was a network of antislavery people in the United States that helped slaves to escape. At the risk of her own life, Tubman led more than 300 slaves to the North and to Canada.

LISTEN closely to the words of "Go Down, Moses."

GO DOWN, MOSES

Freely

African-American Spiritual

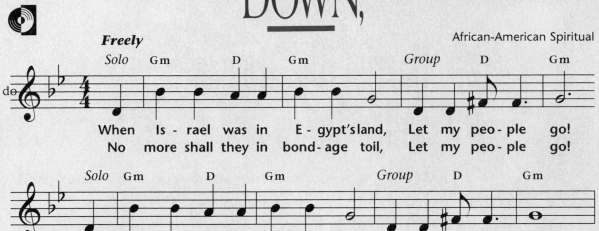

Solo · Gm · D · Gm · Group · D · Gm

When Is-rael was in E-gypt's land, Let my peo-ple go!
No more shall they in bond-age toil, Let my peo-ple go!

Solo · Gm · D · Gm · Group · D · Gm

Op-pressed so hard they could not stand, Let my peo-ple go!
Let them come out with E-gypt's spoil, Let my peo-ple go!

Gm · Cm · Gm

Go down, Mo-ses, 'way down in E-gypt's land.—

Gm · D · Gm

Tell old Phar-oah, to Let my peo-ple go!

The composer Thea Musgrave was inspired by the story of Harriet Tubman. She decided to write an opera about this courageous person. The opera is based on Tubman's life. By weaving spirituals such as "Go Down, Moses" and "Swing Low, Sweet Chariot" into the music, Musgrave established the atmosphere for the opera.

A scene from the opera Harriet, the Woman Called Moses.

LISTENING

Harriet, the Woman Called Moses (excerpts)

by Thea Musgrave

LISTEN to a section from the beginning of the opera.

Harriet, now free, is dreaming about her youth, when enslaved people were forbidden to sing spirituals. As she begins to sing "Go Down, Moses," her brother Benji begins to sing and play the drums. Notice how the composer combines her melodies and harmonies with the spiritual melody.

Why do you think the enslaved Africans were not allowed to sing "Go Down, Moses?"

A successful opera production combines the talents of many people—costume designers, stage set designers, musicians, conductors, and music coaches. The most important part, however, is the singing.

In an opera, there are usually several main characters with different types of voices.

COMPARE the vocal qualities of the singers as you listen.

Harriet mourns the death of her friend Josiah.

A special challenge for the composer of an opera is to give the singers magnificent music to show off their voices. Other challenges are to develop each character and to keep the story moving forward. This requires skill in writing a drama as well as in writing music. Often a composer will work with a **librettist,** a person who writes the **libretto,** or text, to an opera. Thea Musgrave, however, wrote both the music and the libretto for *Harriet, the Woman Called Moses.*

Meet THEA MUSGRAVE

Thea Musgrave was born in Scotland in 1928. As a child she always liked music. However, when she graduated from public school, she enrolled as a pre-medical student at the University of Edinburgh. After a brief period of pre-medical studies, Thea Musgrave knew she could not ignore her first love—music. Three years later, in 1950, she graduated with a music degree. Her decision was wise. Her compositions have received great praise for their dramatic quality and different styles. In addition to composing, Thea Musgrave has conducted a number of her own works. She has received many awards in recognition of her work.

LISTEN to Thea Musgrave talk about her experiences of composing *Harriet, the Woman Called Moses.*

SEA TO SHINING SEA

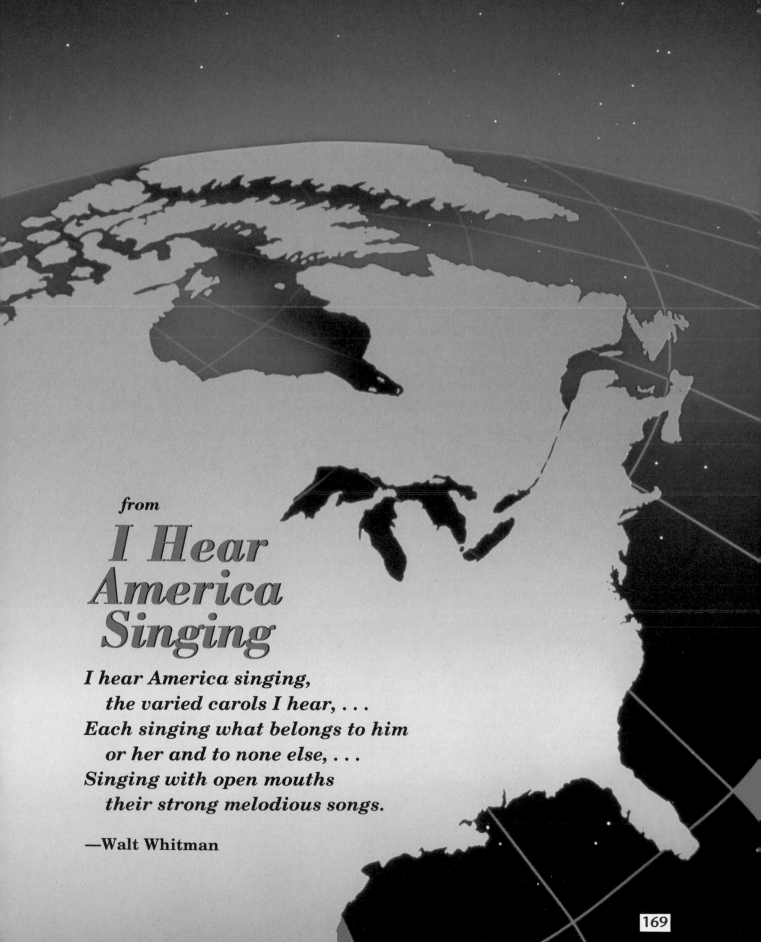

from

I Hear America Singing

I hear America singing,
* the varied carols I hear, . . .*
Each singing what belongs to him
* or her and to none else, . . .*
Singing with open mouths
* their strong melodious songs.*

—Walt Whitman

The United States of America is full of variety. The land changes from flat plains and gentle hills to towering mountains. People from all over the world have made their homes there—in cities, towns, and rural areas. Together they have created some wonderful things.

NAME some of the special things in the United States that make you proud and that you want to protect.

God Bless the U.S.A.

Words and Music by Lee Greenwood

Verse

From the lakes of Min-ne-so-ta, to the hills of Ten-nes-see,___

a-cross the plains of Tex-as, from sea to shin-ing sea.___

From De-troit down to Hous-ton, and New York to L. A.

Well, there's pride in ev'-ry A-mer-i-can heart, and it's

time to stand and say___ That I'm

Refrain

proud   to be an A-mer-i-can___ where at   least I know I'm free.

And   I   won't for-get the men who died, who   gave that right to me.

And I'd glad-ly   stand up,   next to you___ and de-fend her still to-day.

'Cause there ain't no doubt I love this land.___ God bless the U. S. A.

TRAVELING THROUGH

In 1893 Katharine Lee Bates traveled to the top of Pikes Peak in Colorado. As she viewed "the purple mountain's majesty above the fruited plain," she was inspired to write the poem "America, the Beautiful." Later her words were added to a melody composed by Samuel Ward.

SING "America, the Beautiful" and imagine yourself looking at your country from a mountaintop or from space.

Music by Samuel Ward
Words by Katharine Lee Bates

1. O beau - ti - ful for spa - cious skies, for am - ber waves of grain.
2. O beau - ti - ful for pil - grim feet, whose stern im - pass - ioned stress
3. O beau - ti - ful for he - roes proved in lib - er - at - ing strife,
4. O beau - ti - ful for pa - triot dream that sees be - yond the years,

For pur - ple moun - tain maj - es - ties a - bove the fruit - ed plain.
A thor - ough - fare for free - dom beat a - cross the wil - der - ness.
Who more than self their coun - try loved, and mer - cy more than life.
Thine al - a - bas - ter cit - ies gleam un - dim'd by hu - man tears.

172

A - mer - i - ca! A - mer - i - ca! God shed His grace on thee,
A - mer - i - ca! A - mer - i - ca! God mend thine ev' - ry flaw,
A - mer - i - ca! A - mer - i - ca! May God thy gold re - fine,
A - mer - i - ca! A - mer - i - ca! God shed His grace on thee,

And crown thy good with broth - er - hood, from sea to shin - ing sea.
Con - firm thy soul in self - con - trol, Thy lib - er - ty in law.
Till all suc - cess be no - ble - ness, and ev' - ry gain di - vine.
And crown thy good with broth - er - hood, from sea to shin - ing sea.

THE UPS AND DOWNS OF METER

FIND the meter signature in "America, the Beautiful."

Different meters have different patterns of stressed and un-stressed beats. In $\frac{4}{4}$ meter, there is a pattern of one strong beat followed by three weak beats. Bar lines show where these patterns begin and end.

Music can begin with an **upbeat,** or incomplete measure. The upbeat includes one or more notes that occur on a weak beat. The upbeat leads to the **downbeat,** or strong beat. An upbeat can occur in several places in a song. A phrase may start on an upbeat or a downbeat.

FIND each upbeat in "America, the Beautiful."

You may have traveled by bicycle, car, truck, bus, or plane, but have you traveled by song? Many songwriters have made this kind of "travel" possible. In his song "Something to Sing About," Oscar Brand refers to favorite places throughout the United States.

Something To Sing About

Words and Music by Oscar Brand

1. I have wan-dered my way through the won-ders of New York Bay,
2. I have wel-comed the dawn to the high-land of Or-e-gon,

North to Ni-ag-'ra to hear the falls roar,
Seen the moon light up the soft south-ern dew,

Seen the waves tear in vain at the rock-cov-ered coast of Maine,
Where the sweet eve-ning breeze kissed the leaves of the lem-on trees,

Watched them roll back from the New Eng-land shore.
Whis-p'ring the song that I'm shar-ing with you.

Refrain

From the fair Ha-wai-ian is-lands to the Rock-y Moun-tain high-lands,

'Cross the prair-ies, the plains, to the might-y east-ern towers,

From A-las-ka to the great South-west, North to New Eng-land's crest,

Some-thing to sing a-bout, this land of ours.____

3. Yes, we've something to sing about, tune up a string about,
   Call out the chorus, or quietly hum,
   Of a land that's still young, with a ballad that's still unsung,
   Telling the promise of great things to come.

FIND the meter signature and tell what it means. How many phrases start with an upbeat?

THINK IT THROUGH

Have you been to any of the places mentioned in "Something to Sing About"? What places would you include if you wrote a song about your country?

WRITE your own verse for "Something to Sing About."

How would you like to travel by barge? The Erie Canal was built in the early 1800s to transport people and goods between Albany and Buffalo, New York. The canal linked the Hudson River with the Great Lakes. In those days, flat-bottomed boats called barges were towed by mules who walked beside the canal. "Erie Canal" is a song the mule drivers sang.

A **fermata** (⌢) means that the note or rest under it should be held longer than its normal value. Pause on that note or rest before going on.

View on a Canal, 19th-century woodcut

FIND the fermatas in "Erie Canal."

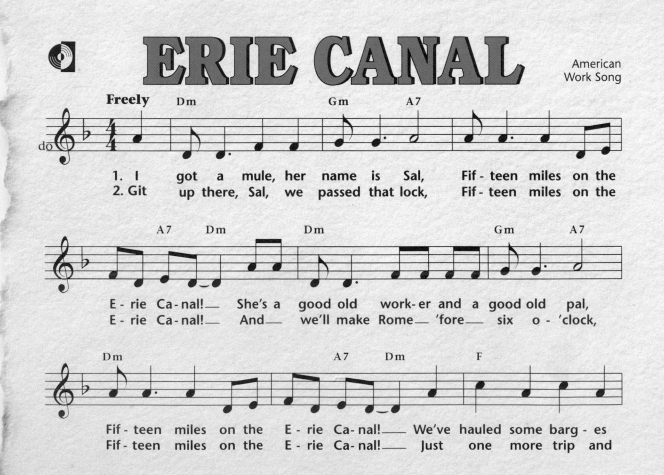

ERIE CANAL

American Work Song

Freely

1. I got a mule, her name is Sal, Fif-teen miles on the
2. Git up there, Sal, we passed that lock, Fif-teen miles on the

E - rie Ca-nal!__ She's a good old work-er and a good old pal,
E - rie Ca-nal!__ And__ we'll make Rome__ 'fore__ six o-'clock,

Fif - teen miles on the E - rie Ca-nal!__ We've hauled some barg-es
Fif - teen miles on the E - rie Ca-nal!__ Just one more trip and

in our day,   Filled with lum-ber, coal and hay,   And   we know ev'-ry

back we'll go,   Through the rain and sleet and snow, 'Cause   we know ev'-ry

inch of the way From Al-ba-ny____ to____ Buf - fa-lo.____

inch of the way From Al-ba-ny____ to____ Buf - fa-lo.____

Refrain

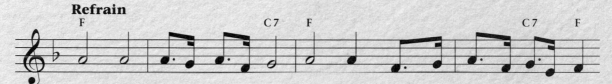

Low bridge, ev'-ry-bod-y down, Low bridge, 'cause we're com-ing to a town;

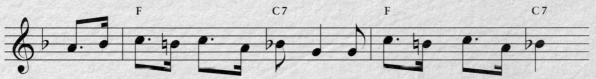

And you'll al-ways know your neigh-bor, You'll al-ways know your pal,

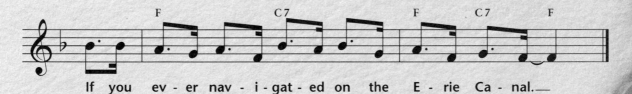

If you   ev-er nav-i-gat-ed on the   E-rie Ca-nal.____

Junction of the Erie & Northern Canals by John William Hill

TRAVELING WITH MUSIC

A Sunday Excursion on the Ohio River, engraving, 1881

If you had lived during the 1800s, you might have traveled by steamboat or barge down the Ohio River from Pennsylvania all the way to Illinois. During your trip, you might have danced to a rollicking tune like "Down the River."

DOWN THE RIVER

American River Chantey

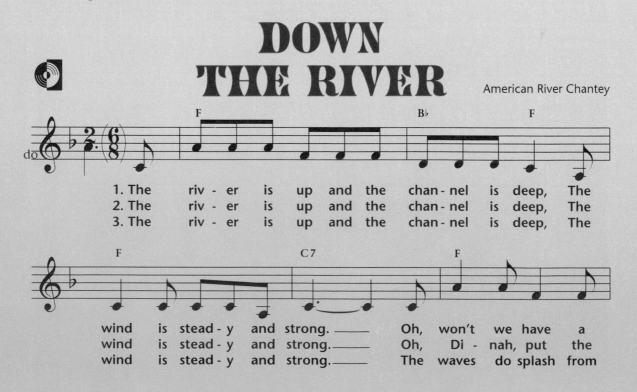

1. The riv-er is up and the chan-nel is deep, The wind is stead-y and strong. _____ Oh, won't we have a
2. The riv-er is up and the chan-nel is deep, The wind is stead-y and strong. _____ Oh, Di-nah, put the
3. The riv-er is up and the chan-nel is deep, The wind is stead-y and strong. _____ The waves do splash from

178

jol - ly good time, As we go sail - ing a - long.
hoe - cake on, As we go sail - ing a - long.
shore —— to shore, As we go sail - ing a - long.

Refrain
Descant
Melody
Down the riv - er, Oh, down the riv - er, Oh,

down the riv - er we go. ————

Down the riv - er, Oh, down the riv - er, Oh,

down the O - hi - o! ————

A **flat** (♭) placed on a note lowers its pitch a half step. A **half step** is the smallest distance between pitches in most music. A flat placed before a note is called an **accidental**. When a flat is placed at the beginning of each staff it is called a **key signature**. This means the flat is in effect throughout the piece of music.

FIND the flat in the key signature of "Down the River."

FOLLOW the pitches of the scale used in "Down the River" on the keyboard as you listen to the scale again.

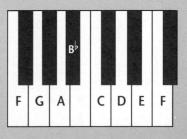

River travel may have been an important means of transportation in the past, but today people are more likely to travel by car or van. You can gather your friends or family, put on a cassette or CD, and you're ready to travel with music.

SING this country music by Willie Nelson.

On the Road Again

Words and
Music by Willie Nelson

1., 3. On the road a-gain._____ Just can't
(2.) road a-gain._____ Go - in'

wait to get on the road a-gain._____ The life I
pla - ces that I've nev - er been._____ See - in'

love is mak-ing mu-sic with my friends, and I can't wait to get
things that I may nev - er see a - gain, and I can't wait to get

on the road__ a - gain.____ 2. On the
on the road__ a - gain.____

On the road a-gain,____

On the road, Like a band of gyp-sies

We're the best of friends,

we go down the high-way._____   On the

road,   In - sist - ing that the   world keep turn - ing   our way,_____

D.S. al Fine
(Go to 𝄉 then to the End)

_____   and   our   way,_____   Is   on   the

Just as the flat (♭) placed on a note lowers its pitch a half step, the **sharp** (♯) raises a pitch a half step. A sharp can be used as an accidental or in a key signature. The key signature of "On the Road Again" has two sharps. The key signature is a written reminder that sharps or flats are needed. A **natural** (♮) is used to cancel a sharp or flat.

FOLLOW the pitches on the keyboard below as you listen to the scale used in "On the Road Again."

D E F# G A B C# D

MOVING ALONG BY STEPS

The major scale is made up of pitches that are a whole step or a half step apart. A half step is the smallest distance between pitches in most music. A **whole step** is twice that distance. Listen to the difference between a whole step and a half step.

Here are two melodic patterns from "Something to Sing About" that use pitches of the C major scale.

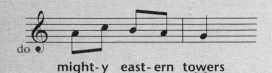

might-y east-ern towers

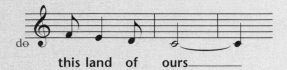

this land of ours_____

SING the melodic patterns with words, with pitch letter names, and with pitch syllables. Then sing the C major scale.

C	D	E	F	G	A	B	C
do	*re*	*mi*	*fa*	*so*	*la*	*ti*	*do'*

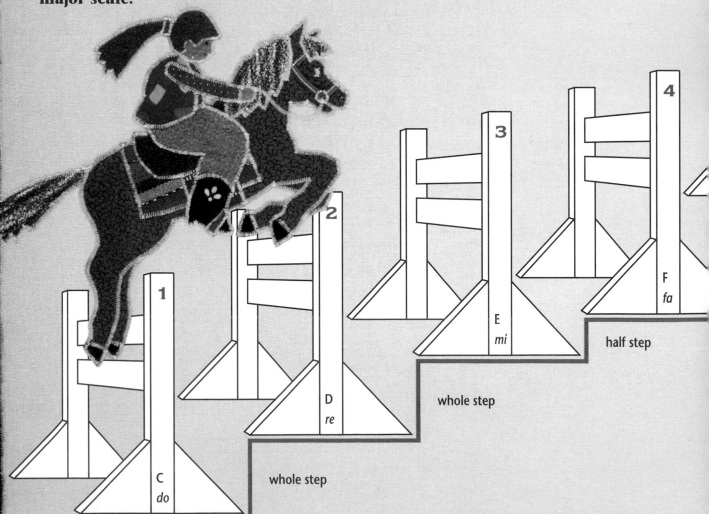

In the major scale, the half steps are between the third and fourth pitches and the seventh and eighth pitches. All the other steps are whole steps.

IDENTIFY the letter names of the pitches that are a whole step apart in the major scale below. Then identify the letter names of the pitches that are a half step apart.

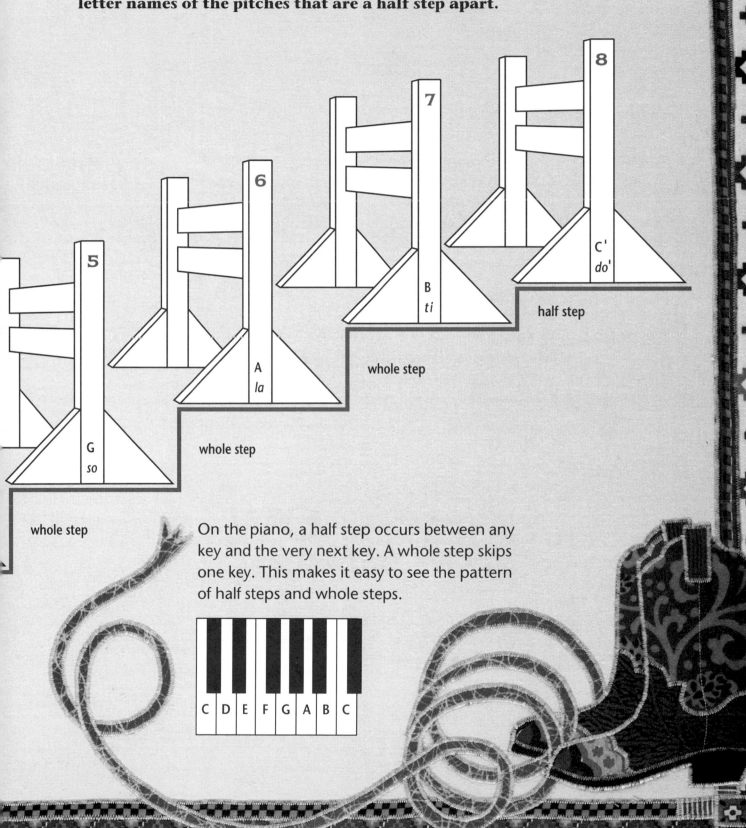

On the piano, a half step occurs between any key and the very next key. A whole step skips one key. This makes it easy to see the pattern of half steps and whole steps.

MOVING THROUGH THE SOUTHLAND

The Ohio River joins the Mississippi River, which flows all the way to New Orleans. "Swing Low, Sweet Chariot" comes from the southern part of our country. It is in **verse-refrain** form. The words to the verse change. The refrain is the part of the song that stays the same.

Find the repeated words in "Swing Low, Sweet Chariot." These words are part of a style called **call and response.** The call is often a solo and the response is sung by a group. The response usually is a repeated phrase.

SWING LOW, SWEET CHARIOT

African American Spiritual

Swing low, sweet char - i - ot,— Com-in' for to car-ry me home,

Swing— low, sweet char - i - ot,— Com-in' for to car-ry me home.

184

Verse

Leader

G   C   D 7

1. I   look'd   o - ver   Jor - dan   an'   what   did   I   see,____
2. If   you   get_____   there_____   be - fore   I_____   do,____
3. I'm   some - times_____   up_____   and some - times_____   down,____ }

Group
G   D 7   *Leader*   G

Com- in'   for   to   car - ry   me   home, { A   band____   of   an - gels
                                              Tell   all____   my   friends I'm
                                              But   still____   my   soul   feels

C   D 7   *Group*   G   D 7   G *D.C. al Fine*

com- in'   af - ter   me,____
com- in' there__   too,____ } Com- in'   for   to   car - ry   me   home.
heav'n - ly__   bound,____

The phrase *comin' for to carry me home* is a repeated musical motive. Make an upward arc with your arm as a "movement motive"
on the words *comin' for to carry me home* in the refrain. Change
the way you do the movement each time by choosing a different
arm, level, or facing.

SING Verse 1 of "When the Saints Go Marching In"
as a partner song with the refrain of "Swing Low,
Sweet Chariot."

A MUSICAL MELTING POT

The Mississippi River flows south to Louisiana. There you might hear **zydeco,** a kind of dance music. Zydeco is a mixture of jazz and blues with Creole music, style, and language. "Et tan' patate là cuite" is in Creole, a language that has French roots.

The accordion, washboard, and fiddle were important in early zydeco music, but today the players may use saxophone, electric guitar, and drums also.

Zydeco band

LISTEN to the zydeco style in "Et tan' patate là cuite" and identify the instruments you hear and recognize.

Sing this traditional Creole song.

CREATE your own dance, following the form of the music.

ET TAN' PATATE LÀ CUITE
POTATO'S DONE

Traditional French Creole Song
English Version by MMH

Lively, With a Solid Beat

Creole: Et tan' pa - tate là cuite, na - nan nan - li na - nan nan - li.
Pronunciation: e tã pa tat la küit na nã nã li na nã nã li
English: Po - ta - to's done, it's time to eat it, time to eat it now!

Et tan' pa - tate là cuite, na - nan nan - li na - nan nan - li.
e tã pa tat la küit na nã nã li na nã nã li
Po - ta - to's done, it's time to eat it, time to eat it now!

Even though "Et tan' patate là cuite" and "Swing Low, Sweet Chariot" are very different in style, they have something in common. Each song has two contrasting sections.

DESCRIBE the forms of "Swing Low, Sweet Chariot" and "Et tan' patate là cuite."

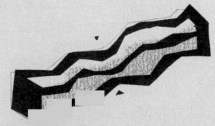

You Can't Go Far
WITHOUT METER

Traveling west from New Orleans, you would soon hit Texas. At one time, Texas belonged to Mexico. Some think the composer of "The Yellow Rose of Texas" was a volunteer in the Texan war for independence.

SING this famous Texas song and imagine the excitement you would feel if you returned to your home and family after being gone for a long time.

Music Adapted by Jay Arnold
Words Adapted by
Jay Arnold and Marilyn Davidson

1. There's a Yel-low Rose in Tex-as I'm go-ing home to see.
2. Where the Ri-o Grande is flow-ing, and stars are shin-ing bright,
3. Now I'm go-ing back to find her, my heart is full of woe.

   I miss that lit-tle la-dy, I'm sure she miss-es me.
We walked a-long the riv-er one qui-et sum-mer night.
We'll sing the songs to-geth-er we sang so long a-go.

188

She   cried so when I   left her,   it   al-most broke my heart;
I   know that she re - mem-bers   our   part-ing long   a - go.
I'll   pick the ban-jo   gai-ly,   just   like I   did be-fore.

And   ver - y   soon we'll meet a - gain   and nev - er,   nev - er   part.
I   prom-ised to   re-turn to her   and nev - er   let   her go.
The   Yel - low Rose of   Tex-as shall   be mine for-ev - er-more.

Refrain

She's the sweet-est lit - tle   la-dy   that   Tex - as   ev - er   knew.

Her   eyes are bright as   dia-monds; they spar-kle like   the dew.

You may find   a   lot   of   pret-ty girls wher - ev - er you   may be,

But the Yel - low Rose of   Tex-as   is   the on - ly one   for me.

What is the meter signature of "The Yellow Rose of Texas"?
Explain what the meter signature tells you.

BE A METER READER

In $\frac{2}{4}$ ($\frac{2}{\downarrow}$) meter, the quarter note (♩) stands for one beat. Each measure has two beats. The quarter note can be divided into two eighth notes. ♩ = ♫ or ♪ ♪

In $\frac{6}{8}$ ($\frac{2}{\downarrow.}$) meter, the dotted quarter note (♩.) lasts for one beat. Each measure has two beats. The dotted quarter note can be divided into three eighth notes. ♩. = ♫♪ or ♪ ♪ ♪ There are six eighth notes in a measure.

PERFORM rhythm patterns in $\frac{2}{4}$ and $\frac{6}{8}$.

In the 1800s, a railroad was built that went from coast to coast across the United States. Many immigrants from Europe and China helped to build this and other railroads. The photograph shows the celebration that took place at Promontory Point, Utah, when the railroad was completed.

SAY and clap these $\frac{6}{8}$ patterns. Find the same rhythm sequence in "Pat Works on the Railway."

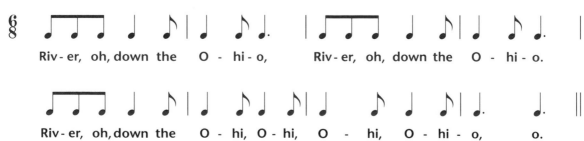

Riv- er, oh, down the O - hi - o, Riv- er, oh, down the O - hi - o.

Riv- er, oh, down the O - hi, O - hi, O - hi, O - hi - o, o.

This song is about one of the Irish railway workers.

PAT WORKS ON THE RAILWAY

American Railroad Song

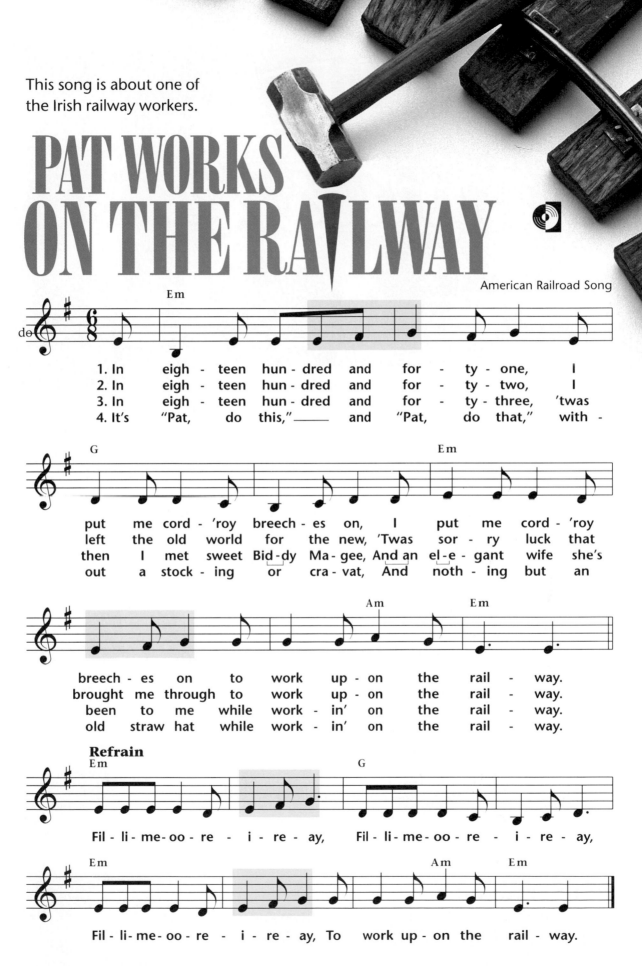

1. In eigh - teen hun - dred and for - ty - one, I
2. In eigh - teen hun - dred and for - ty - two, I
3. In eigh - teen hun - dred and for - ty - three, 'twas
4. It's "Pat, do this," ——— and "Pat, do that," with -

put me cord - 'roy breech - es on, I put me cord - 'roy
left the old world for the new, 'Twas sor - ry luck that
then I met sweet Bid - dy Ma - gee, And an el - e - gant wife she's
out a stock - ing or cra - vat, And noth - ing but an

breech - es on to work up - on the rail - way.
brought me through to work up - on the rail - way.
been to me while work - in' on the rail - way.
old straw hat while work - in' on the rail - way.

Refrain

Fil - li - me - oo - re - i - re - ay, Fil - li - me - oo - re - i - re - ay,

Fil - li - me - oo - re - i - re - ay, To work up - on the rail - way.

WESTWARD BOUND ON A TRAIL OF music

Songs about America, work songs, songs for entertainment, and songs which express feelings—your musical journey has included all of these and more. Just as the world is filled with many different people, there are many different kinds of songs, each one with a special meaning for its time and place.

LISTEN to beginnings of songs you have learned and tell the name of each one. Find their locations on the map.

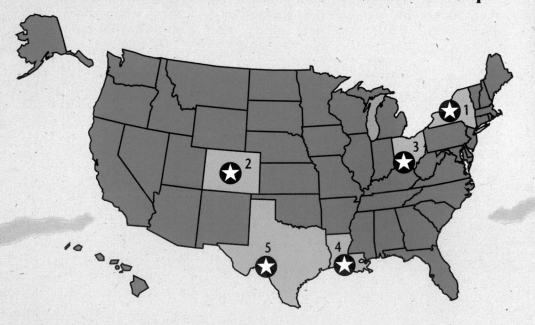

THINK IT THROUGH

"Erie Canal" and "Pat Works on the Railway" are both work songs. How are they alike? How are they different?

MIND YOUR MINOR

You probably realized the first time you heard "Pat Works on the Railway" that it has a minor sound. What makes music sound minor? It's because the melody is based on pitches in the minor scale and the tonal center is *la*. Just as you learned the arrangement of half steps and whole steps for the major scale, you can learn a different arrangement for the minor scale.

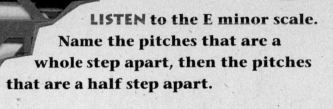

LISTEN to the E minor scale. Name the pitches that are a whole step apart, then the pitches that are a half step apart.

E *la* — whole
D *so* — whole
C *fa* — half
B *mi* — whole
A *re* — whole
G *do* — half
F♯ *ti₁* — whole
E *la₁*

FOLLOW the pattern of half steps and whole steps on the piano keyboard.

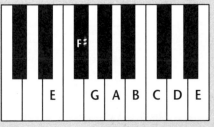

¡HOLA, AMIGO!

Throughout the Southwest, Spanish is often spoken and Spanish songs such as "Campanas vespertinas" are sung with beautiful harmony.

Before the wristwatch was invented, people often depended on the sound of church bells to tell the time of day. The sound of large bells can be heard from quite a distance.

LISTEN for the contrast between unison and two-part singing in this song about bells.

CAMPANAS VESPERTINAS
EVENING BELLS

Music by Julio Z. Guerra
Words by Juana Guglielmi
English Words by MMH

Andante

Spanish: Las cam - pa - nas de la_i - gle - sia dan el to - que de_o - ra - ción
Pronunciation: las kam pa nas de la i gle sya dan el to ke ðeo ɾa syon
English: Hear the ring - ing of the church- bells, hear them call - ing, hear the sound.

Y la luz del sol que mue - re a_o-tro mun - do_i - rá a-lum-brar.
i la lus ðel sol ke mwe ɾe ao tɾo mun doi ɾaa lum bɾaɾ.
See the sun - light slow-ly dy - ing, as the eve - ning comes a-round.

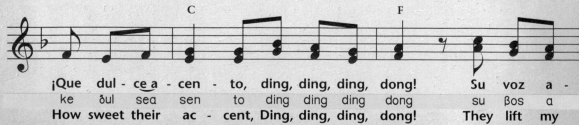

¡Que dul - ce_a - cen - to, ding, ding, ding, dong! Su voz a -
ke ðul sea sen to ding ding ding dong su ßos a
How sweet their ac - cent, Ding, ding, ding, dong! They lift my

le - gra mi co - ra - zón. ¡Ding ding ding dong!
le gɾa mi ko ɾa son ding ding ding dong
heart with their e - ven - song. Ding ding ding dong!

le - gra mi co - ra - zón. ¡Ding ding ding
le gɾa mi ko ɾa son ding ding ding
heart with their e - ven - song. Ding ding ding

Su voz a - le - gra mi co - ra - zón.
su βos a le gɾa mi ko ɾa son.
They lift my heart With their e - ven - song.

dong! Ay, mi co - ra - zón.
dong ai mi ko ɾa son.
dong! With their e - ven - song.

Taos Pueblo, New Mexico

A MUSICAL GAME FROM THE PLAINS

Eka Muda **Comanche Hand-Game Song**

Native Americans knew how beautiful this land was long before it was called America. The many Native American nations stretch "from sea to shining sea." Each has its own culture, language, and customs.

"Eka Muda" has been a popular hand-game song of the Comanches for many years. The game is played by people of all ages. In the Comanche language, eka muda means "You're no smarter than a red mule." The words are sung to tease members of the other team as the hand game is played.

LISTEN to "Eka Muda" as it is sung in the traditional style of the Plains Indians. Describe the vocal quality, mood, and instruments used in the accompaniment.

LISTEN to the song sung by students. Find the places where the voices slide up to the pitch (⌣).

196

EKA MUDA

Comanche: E - ka mu - da,⎯ E - ka mu - da,⎯ He hai - ya
Pronunciation: e ka mu da e ka mu da he hai ya

E - ka mu - da, He hai - ya E - ka mu - da.
e ka mu da he hai ya e ka mu da

A COMANCHE VILLAGE

A Comanche Village shows Comanche women curing buffalo hides. Buffalo skins were used for many purposes, including clothing and tepees, until the buffalo became scarce. George Catlin, the artist, spent several summers in the 1830s among various Indian groups.

Hide painted by Comanche women
Sioux beaded ball and doll

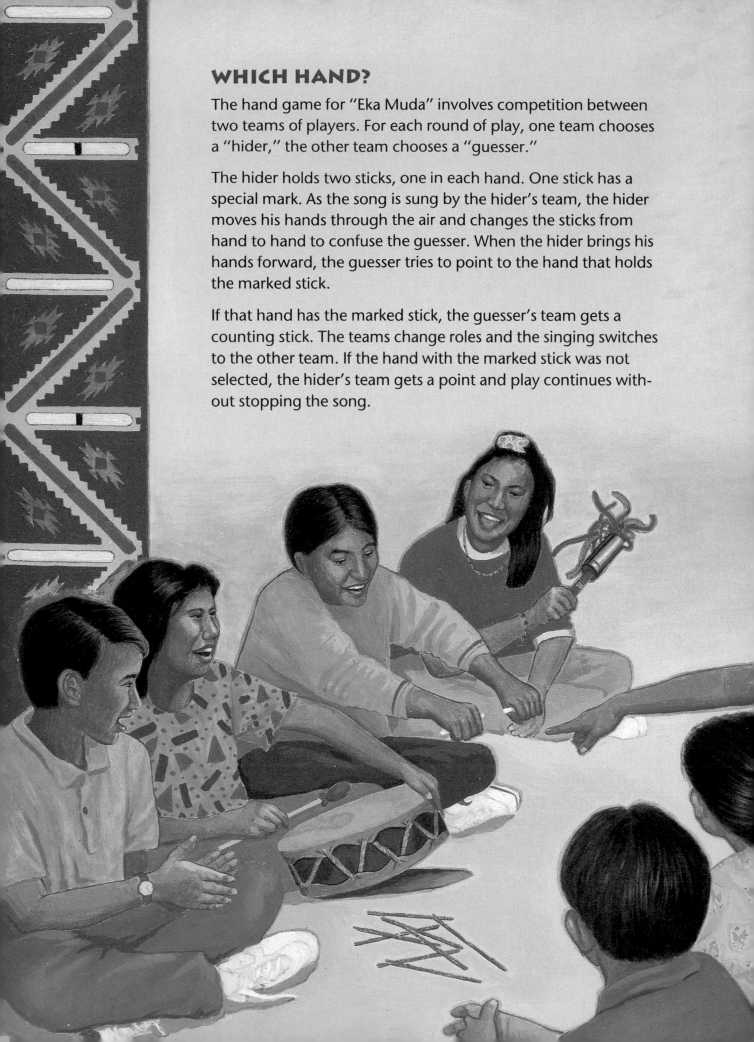

WHICH HAND?

The hand game for "Eka Muda" involves competition between two teams of players. For each round of play, one team chooses a "hider," the other team chooses a "guesser."

The hider holds two sticks, one in each hand. One stick has a special mark. As the song is sung by the hider's team, the hider moves his hands through the air and changes the sticks from hand to hand to confuse the guesser. When the hider brings his hands forward, the guesser tries to point to the hand that holds the marked stick.

If that hand has the marked stick, the guesser's team gets a counting stick. The teams change roles and the singing switches to the other team. If the hand with the marked stick was not selected, the hider's team gets a point and play continues without out stopping the song.

Potawatomi hand drum, ca. 1875-1900
Fox tortoise-shell rattle, ca. 1920

Philbrook Museum of Art, Tulsa, Oklahoma

WINTER GAMES OF THE CHEYENNE

Winter Games of the Cheyenne by Dick West (Wah-pah-nah-yah) shows many Native American games. Find the people playing a stone-tossing game and "stick in the hoop." There is also wrestling, kickball, "snow snake" javelin throwing, tobogganing, and a game of "shinny."

"In New Mexico the land is made of many colors. When I was a boy I rode over the red and yellow and purple earth to the West Jemez Pueblo. My horse was a small red roan, fast and easy-riding. I rode among the dunes, along the bases of mesas and cliffs, into canyons and arroyos. I came to know that country, not in the way a traveler knows the landmarks he sees in the distance, but more truly and intimately, in every season, from a thousand points of view. I know the living motion of a horse and the sound of hooves. I know what it is, on a hot day in August or September, to ride into a bank of cold, fresh rain."

—from The Way to Rainy Mountain
by N. Scott Momaday, Kiowa

On the Trail
from *Grand Canyon Suite*
by Ferde Grofé

Just as Pikes Peak inspired Katharine Lee Bates to write the poem "America, the Beautiful," the Grand Canyon has inspired many others to create works of art, poetry, and music.

One composer who was inspired by the Grand Canyon was Ferde Grofé. Each movement of his *Grand Canyon Suite* tells a story: "Sunrise," "Painted Desert," "On the Trail," "Sunset," and "Cloudburst."

In "On the Trail," Grofé creates a musical image of the trip down into the canyon on the back of a mule. You can almost hear the sound of hooves on the stone and feel the rocking motion of the ride.

This type of story-telling or image-making music is called **program music.** Can you name another example of program music that you heard earlier this year?

GETTING TO THE

PAT the rhythm of Theme 1 in "On the Trail" with alternating hands.

Theme 1

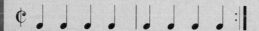

To accompany Theme 1, Grofé used a steady "clip-clop" played on coconut shells. This part is written in **cut time** (¢ or ²⁄₂). In cut time, the half note gets one beat. There are two beats in a measure.

CLAP the clip-clop part with Theme 1 as you listen to these parts.

TRACE the melody of Theme 2 as you listen.

Theme 2

LISTENING MAP *Listen for the two themes in "On the Trail" as you follow the map.*

Listening Map concept by Kay Greenhaw

PUT YOUR SKILLS TO WORK

Clap the patterns below to check your reading skill.

CREATE an accompaniment for "Et tan' patate là cuite" or "Pat Works on the Railway" using rhythm patterns in $\frac{2}{4}$ or $\frac{6}{8}$. Work in a group to choose the song and create an eight-beat pattern in the meter of the song. How many patterns are needed to fit the form of the song?

CHOOSE percussion instruments and play your accompaniment as you sing the song.

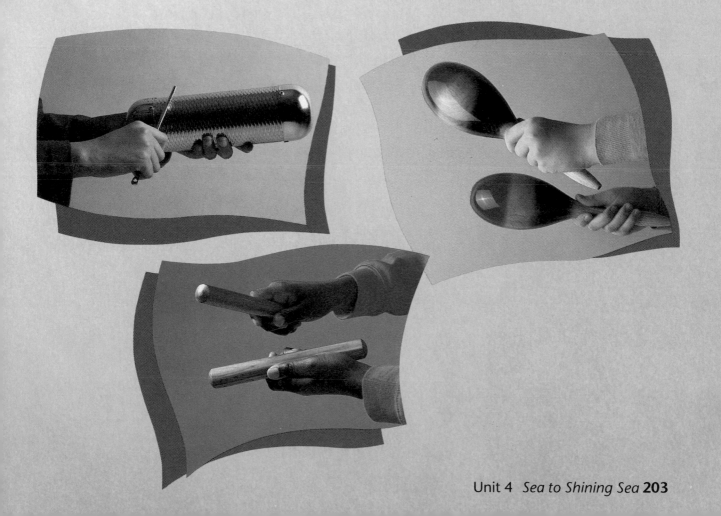

Journey's End

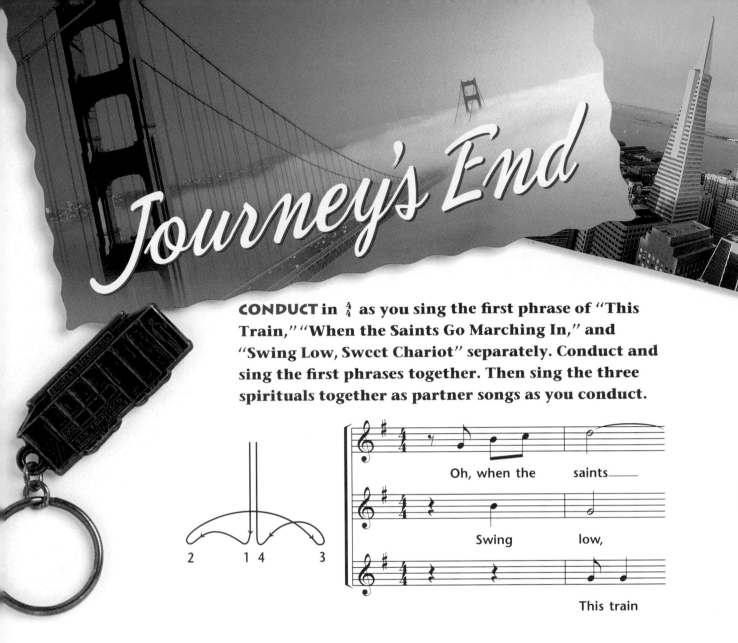

CONDUCT in $\frac{4}{4}$ as you sing the first phrase of "This Train," "When the Saints Go Marching In," and "Swing Low, Sweet Chariot" separately. Conduct and sing the first phrases together. Then sing the three spirituals together as partner songs as you conduct.

Oh, when the saints

Swing low,

This train

California, here we come! Our destination is San Francisco, home of the Golden Gate Bridge. This city has inspired many songwriters.

San Francisco

Music by Bronislaw Kaper
and Walter Jurmann
Words by Gus Kahn

Moderato

San Fran - cis - co, o - pen your gold - en gate.

You let no stran - ger wait out - side your door.

San Fran - cis - co, here is your wan - dering one

Say - ing, "I'll wan - der no more."

Oth - er plac - es on - ly make me love you best.

Tell me you're the heart of all the gold - en west.

2nd time ritard

San Fran - cis - co, wel - come me home a - gain.

2nd time molto rit.

I'm com - ing home to go roam - ing no more. more.

FIND the meter signature in "San Francisco" and explain the meter to a friend.

CONDUCT in cut time as you sing "San Francisco."

1 2

Visit San Francisco

SAN FRANCISCO

ALOHA!

When Katharine Lee Bates wrote her famous poem "America, the Beautiful," our country was the land from the Atlantic Ocean to the Pacific Ocean—"from sea to shining sea." That changed in 1959, when Hawaii became our fiftieth state.

Your musical journey would not be complete without a song from Hawaii, where ocean fishing is popular. A *hukilau* is a fish feast. The people of a village catch a hundred or so fish in a huge circular net, then cook and eat them.

The Hukilau Song

Words and Music by
Jack Owens

Eng./Hawaiian: Oh, we're go - in' to the hu - ki - lau,
Pronunciation: hu ki lau

hu - ki, hu - ki, hu - ki, hu - ki, hu - ki, hu - ki - lau,
hu ki hu ki hu ki hu ki hu ki hu ki lau

Ev' - ry - bod - y loves the hu - ki - lau,
hu ki lau

where the lau - lau is the kau - kau at the hu - ki - lau.
lau lau kau kau hu ki lau

Oh, we throw the net out in - to the sea,____

and all the a - ma a - ma come a - swim-min' to me.____
a ma a ma

Oh, we're go - in' to the hu - ki - lau,
hu ki lau

hu - ki, hu - ki, hu - ki, hu - ki, hu - ki - lau.
hu ki hu ki hu ki hu ki hu ki lau

As I Row

As I row over the plain
Of the sea and gaze
Into the distance, the waves
Merge with the bright sky.

—Fujiwara No Tadamichi

ACROSS THE COUNTRY IN SONG

The United States of America *from California to the New York island, from sea to shining sea*—this is a great land with great people. Sing "Something to Sing About" and recall all the places you sang about in Unit 4.

In the early days of the United States, the waterways were our lifelines. Sing "The Erie Canal," and imagine that you are making the long trip from Albany to Buffalo by barge.

Probably the most important river to the new nation was the Mississippi with its tributaries such as the Ohio. Boats of all shapes and sizes still go "Down the River."

Each state has its own history and traditions. When you travel across Texas, you can get a sense of how large our country is. Sing "The Yellow Rose of Texas" as you imagine traveling across Texas on horseback at the time this song was written.

People have come from all over the world to make new homes in the United States. In the mid-1800s, people came from Europe as well as from Asia to help build the Transcontinental Railway. Sing "Pat Works on the Railway," a song that tells the story of railway workers from Ireland.

The personality of different parts of the country comes from the people who lived there in the past as well as from the people who live there today. The Southwest has a Spanish flavor because the first Europeans who settled there were from Spain. Sing "Campanas vespertinas."

This vast land of ours, with its cities and towns, deserts, mountains, rivers and lakes, and its rich variety of people surely is "America, the Beautiful."

SING "On the Road Again" and "America, the Beautiful."

CHECK IT OUT

1. Choose the meter you hear.

   a. $\frac{4}{4}$ b. $\frac{6}{8}$

2. Which of the following examples shows what you hear?

   a.   b.

3. Which of the following examples shows what you hear?

   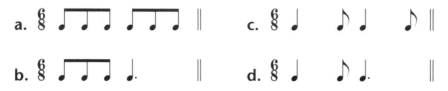

   a.   b.

4. Choose the $\frac{6}{8}$ pattern you hear.

   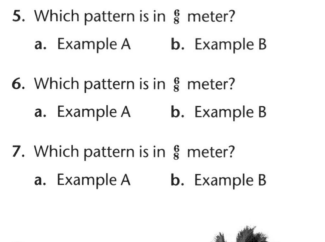

   a. $\frac{6}{8}$ c. $\frac{6}{8}$

   b. $\frac{6}{8}$ d. $\frac{6}{8}$

5. Which pattern is in $\frac{6}{8}$ meter?

   a. Example A   **b.** Example B

6. Which pattern is in $\frac{6}{8}$ meter?

   a. Example A   **b.** Example B

7. Which pattern is in $\frac{6}{8}$ meter?

   a. Example A   **b.** Example B

CREATE

Plan and Perform a Program

Plan a program around the theme "Sea to Shining Sea."
Review songs, dances, and poetry learned in this unit, and
select some of them for performance. The beginning song
should set the mood and the ending song should reinforce
or sum up the theme.

Create a script from information in your book as well as
additional research.

**PRACTICE the program and then present it to an
audience.**

Write

Which place in the United States would you
most like to visit? Write an essay or poem
about this place. Tell what type of music
you might hear in your chosen place.

Theme from NEW YORK, NEW YORK

Music by John Kander
Words by Fred Ebb

Moderately, with Rhythm

Start spread-in' the news, I'm leav-ing to - day,

I wan - na be a part— of it, New York, New York.

These vag - a - bond shoes are long-ing to stray,

And step a - round the heart— of it, New York, New York.

I wan - na wake up in the cit - y that does - n't sleep

212

To find I'm king of the hill,_____ top of the heap.

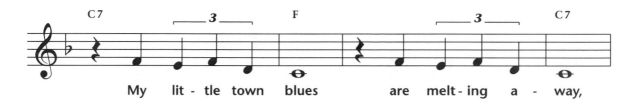

My lit - tle town blues are melt - ing a - way,

I'll make a brand new start__ of it in old New York.

If I can make it there,__ I'd make it an - y - where,__ It's up to

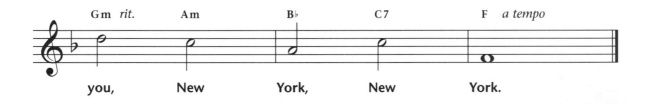

you, New York, New York.

Encore

SIMPLE GIFTS
The World of the Shakers

Look at the pictures on this page. What do they tell you about the people who created these objects?

The Shakers are a religious group, founded in this country in 1774. Their small communities were in northern New York state, New England, and the Midwest. The scenes on these pages show their fine crafts. Although today their population is very small, the Shaker way of life and the high quality of their crafts are still much admired.

DESCRIBE the kind of music you think Shakers might have created. Listen to the song. Were you correct?

SIMPLE GIFTS

Shaker Song

'Tis the gift to be sim - ple, 'tis the gift to be free,

'Tis the gift to come down where we ought to be.

And when we find our - selves in the place just right,

'Twill be in the val - ley of love and de - light.

When true sim - pli - ci - ty is gained,

To bow and to bend we shan't be a - shamed.

To turn, turn will be our de - light,

Till by turn - ing, turn - ing we come 'round right.

Variations on Simple Gifts from *Appalachian Spring*
by Aaron Copland

Aaron Copland chose "Simple Gifts" to use in his music for the ballet Appalachian Spring. *Even though the Shakers are not in his ballet, Copland felt that the song expressed the spirit of all early settlers. The ballet is about a pioneer celebration of a recently married couple at a newly built farmhouse in Pennsylvania.*

LISTEN for the melody in its original form and in *augmentation,* a technique in which all of the note values are doubled.

LISTENING MAP *As you listen to "Variations on Simple Gifts," follow the pictures that represent the variations. Each picture shows an everyday activity with friends and relatives helping out.*

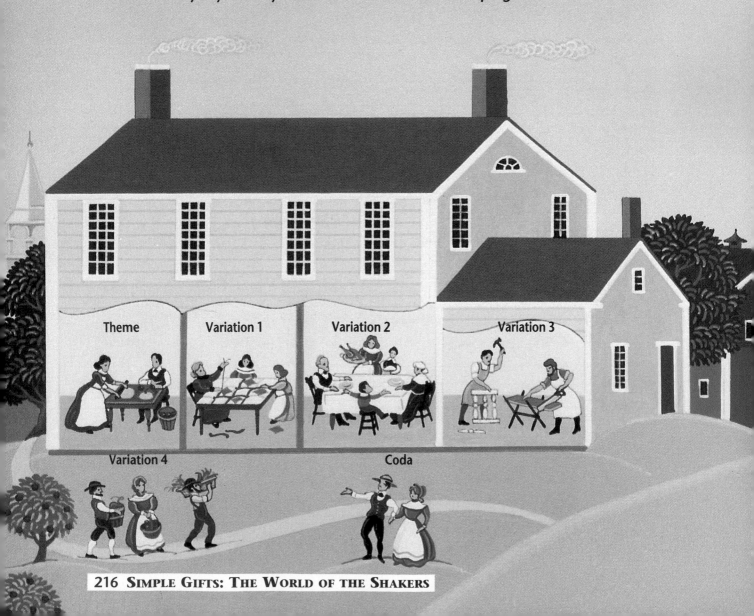

Theme   Variation 1   Variation 2   Variation 3

Variation 4   Coda

QUILTS
An American Folk Tradition

Most early American settlers made all of their own cloth. They wove the cloth themselves and dyed it with dyes made from flowers, leaves, or berries from their own gardens. From the cloth, they made bed linens, quilts, and clothing.

The quilts made by the early settlers were often beautifully designed. People still enjoy making quilts today. Square scraps of cloth are sewn together to form colorful patterns. The stitching itself is frequently done so well that it adds to the beauty of the quilt. Often, several friends will work together to make a quilt. The pleasure of their combined efforts adds to their satisfaction in accomplishment.

LOOK at the quilts below. In what way is making a quilt like creating a rhythm or melody pattern?

Expressions of Style

Music

Music is a tale told in sounds
Of such infinite reach
All time, all life, all tongues
Are in its speech.
Music is the sound of events
So moving, in its classic or its blue,
The heart nods recognition: "I was there.
And I have felt that, too . . ."

—Mary O'Neill

A song expresses feelings, ideas, pictures, and stories in ways that words alone cannot express. The same song may express something quite different when parts of the music are changed.

DESCRIBE the four ways "The Music Is You" is performed.

SING each version of the song in unison and as a canon.

The Music Is You

Words and Music by John Denver

Mu - sic makes pic - tures and of - ten tells sto - ries,

All of it mag - ic and all of it true. And

all of the pic - tures and all of the sto - ries and

last time

all___ of___ the mag-ic, The mu - sic is you.

220

John Denver in performance

The Music is You

Words and Music by John Denver
Arranged by Connie Heidt

Mu - sic makes pic - tures__ and of - ten tells sto - ries,__

All of it mag - ic__ and all of it true.__ And

all of the pic - tures__ and all of the sto - ries__ and

all of the mag - ic,__ the mu - sic is you.__

A Musical Style Show!

The many kinds of music reflect the ideas of the people who created them. Musical styles reflect the dreams and feelings of people from near and far, from the past and the present.

The elements of music are rhythm, pitch, harmony, texture, dynamics, tempo, and tone color. The distinct ways that people use these elements to express themselves create a **style** of music. The time, place, and purpose of the music also affect its style.

LISTENING

Pitched Percussion Montage

LISTEN to "Pitched Percussion Montage" and think about how to describe the different styles. Follow the pictures as you listen. How are the instruments alike or different? Which instruments are familiar?

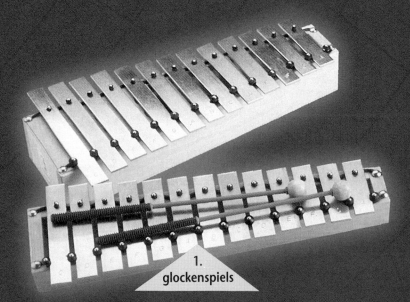

3.
angklung

2.
cloud
chamber bowl

1.
glockenspiels

222

5. steel drum

4. stone chimes

AMERICAN POPULAR STYLE

"Music! Music!" is in a style you've heard before. It is in an American popular song style.

DESCRIBE the musical elements as they are used in this song. What do you think makes it sound like a popular song?

MUSIC! MUSIC!

Words and Music by
Frederick Silver

1. Ev' - ry - bod - y's got some___ rhy - thm in___ them.
2. Ev' - ry - one on earth is an in - stru - ment,___ some

Ev' - ry - thing has got its song___ to sing.___
play - ing in a way that might___ seem strange.___

Noth - ing in the u - ni - verse is si - lent.
Ev' - ry - one of us has a dif - f'rent sound, a

C7   F   D7   G

There's a mel - o - dy in ev' - ry - thing.___
dif - f'rent___ look, a dif - f'rent range.___ If

Gm   C7   Fm   B♭

Ev' - ry - thing ce - les - tial___ is or - ches - tral.
ev' - ry - thing we played were the same old col - or, the

E♭m   A♭   Fm   G7

All the stars and plan - ets___ have a voice.
mu - sic that we made sim - ply could-n't be dull - er.

C   C7   D7

Mu - sic of the spheres can fill our ears and
Deep in you and me is a sym - pho - ny, a

G7   C

make our hearts___ re - joice!
sym - pho - ny___ of life.

Refrain

Em   Am   F   Dm

Mu - sic! Mu - sic! Lis - ten to the mu - sic!

Any sharp (♯), flat (♭) or natural (♮) that does not appear in the key signature is called an accidental.

NOTICE the accidentals as you sing "Music! Music!" How many accidentals can you find in "Music! Music!"?

JUST FOR THE FUN OF IT

Have you ever sung around a campfire or been part of a group that enjoyed singing together just for entertainment and fun? Songs enjoyed in this way are often **folk songs.** These songs have been passed on from one person to another for such a long time that no one knows who composed them.

There are many styles of folk music. No matter where you go, however, you may hear nonsense songs. "Chumbara" doesn't mean anything, but it's fun to sing!

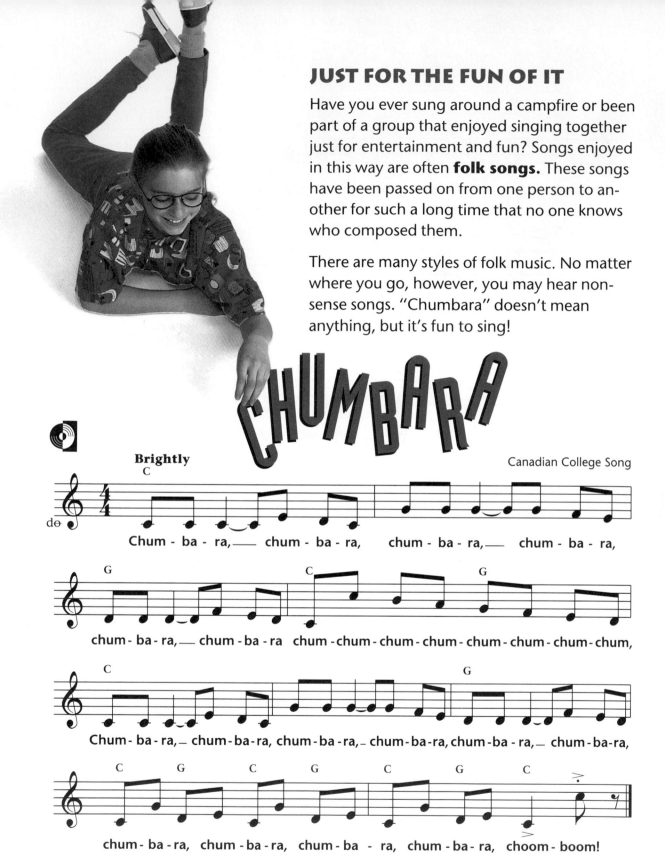

CHUMBARA

Brightly

Canadian College Song

Chum - ba - ra,— chum - ba - ra, chum - ba - ra,— chum - ba - ra,

chum - ba - ra,— chum - ba - ra chum - chum - chum - chum - chum - chum - chum - chum,

Chum - ba - ra,— chum - ba - ra, chum - ba - ra,— chum - ba - ra, chum - ba - ra,— chum - ba - ra,

chum - ba - ra, chum - ba - ra, chum - ba - ra, chum - ba - ra, choom - boom!

The two phrases of "Chumbara" are connected by a scale.
The scale is part of what makes this song fun to sing.

FIND the major scale in the song.

226 A MUSICAL STYLE SHOW!

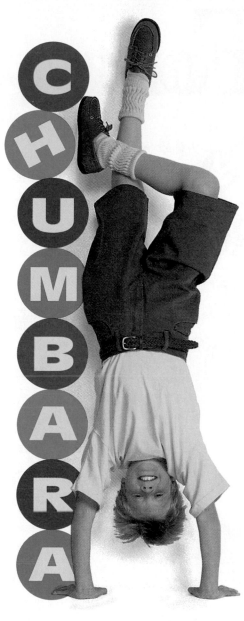

C
H
U
M
B
A
R
A

CHORDS CREATE HARMONY

When you hear music, you often hear more than one pitch at a time. This is called harmony. One way to create harmony is with chords. A **chord** is made up of three or more pitches sounding together. People who play instruments such as guitar and keyboards use chords to accompany their melodies.

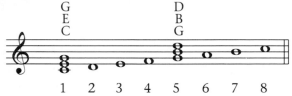

The pitch on which the chord is built is called its **root.** It is often the lowest pitch of the chord. Chords can be named by the letter of the chord root, for example, C chord or G chord. Another way to name chords is by the position of the chord root in the scale.

For example, the chord based on the first step of the scale is also called the I ("one") chord. The chord based on the fifth step of the scale is also called the V ("five") chord. You can accompany many songs, including "Chumbara," with just these two chords.

FIND the chord symbols C and G in "Chumbara." Play the chords on the resonator bells.

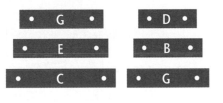

What pitch is in both chords?

SING "Chumbara" as some students play the chords.

mbara

FOLK STYLES FROM THE PAST

Go to a Mexican festival and you might sing and dance to "La bamba." This song, which comes from Veracruz, has a catchy rhythm that never fails to get people up on their feet. On this recording you will hear traditional Mexican instruments.

LA BAMBA

Mexican Folk Song

Spanish: 1. Pa - ra bai - lar la bam - ba, pa - ra bai - lar la
Pronunciation: pa ɾa βai laɾ la bam ba pa ɾa βai laɾ la
(2.) cie - lo, pa - ra su - bir al
sye lo pa ɾa su βiɾ al

bam - ba se ne - ce - si - ta u - na po - ca de gra - cia,
bam ba se ne se si ta u na po ka ðe gɾa sia
cie - lo se ne - ce - si - ta u - na es - ca - le - ra gran - de,
sye lo se ne se si ta u naes ka le ɾa gɾan de

228

u - na po - ca de gra - cia y o - tra co - si - ta y a - rri - ba y a - rri - ba,
u na po ka ðe gɾa sia yo tɾa ko si ta ya ɾi βa ya ɾi βa

u - na es - ca - le - ra gran - de y o - tra chi - qui - ta y a - rri - ba y a - rri - ba,
u naes ka le ɾa gɾan de yo tɾa chi ki ta ya ɾi βa ya ɾi βa

y a - rri - ba y a - rri - ba y a - rri - ba i - ré, por ti se - ré, por ti se - ré,
i a ɾi βa ya ɾi βa ya ɾi βai ɾe poɾ ti se ɾe poɾ ti se ɾe

Bam - ba, bam - ba. Bam - ba, bam - ba.
bam ba bam ba bam ba bam ba

Bam - ba, bam - ba. Bam - ba, ba. 2. Pa - ra su - bir al
bam ba bam ba bam ba ba pa ɾa su βiɾ al

Bam - ba, bam - ba. Bam - ba.
bam ba bam ba bam ba

PAT-CLAP to the beat and silently count *1–2*. Pat to the beat as you say *Ba-ma-la-ma Bam!* Then tell which beat has four sounds.

PAT the rhythm of *Ba-ma-la-ma Bam!* during the last three lines of "La bamba."

"Oh, my darling, Oh, my darling, Oh, my darling Clementine. . . ." You may have already sung about Clementine, but do you remember when you first heard this song?

The words to "Oh, My Darling, Clementine" mention a "forty-niner," or gold miner from the days of the California Gold Rush, so it might have first been sung around that time. Today it's part of our American folk heritage.

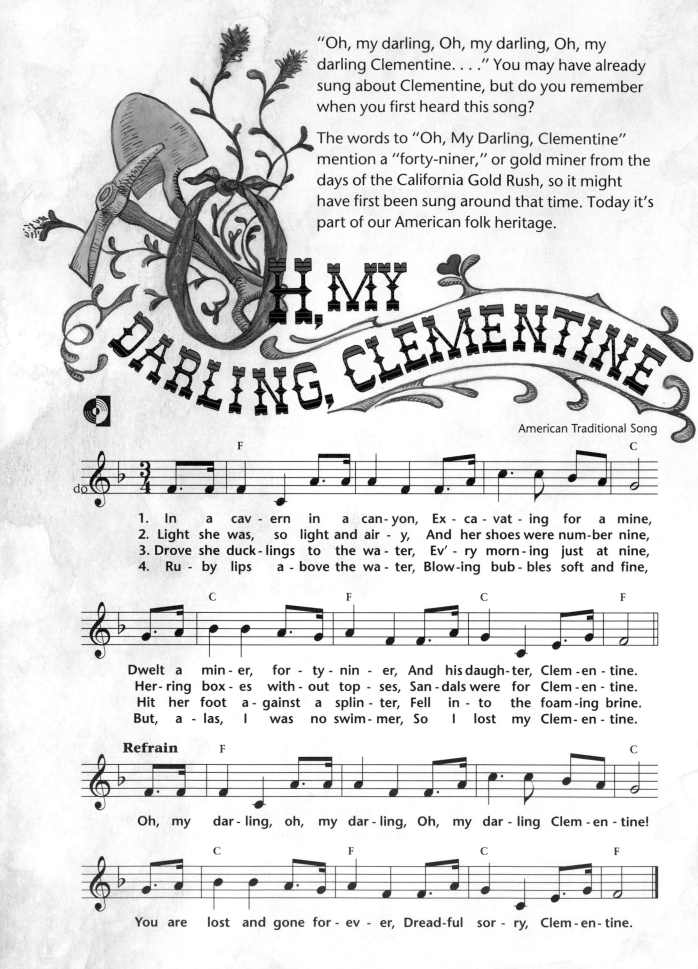

American Traditional Song

1. In a cav-ern in a can-yon, Ex-ca-vat-ing for a mine,
2. Light she was, so light and air-y, And her shoes were num-ber nine,
3. Drove she duck-lings to the wa-ter, Ev'-ry morn-ing just at nine,
4. Ru-by lips a-bove the wa-ter, Blow-ing bub-bles soft and fine,

Dwelt a min-er, for-ty-nin-er, And his daugh-ter, Clem-en-tine.
Her-ring box-es with-out top-ses, San-dals were for Clem-en-tine.
Hit her foot a-gainst a splin-ter, Fell in-to the foam-ing brine.
But, a-las, I was no swim-mer, So I lost my Clem-en-tine.

Refrain

Oh, my dar-ling, oh, my dar-ling, Oh, my dar-ling Clem-en-tine!

You are lost and gone for-ev-er, Dread-ful sor-ry, Clem-en-tine.

"CLEMENTINE" MOVES IN THREES

Find the ¾ meter signature in "Oh, My Darling, Clementine."

The ¾ meter signature in this song means that there are three beats in a measure. The first beat is stressed, followed by two unstressed beats. The quarter note is the symbol for one beat.

Does "Oh, My Darling, Clementine" begin with an upbeat? How many measures are there in each verse up to the refrain?

PRACTICE this ostinato with "Oh, My Darling, Clementine." Snap your fingers on the first two notes. Brush your palms together for the last four notes.

Snap,   snap,   brush brush brush brush.

PLAY the ostinato on instruments. Use two different sounds.

RHYTHM GIVES STYLE

"La bamba" is sung in Spanish. Instruments used to accompany the folk song include the jarocha (Mexican folk harp), a requinto (four-stringed guitar), and a jarana (eight-stringed guitar). These instruments form a conjunto jarocho, a typical ensemble from the port of Veracruz. Percussion effects come from the footwork of the dancers.

232

ADD AN ACCOMPANIMENT

Here are rhythm patterns to accompany
"La bamba."

**PRACTICE the patterns, then play
them together with the song.**

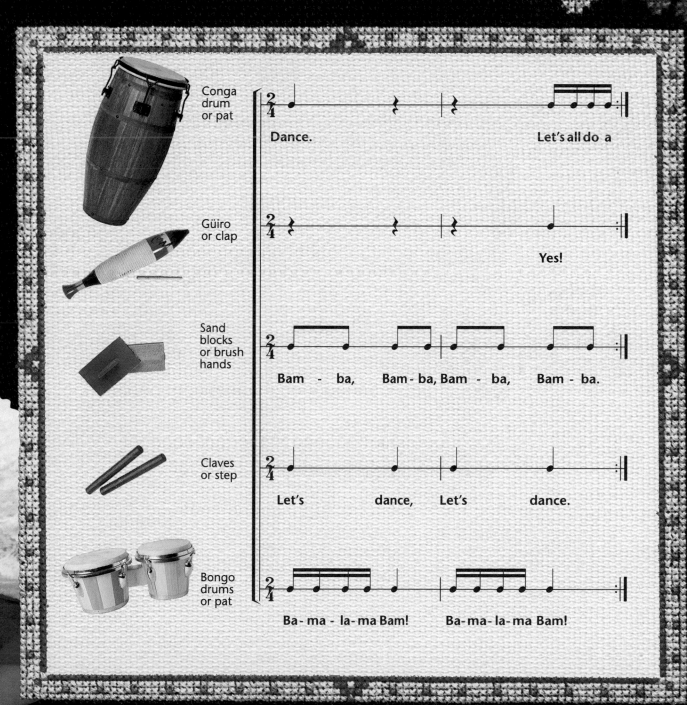

Flower and leaf pattern is based on embroidery from Veracruz.

CALYPSO STYLE

"Yellow Bird" sounds like a folk song but it is not. Instead, it is a song composed in a folk style called **calypso.** The composer combined typical Caribbean instruments, syncopated rhythms, and harmonies to give "Yellow Bird" its calypso sound.

Yellow Bird

Music by Norman Luboff
Words by Marilyn Keith and
Alan Bergman

Refrain

Yel - low bird, up high in— ba - nan - a tree.

Yel - low bird, up high in— ba - nan - a tree.

Yel - low bird, you sit all— a - lone like me.

Yel - low bird, you sit all— a - lone like me.

LISTENING

Intrada für Pauken, Trompeten, und Flöten
by Gunild Keetman

*An **intrada** is an opening piece that is festive or marchlike.*

LISTEN for these musical elements in the first section: higher and lower pitches and patterns with four sounds to a beat. Then listen for these differences in tone color and texture in the next sections.

> **Trumpeten und Pauken**
> **Flöten und Trompete**
> **Flöten, Trompeten, und Pauken**

Name the pitched percussion instrument that is used both in "Intrada für Pauken, Trompeten, und Flöten" and "Fanfare for the Common Man."

SPOTLIGHT ON

GUNILD KEETMAN

Gunild Keetman (1904–1990) was a German composer, music educator, and dance teacher. She studied music and dance with Carl Orff, another German composer, and then worked with him to develop materials for teaching music. Her compositions include works for voice, body percussion, Orff instruments, and recorders. Most of her music is found in volumes written especially for students studying music and dance through Orff's philosophy of music education, called Orff-Schulwerk. Throughout her life, Keetman combined teaching music and dance with composing.

Chord Connections

When you learned "Chumbara" you played two chords, C and G—the I and V chords—in the key of C. You can learn to play the I and V chords in other keys and use them to accompany many folk songs.

The I and V chords in the key of F can be played on the resonator bells using the pitches shown.

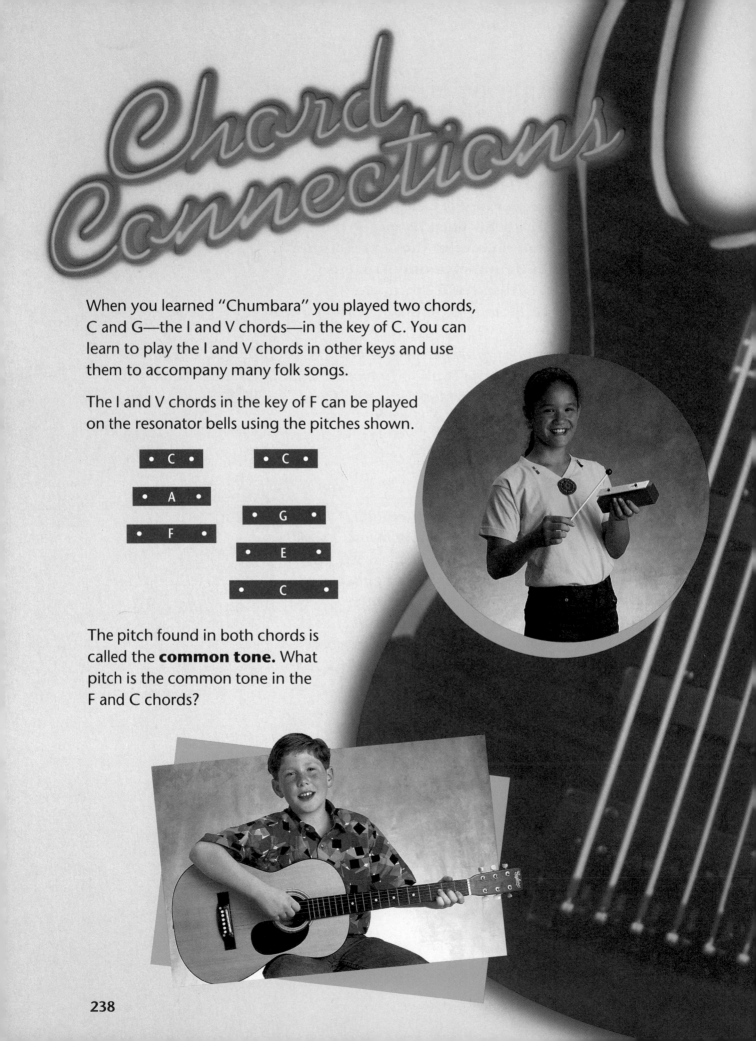

The pitch found in both chords is called the **common tone.** What pitch is the common tone in the F and C chords?

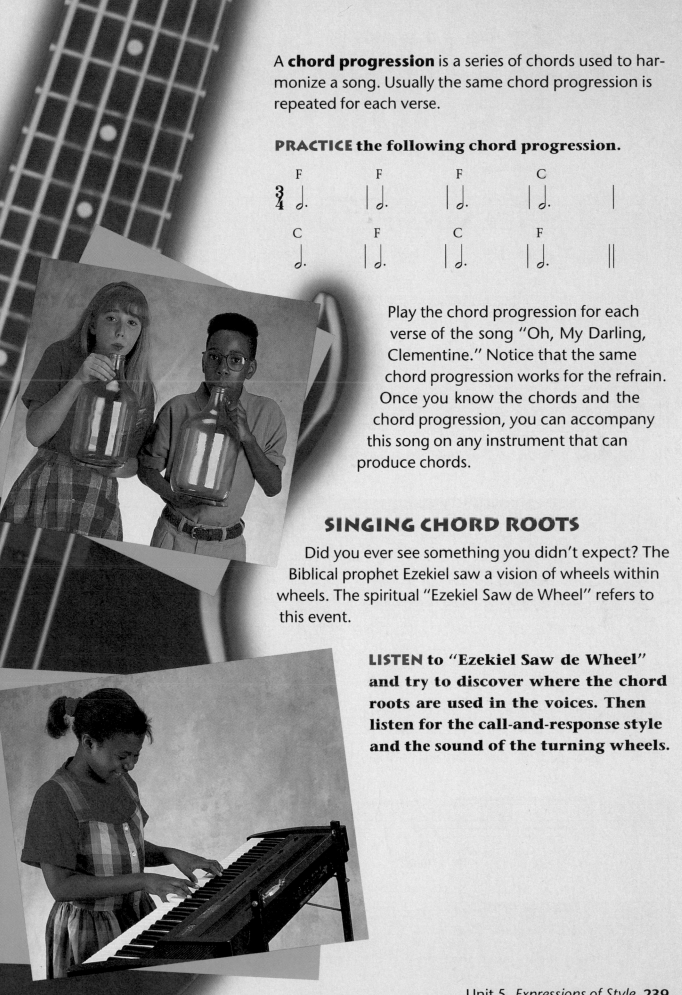

A **chord progression** is a series of chords used to harmonize a song. Usually the same chord progression is repeated for each verse.

PRACTICE the following chord progression.

| F | F | F | C |
| C | F | C | F |

Play the chord progression for each verse of the song "Oh, My Darling, Clementine." Notice that the same chord progression works for the refrain. Once you know the chords and the chord progression, you can accompany this song on any instrument that can produce chords.

SINGING CHORD ROOTS

Did you ever see something you didn't expect? The Biblical prophet Ezekiel saw a vision of wheels within wheels. The spiritual "Ezekiel Saw de Wheel" refers to this event.

LISTEN to "Ezekiel Saw de Wheel" and try to discover where the chord roots are used in the voices. Then listen for the call-and-response style and the sound of the turning wheels.

EZEKIEL SAW DE WHEEL

Allegro Moderato

African American Spiritual

Leader

E - ze - kiel saw de wheel

simile

Mid - dle of the, mid - dle of the, mid - dle of the, mid - dle of the,

Group

'way up in de mid'l of de air. E-

middle of the, mid - dle of the, mid - dle of the air.

ze - kiel saw de wheel

Mid - dle of the, mid - dle of the, mid - dle of the, mid - dle of the,

Group

'way in de mid'l of de air. De

mid - dle of the, mid - dle of the air.

ARRANGING Rhythms

There are many kinds of careers in music. An **arranger** takes a piece of folk or composed music and makes decisions about how style, instrumentation, tempo, harmony, and dynamics can be changed.

THINK IT THROUGH
How is the work of a composer different from that of an arranger?

LISTENING

Ezekiel Saw de Wheel

Spiritual Arranged by William Dawson

A number of musicians have created their own arrangements of "Ezekiel Saw de Wheel" so that it can be performed in different ways. William Dawson arranged this spiritual for a cappella choir.

COMPARE William Dawson's arrangement of "Ezekiel Saw de Wheel" to the arrangement in your book.

How did William Dawson imitate the sound of wheels turning in his arrangement of "Ezekiel Saw de Wheel"?

TAP the beat and say *doom-a-loom-a* **over and over. How many sounds are there to a beat?**

242

Spotlight on William Dawson

William Dawson (1899–1990) was an important American musician. When he was 13, he sold his bicycle for $6.00 to go to Tuskegee Institute in Alabama to learn music. He earned tuition money by working on the school farm. His musical career included being a teacher, conductor, composer, and arranger. Dawson set high standards for himself and insisted on quality performances from his students. He helped others to understand and preserve the African American spiritual.

William Dawson and the Tuskegee Institute Choir, 1932

When there are four sounds to a beat, each sound is represented by a sixteenth note (♪). The sixteenth note has two flags. Sixteenth notes in groups of four have a double beam (▯▯▯▯). A **sixteenth rest** (𝄿) is the same length as a sixteenth note. How did you imitate the sound of wheels turning when you sang "Ezekiel Saw de Wheel" in two parts?

How would eight sounds to a beat be notated? What would be the name of each of the notes?

NEW RHYTHM COMBINATIONS

Eighth notes and **eighth rests** can be combined with sixteenth notes and sixteenth rests. This makes different rhythm combinations possible. Review these notes and rests.

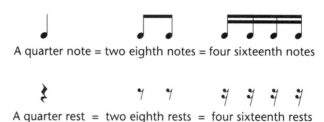

A quarter note = two eighth notes = four sixteenth notes

A quarter rest = two eighth rests = four sixteenth rests

TRY each of these combinations.

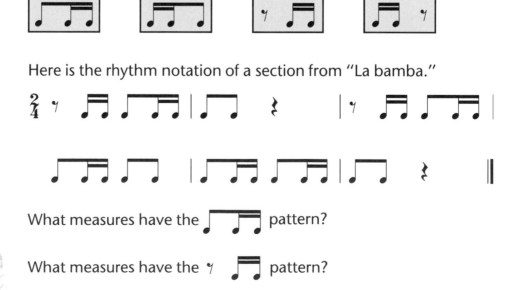

Here is the rhythm notation of a section from "La bamba."

What measures have the ▯ ▯▯ pattern?

What measures have the 𝄿 ▯▯ pattern?

The painting *American Gothic*, 1930, (far left) is by Grant Wood. Other artists have created new versions of this farm family. Notice the differences and similarities of these pictures.

BE AN ARRANGER

By combining rhythms in your own way, you can experiment with one element of musical style.

CREATE a four-beat pattern with ♩, ♫♫, ♩♪, and 𝄽. Play your pattern as an accompaniment to "La bamba" or "Ezekiel Saw de Wheel."

THINK IT THROUGH

What other changes could you make to create a new arrangement of "La bamba" or "Ezekiel Saw de Wheel"?

TONE COLORS FROM

The verse of "Chan mali chan" tells about a baby goat who meets people on the road to Kota Bharu. He says, "Love me who has a blue shirt. Love me who has no teeth." It's all in fun! The words *chan mali chan* don't mean anything. People in Asia enjoy this nonsense song just as people in North America enjoy "Chumbara" or "Oh, My Darling, Clementine."

CHAN MALI CHAN

Refrain

Singaporean Folk Song

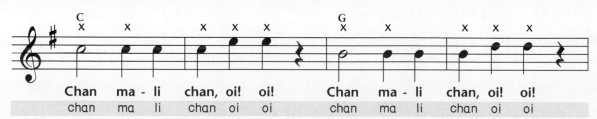

THE FAR EAST

Verse

G · · · C · · · G

1. Di - ma - na di - a   a - nak kam-bing sa - ya
   di ma na di   a   a   nak kam bing sa   ya
2. Di - ma - na di - a   a - nak kam-bing sa - ya
   di ma na di   a   a   nak kam bing sa   ya

D · · · G

A - nak kam-bing sa - ya   per - gi   ke   Ko - ta Bha - ru;
a   nak kam bing sa   ya   pə   gi   kə   ko   ta ba   ru
A - nak kam-bing sa - ya   ma - kan   te - pi   pe - ri - gi;
a   nak kam bing sa   ya   ma kan   tə   pi   pə   īi   gi

G · · · C · · · G

Di - ma - na di - a   chin - ta   ha - ti   sa - ya
di ma na di   a   chin   ta   ha   ti   sa   ya
Di - ma - na di - a   chin - ta   ha - ti   sa - ya
di ma na di   a   chin   ta   ha   ti   sa   ya

D · · · G   *D.C. al Fine*

chin   ta ha - ti   sa - ya   yang pa - kal ba - ju   bi - ru.
chin   ta ha ti   sa   ya   yang pa   kai ba   ju   bi   ru
chin   ta ha - ti   sa - ya   yang ti - dak   a - da   gi - gi.
chin   ta ha ti   sa   ya   yang ti   dak   a   da   gi   gi

The angklung is a pitched percussion instrument
used in Singapore. It is made of one or more
tuned bamboo tubes set loosely in a frame. The
angklung player shakes a tube to produce a
specific pitch.

LISTEN for the angklung in
"Chan mali chan."

A FOLK SONG FROM KOREA

"Arirang" is one of the most well-known songs from Korea. The song is about the Arirang hill outside of the east gate of Seoul, the capital city of South Korea.

1 3   2

CONDUCT in ¾ as you listen to "Arirang."

ARIRANG

Korean Folk Song
English Words by
Marilyn Davidson

Korean: 아 리 랑 아 리 랑 아 라 리 요
Pronunciation: a ɾi ɾang a ɾi ɾang a ɾa ɾi yo
English: A - ri- rang,— A - ri- rang,— A - ra - ri - yo.—

아 리 랑 고 개 를 넘 어 간 다
a ɾi ɾang go ge ɾʉl nɔ mɔ gan da
You are go-ing far a-way— o-ver A - ri-rang hill.

나 를 버 리 고 가 시 는 님 은
na ɾʉl pɔ ɾi go ga shi nʉn ni mʉn
Oh, my friend, if you leave me— here a-lone,— may your

십 리 도 못 가 서 발 병 난 다
shim ni do mo ka sɔ bal pyɔng nan da
feet be-gin to hurt be-fore you've e - ven walked the first mile!

The ornamented version of "Arirang" below includes a changko, which is a Korean drum. The drum has a waist, which means it gets narrow in the center. The body is lacquered wood and the two heads are laced together.

LISTENING

Arirang Ornamented Version
Korean Folk Song

Folk songs are passed on from one person to another through singing. In Korea, where "Arirang" is a well-known song, the singer is expected to ornament, or decorate, the melody. The ornamentation is different each time, depending on the skill and mood of the singer.

LISTEN to the ornamented version of "Arirang." The basic melody is the same, but the singer has added extra notes. Then describe how the style of this "Arirang" is different from the one you sang.

AN ACCOMPANIMENT TO "ARIRANG"

CHOOSE three of the rhythm patterns below. Then decide which one to use twice. Place the patterns in any order you like.

Explore drum sounds. Find three different sounds on a drum. Decide how to use these three sounds to perform your four-measure rhythm sequence. Use it to accompany "Arirang."

XYLO-Mania

African musicians use many traditional and modern instruments. Some of the traditional pitched percussion instruments were part of African cultures long before the present-day xylophone was developed.

An amadinda is a traditional log xylophone from Uganda. It is made up of 12 wooden slabs placed horizontally on two logs. Each slab is tuned to a different pitch. The amadinda belongs to the Baganda people who live in the south-central region of Uganda. They play the amadinda on special occasions and during sports and games.

LISTEN to James Makubuya as he speaks about and plays the amadinda and performs "Baamulijja."

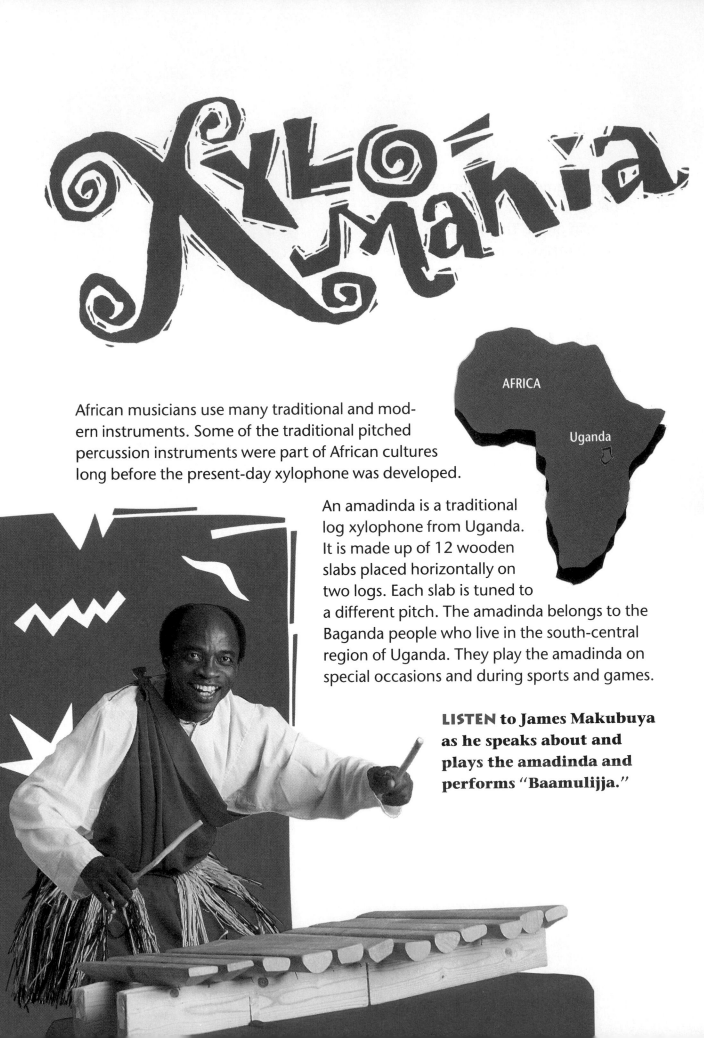

AFRICA

Uganda

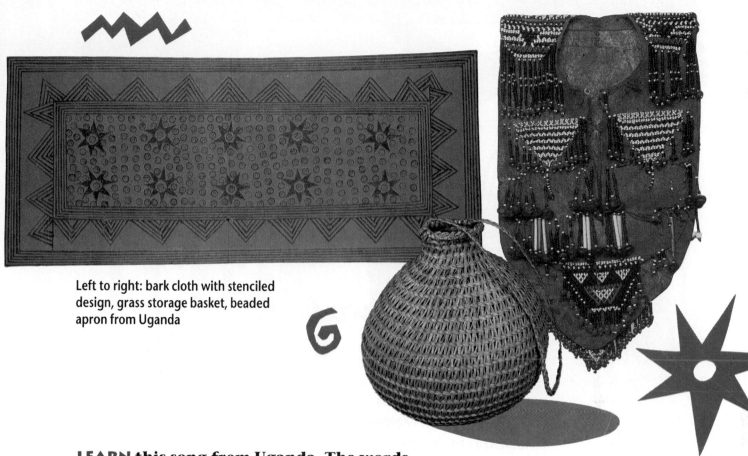

Left to right: bark cloth with stenciled design, grass storage basket, beaded apron from Uganda

LEARN this song from Uganda. The words are in Luganda, the language of the Baganda.

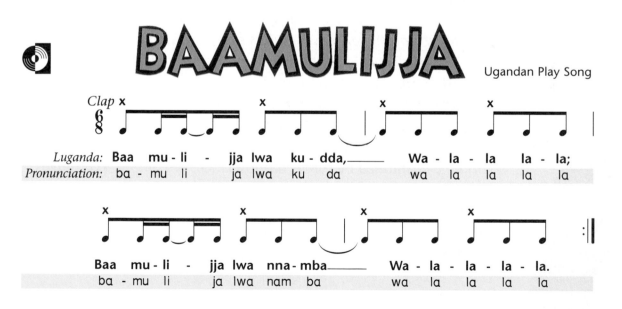

BAAMULIJJA

Ugandan Play Song

Clap

Luganda: Baa mu - li - jja lwa ku - dda,_____ Wa - la - la la - la;
Pronunciation: ba - mu li ja lwa ku da wa la la la la

Baa mu - li - jja lwa nna - mba_____ Wa - la - la - la - la.
ba - mu li ja lwa nam ba wa la la la la

The words to "Baamulijja" mean: "Be careful; for if you challenge your enemies, make sure you have enough strength to drive them away; otherwise they might destroy you."

Spotlight on Johann Sebastian Bach

Johann Sebastian Bach (1685–1750) was born over 300 years ago in Germany. Members of Bach's family had been professional musicians for many years. Bach began his musical career at the age of 18, when he took his first job as an organist.

For most of his life, Bach lived quietly and worked very hard at composing music. Most of Bach's compositions were vocal works written for Protestant church services. At one period in his life, he wrote new music for these services every week. In addition, he wrote music for solo instruments such as the violin, flute, and harpsichord, and concertos and suites for orchestras.

Bach had a reputation of being a skilled performer, improviser, and composer during his lifetime. He was not, however, a world-wide celebrity during his lifetime. His music was considered heavy and old-fashioned by some composers. Other composers studied Bach's music for its skilled construction. Years later, his music was "rediscovered" by Felix Mendelssohn and other composers of the 1800s. Today, Bach's music is very popular, and he is considered to be one of the greatest composers who ever lived.

LISTENING

Musette Harpsichord and Percussion Versions

by Johann Sebastian Bach

Arrangers enjoy giving music a different sound by changing the instruments, rhythms, or harmonies. The music of Johann Sebastian Bach has been arranged in many different ways over the years.

Listen to two versions of "Musette." First, you will hear it on a harpsichord, an instrument used in Bach's time. Then you will hear a new version of the same piece arranged for pitched and unpitched percussion instruments, including the xylophone.

PLAY this "Musette" accompaniment on an unpitched instrument.

The Importance of

Style

In every culture, people express their feelings through their own music, art, dance, and poetry. The poem "We Return Thanks" is an Iroquois prayer which has been handed down from generation to generation.

WE RETURN THANKS

We return thanks to our Mother, the Earth,
who sustains us—
to the rivers and streams,
that run upon the bosom of the Earth—
to the Three Sisters—corn, beans, and squash—
that support our lives—
to the winds,
that move the air, banishing disease—
to the descending rains,
that give us water and cause all plants to grow—
to the moon and stars,
that give us light when the sun is gone.
We return thanks to the sun,
who looks upon the Earth with a fatherly eye.

—Prayer which opens and closes Iroquois spiritual
  and political gatherings.

THINK IT THROUGH

How can learning poetry and music help you understand people from cultures that are different from your own? What does "We Return Thanks" tell you about the Iroquois culture?

"Tsiothwatasè:tha" is a round dance that came from the tribes of the Plains region to the Iroquois in New York. The Iroquois adapted it to fit their style. The dancers form a circle and alternate movement to the right with movement to the left. Movement to the right stands for good and positive things. Movement to the left symbolizes negative things such as sadness, grief, or anger. According to Iroquois belief, the good always triumphs over the bad and the dance always ends moving to the right.

Tsiothwatasè:tha
ROUND DANCE

Iroquois Social Song
and Dance As Sung by
Members of the Mohawk Nation

(a)

Mohawk: he   yo   he   yo   ha   hi   yo   ha   ya
Pronunciation: he yo   he   yo   ha   hi   yo   ha   ya

(b)

(c)

he   yo   ha   hi   yo   ha   ya   he   yo   ha   hi   yo   ha   ya
he   yo   ha   hi   yo   ha   ya   he   yo   ha   hi   yo   ha   ya

(d)

(e)

he   yo   ha   hi   yo   ha   ya   he   yo   ha   hi   yo   ha   ya
he   yo   ha   hi   yo   ha   ya   he   yo   ha   hi   yo   ha   ya

(f)

ho   ya   he   ya   ha   ho   ya   he   ya   ha   yo - e   (pitch fall off)
ho   ya   he   ya   ha   ho   ya   he   ya   ha   yo   e

Top left: Turtle Pendant, by Julius Cook, Mohawk Nation (symbolizes story of how the earth, good/evil, and the gifts of the earth came to be). Bottom: Corn Spirit, by Tammy Tarbell, Mohawk Nation. Top right: Water drum and stick, Onondaga Nation.

STYLE BRINGS IT ALL TOGETHER

Styles in music are as different as the earth's peoples. Many factors influence styles, including differences in people, countries, and time periods. In the past, before television, radio, and recordings were invented, people didn't have the opportunity to hear many different styles. Today we can enjoy musical styles from all over the world.

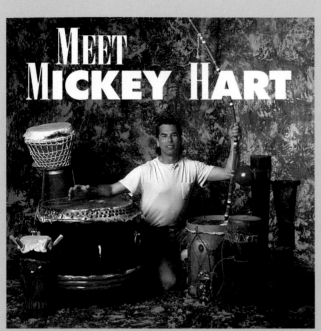

Mickey Hart began drumming at an early age. Both of his parents were drummers. Hart played in rock-and-roll bands, jazz bands, and the Air Force marching band. Since 1967 he has been the percussionist for the rock band **The Grateful Dead.** *Percussion from around the world has become of special interest to him. He has collected percussion instruments as well as the lore and history of drumming in many cultures.*

LISTEN to Mickey Hart as he speaks on music of different cultures and the value of all different styles.

"What we call world music really is all the world's music. It's a reflection of our dreams, our lives.... Underneath the world's extraordinary musical diversity is another, deeper realm in which there is no better or worse, no modern or primitive, no art music versus folk music ... but rather a [desire] to translate ... being alive into sound, into rhythm, into something you can dance to."

—*Mickey Hart,* The Planet Drum

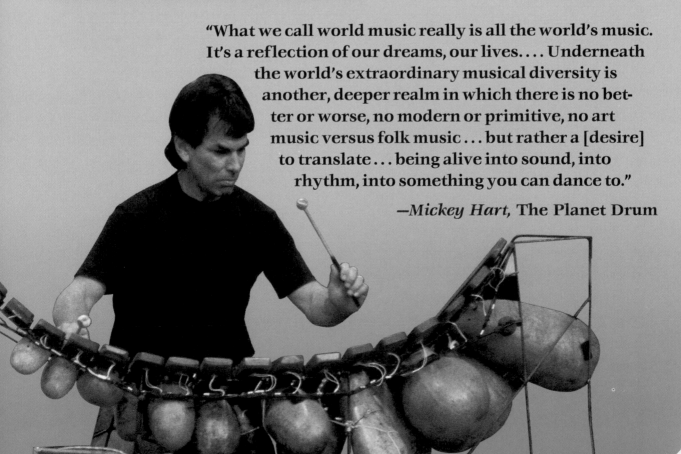

Architecture exists in as many styles as music. Notice the variety of forms, colors, and decoration used in these homes. What similarities and differences can you find in the styles of these homes? What other styles of homes have you seen?

SINGING IN STYLE

Imagine that you're on a long hike or car trip with your family or friends. You might enjoy singing a song like "Chumbara" to help pass the time. Listen for the descending major scale as you sing this song.

Another type of folk song is the nonsense ballad. A nonsense ballad tells a story (but not too seriously) and usually there's only a shred of truth in it. "Oh, My Darling, Clementine" is this kind of song. Folk songs are often accompanied by a guitar or banjo strumming chords. Listen for the I and V chords in "Oh, My Darling, Clementine" as you sing it.

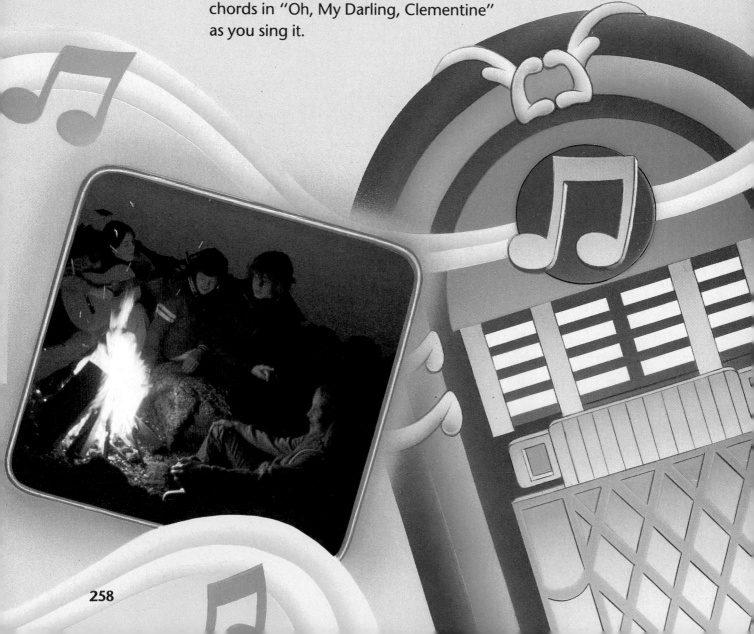

Many folk songs are more serious in style. African American spirituals, for example, are songs of faith that originally were often sung a cappella. Today spirituals are sung in a variety of styles. Sing "Ezekiel Saw de Wheel" and think of the qualities that have made spirituals such a valuable part of our American folk heritage.

If you come across Latin American music on the radio, you will probably recognize its distinctive styles. There is a unique character to the way the rhythm, melody, harmony, and tone color are put together and performed. "La bamba" has the added feature of being a dance.

IMPROVISE a dance with a partner using step-touches, turns, and snaps, as you sing "La bamba."

Every one of us has a different sound. This line from "Music! Music!" gives us a clue to the reason that there are so many kinds of music. Sing this song and think about your own musical style. Will it be the same tomorrow as it is today?

CHECK IT OUT

1. Which meter do you hear?
   a. $\frac{3}{4}$ b. $\frac{4}{4}$ c. $\frac{6}{8}$

2. Which meter do you hear?
   a. $\frac{3}{4}$ b. $\frac{4}{4}$ c. $\frac{6}{8}$

3. Which meter do you hear?
   a. $\frac{3}{4}$ b. $\frac{4}{4}$ c. $\frac{6}{8}$

4. Choose the pattern you hear.

5. Choose the pattern you hear.

6. Choose the pattern you hear.

7. Which chord progression do you hear?
   a. I I V I b. I V I V c. I V V I d. I I I V

260

CREATE

Create an Accompaniment

CREATE accompaniments to "Oh, My Darling, Clementine." Use the chord progression from the song.

Choose a rhythm pattern for the chords. Use one or more of the following patterns or make up your own.

Sing a harmony part. Use the chord roots in the chord progression and add words, for example:

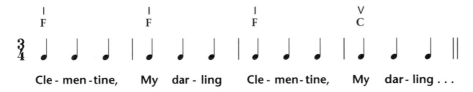

Cle - men - tine,   My   dar - ling   Cle - men - tine,   My   dar - ling . . .

Create and play a countermelody using pitches from the chord progression.

Create a rhythmic ostinato to go with the song. Perform the accompaniments as you sing the song.

Write

Which style of music do you like best? Write a brief paragraph explaining why.

Turn the World Around

Music by Robert M. Freedman
Words by Harry Belafonte
Arranged by Lynn Johnson, adapted

Refrain

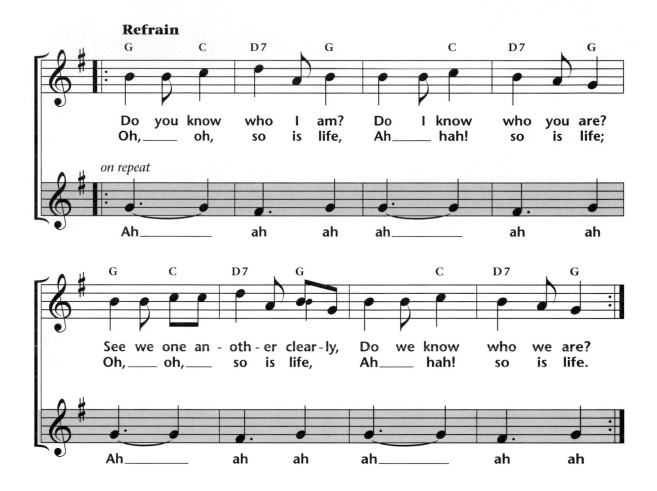

on repeat

Do you know who I am? Do I know who you are?
Oh,____ oh, so is life, Ah____ hah! so is life;

Ah_____ ah ah ah_____ ah ah

See we one an - oth - er clear - ly, Do we know who we are?
Oh,____ oh,____ so is life, Ah____ hah! so is life.

Ah_____ ah ah ah_____ ah ah

ENCORE DRUMMIN'

Have you ever started your own jam session? Perhaps you and several friends began by rapping on a table. Some of you may have slapped your hands on your thighs and perhaps others stomped their feet in a rhythmic pattern against the floor. You created an instant percussion band. Percussion instruments are those that produce sound when they are struck or shaken.

The drum is, perhaps, the most popular percussion instrument. All cultures have some form of drum. Drums vary greatly in shape, size, and method of playing. Some drums are struck with the fingers, others are shaken, and still others are rattled. The sound of the drum is affected by the material of the drumhead and the kind of wood used for the frame. In some cultures, the drum solo is the most important part of a performance.

G ALONG

Indian tablas

African talking drum

Korean changko

Middle-Eastern dumbek

Frame drums are portable instruments with circular frames. They are small enough to be held in one hand and struck with the other.

The tambourine, which originated in Southwest Asia, is a very simple and versatile instrument. It is one of the more popular frame drums. In addition to a drum head, the tambourine has jingles on it that ring when the instrument is struck.

The riq, a drum from Egypt, resembles the tambourine. It is used in dance music, concert music, and religious music. The pitch of this drum can be raised or lowered.

Popular for more than a hundred years, the bodhran is a frame drum from Ireland. It has a low, deep sound, but brighter, ringing sounds can be drawn from it as well. Traditionally, this drum is played with a double-headed stick and is used in Irish folk music.

Meet
GLEN VELEZ

Glen Velez, who first started studying the drums with his uncle at the age of eight, is an internationally known drummer, composer, scholar, and teacher. He has combined his background in Western percussion with the study of tambourine performance styles from around the world. For 15 years, Velez performed with the Steve Reich ensemble. He has been the percussionist with the Paul Winter Consort since 1983.

LISTEN to Glen Velez talk about his career and demonstrate some of the drums he has collected from around the world.

The Yesterdays and the Tomorrows

No year stands by itself,
any more than any day stands alone.
There is the continuity of all the years
in the trees,
the grass,
even in the stones on the hilltops.
Even in man.
For time flows like water,
eroding and building,
shaping and ever flowing;
and time is a part of us,
not only our years, as we speak of them,
but our lives,
our thoughts.
All our yesterdays are summarized in our now,
and all the tomorrows are ours
to shape.

—Hal Borland

LOOKING BACK

LOOKING FORWARD

"Yesterday" was composed by John Lennon and Paul McCartney, two members of the Beatles. Sometimes your yesterdays appear better than the present, as expressed in the words of the song. You can also take the present and work to shape it into something good.

How many different sections are in the song?

Yesterday

Words and Music by
John Lennon and Paul McCartney

C   Bm7   E7   Am

Yes - ter-day,___ all my trou-bles seemed so far a - way.___
Sud-den-ly,___ I'm not half the man_ I used to be.___

F   G   F   C   G

Now it looks as though___ they're here to stay,___
There's a shad-ow hang - ing o - ver me,___

Am7   D7   F   C

oh I be - lieve___ in yes - ter - day.___
oh yes - ter - day___ came sud - den - ly.___

270

Why she had to go, I don't know, she would-n't say.____

I said some-thing wrong, now I long for yes-ter-day.

Yes-ter-day,____ love was such an eas - y game to play.____

Now I need a place to hide a-way,____

oh I be - lieve____ in yes-ter-day.____

Mm mm mm mm mm.____

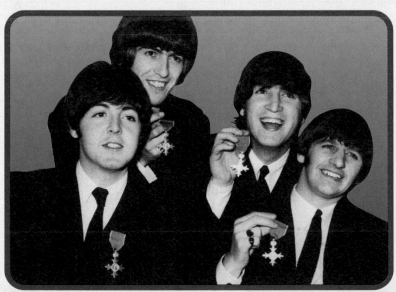

The Beatles, 1965 L to R: P. McCartney, G. Harrison, J. Lennon, R. Starr

FORMING THE FUTURE

Looking back on music from earlier times can help you better understand music of both today and yesterday. Listen for ways that music of long ago is like music that was written recently. Think about how music may change in the future. One of the elements of music that you find in every time period is **form,** the way a composer organizes musical material.

LOOK for form in "Young People of the World." Locate the two main sections and the canon at the end.

Young People of the World

Words and
Music by
Glen Everhart

Ⓐ Em / D

1. Young peo-ple of the world, put your hands to-geth-
2. Young peo-ple of the world, put your minds to-geth-

Em / D / Em

- er, put your hands to-geth - er, young peo-ple.
- er, put your minds to-geth - er, young peo-ple.

Em / D

Young peo-ple of the world, put your hearts to-geth-
Young peo-ple of the world, put your dreams to-geth-

er, put your hearts to - geth - er, young peo - ple.
er, put your dreams to - geth -

er, young peo - ple. Got - ta shout! up to the sky,

you got - ta show ev' - ry - bod - y there's a rea - son why,

you got - ta raise your voi - ces all o - ver the world

D.C. (2nd time to Canon)

and let your spir - it shine!

Canon

Young peo - ple of the world, put your { hands hearts minds dreams } to - geth -

er, put your { hands hearts minds dreams } to - geth - er, young peo - ple. Shout!

LISTENING

String Quartet

Op. 33, No. 3, Fourth Movement

by Franz Joseph Haydn

The string quartet is made up of two violins, a viola, and a cello. Composers started writing for this combination in the 1700s. Franz Joseph Haydn developed the string quartet into its distinctive form and wrote over 80 string quartets.

*Composers use repetition and contrast to make their music interesting. **Rondo** is a musical form based on these ideas of same and different. The sections of a rondo may be organized as:* A B A C A *or* A B A C A B A *or* A B A C A D A.

The Granger Collection

Lithograph from the 1800s, showing an 18th century Austrian string quartet

LISTEN for repetitions of the A section and the contrasting B and C sections in the fast-moving Fourth Movement from String Quartet Op. 33, No. 3.

274   FORMING THE FUTURE

This song is an interesting mix of past and present. It is sung both in Samoan, a traditional Polynesian language, and in English, a language that is relatively new to the islands. "Savalivali" is used today in Samoan schools where students are learning English.

LISTEN closely to how "Savalivali" is performed. What musical form is used in this song?

Savalivali

Samoan Folk Song
Collected and
Transcribed by
Kathy B. Sorensen

Samoan/English: Sa - va - li - va - li means go for a walk,_____
Pronunciation: sa va li va li

Tau - ta - la - ta - la means too much talk._____
tau ta la ta la

A - lo - fa ia te oe means I love you,
ʌ lo fa ya te oe

Take it ea - sy, fai fai le mu.
fai fai le mu

NOTICE the dotted eighth and sixteenth rhythm (♪.). A *dotted eighth note* lasts as long as three sixteenth notes tied together. What other song in this lesson uses ♪. ?

BLUES, HOW DO YOU DO?

Did you ever use the expression "I'm feeling blue"? It means that you're not happy. A style of music called the **blues** grew out of the sorrow and troubled feelings of Africans who were enslaved and brought to this country. Music in the blues style started in the early 1900s and is still popular today.

LISTENING

Good Mornin', Blues *by Huddie Ledbetter*

Like many other blues singers, Huddie Ledbetter often played the guitar to accompany his singing.

LISTEN to Ledbetter sing "Good Mornin', Blues."

Spotlight on LEADBELLY

"Singin' the blues" came naturally to Huddie Ledbetter (1885–1949), better known as "Leadbelly." Leadbelly had a hard life. By the age of 15 he had learned to play a twelve-stringed guitar and was supporting himself by singing on the streets of Dallas, Texas. He memorized hundreds of work and game songs, field hollers, ballads, and other songs. Leadbelly was first "discovered" in the early 1930s and from then until the time of his death, he performed these same traditional songs.

GOOD MORNIN', BLUES

Words and Music by
Huddie Ledbetter

1. Good morn - in', blues;____
2. I lay down last night,____

Blues, how do you do?____
turn-in' from side to side.____

Good morn - in', blues;__ Blues, how do you do?__
Yes, I was turn-in' from side to side.__

I'm do - ing all right,__ good morn - in', how are you?
I was not__ a - sleep,__ but I was dis - sat - is - fied.

A SOUND AND A STYLE

The blues style is more than just singing about sad times. The blues have a distinctive musical flavor that is created by singing or playing pitches that have been "bent." These are called **blue notes.** Most people who sing the blues never give a thought to these blue notes; they just sing them automatically. Those who want to write down these notes show the altered pitches with accidentals.

The flatted blue notes create the sound of the blues scale. This scale is somewhat like a major scale with two or three added notes. The lowered third, seventh, and sometimes fifth degrees of the scale are the most commonly used blue notes.

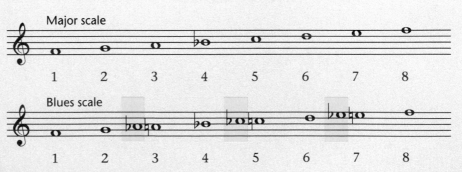

Major scale

1   2   3   4   5   6   7   8

Blues scale

1   2   3   4   5   6   7   8

IDENTIFY the blue note in the melody of "Good Mornin', Blues."

The blues continue to influence jazz and much popular music. Here, for example, is "Jazz Round." What blue notes and other accidentals do you find in this song?

Words and Music by John Coates

Notice the unusual words for this song. These nonsense words, called **scat syllables,** are popular with jazz singers. They allow the singers to use their voices like instruments.

THINK IT THROUGH

"Jazz Round" has a flatted third and seventh step of the scale. Does that mean that it is in the blues style?

Manhattan Transfer uses scat syllables in some of their songs.

TEMPO TRAVELS

Chamber music is music usually played by a small ensemble. Chamber ensembles come in different sizes and are made up of different instruments. Here is a **woodwind quintet**. How is it different from a string quartet? Is there any similarity between the two chamber ensembles?

flute

oboe

French horn

bassoon

THINK IT THROUGH
Why do you think the French horn is part of a "woodwind" ensemble?

LISTENING

Suite for Wind Quintet

First Movement
by Ruth Crawford-Seeger

The first movement of "Suite for Wind Quintet" has three sections: A B A. This pattern occurs in each section.

$$\frac{10}{8}\left(\frac{6}{8}+\frac{2}{4}\right)$$

Listen for these changes.

A   *Pattern acts as an ostinato in the bassoon*

B   *Instruments play modified pattern in octaves*

A   *Transformation of the pattern in the oboe, then flute, and finally the bassoon*

There is something more than just a change in instruments that marks off these three sections. What is it?

SPOTLIGHT ON
Ruth Crawford-Seeger

clarinet

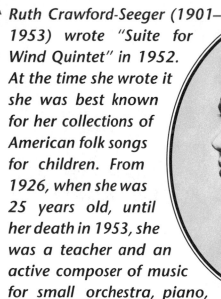

Ruth Crawford-Seeger (1901–1953) wrote "Suite for Wind Quintet" in 1952. At the time she wrote it she was best known for her collections of American folk songs for children. From 1926, when she was 25 years old, until her death in 1953, she was a teacher and an active composer of music for small orchestra, piano, chamber ensembles, and voice. Her music was ahead of its time because of her bold technique and was rarely performed during her lifetime. Only since her death have her compositions been widely recognized.

Tempo is an Italian word that means "the speed of the beat." Tempo markings are used to describe the tempo the composer wants for a particular piece of music. These words are often found above the first line of music and anywhere the tempo changes. Tempo markings are most often found in Italian. Other languages such as German, English, and French, are also used. Look for tempo markings in music you perform.

belebt
(brisk)

moderato
(moderate)

largo
(broad)

accelerando
(quickening)

ritardando
(slowing)

adagio
(at ease)

allegro
(fast)

andante
(walking)

plodding

allegretto
(lively)

lento
(slow)

THINK IT THROUGH
What other words besides the ones on this page could be used as tempo markings?

REVIEW "Tsiothwatasè:tha" and describe the tempo.

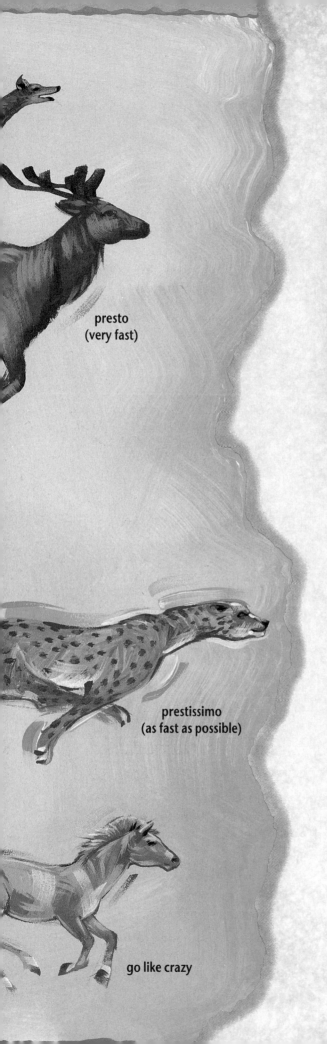

presto
(very fast)

prestissimo
(as fast as possible)

go like crazy

Meet
ARLIENE NOFCHISSEY WILLIAMS

Arliene Nofchissey Williams is a Navaho from Arizona. In 1967, she and Carnes Burson, a Ute, composed the song "Go, My Son" while they were attending Brigham Young University. They wrote it for a Native American student touring group.

Williams explains that "Go, My Son" was written to encourage Native American youth to continue their education past high school. She says that education for Native Americans is also in nature, where they can learn from the trees, the mountains, the sun, the rain, the wind, and all the elements.

LISTEN as Arliene Nofchissey Williams tells about the meaning of "Go, My Son."

FIND the tempo markings in the notation of "Go, My Son" and use both of them when you perform the song. *Andante* means "at a moderate walking tempo," and *ritardando* (*rit.*) means "to slow down."

This silver-and-turquoise necklace was made in 1992 by Alice Blackgoat, a Navaho. The skills to make this squash-blossom necklace have been passed from generation to generation.

GO, MY SON

Words and Music by
Carnes Burson and
Arliene Nofchissey Williams

Andante

1. Go, my son, go and climb the lad-der. Go, my son,
2. Work, my son, get an ed-u-ca-tion. Work, my son,
(3.) on the lad-der of an ed-u-ca-tion, You can see to

go and earn your fea-ther. Go, my son,
learn a good vo-ca-tion and Climb, my son,
help your In-dian na-tion then Reach, my son, and

make your peo-ple proud of you.
go and take a loft-y
lift your peo-ple up with

view. 3. From you.
Go, my son,
on the lad-der

go and climb the lad-der. Go, my son, go and earn your fea - ther.
of an ed-u-ca-tion, You can see to help your In-dian na-tion, then

Second time to Coda

Go, my son, make your peo-ple proud of you. From

Coda

Reach, my son and lift your peo-ple up with you.

LISTENING

Musette

(performed by Yo-Yo Ma and Bobby McFerrin)

by Johann Sebastian Bach

"Musette" is performed by a cellist and singer. Think back and remember this music, but look forward to a new sound!

SHOW the tempo as you listen to "Musette."

What happened to the tempo? How did Bobby's voice change in the song?

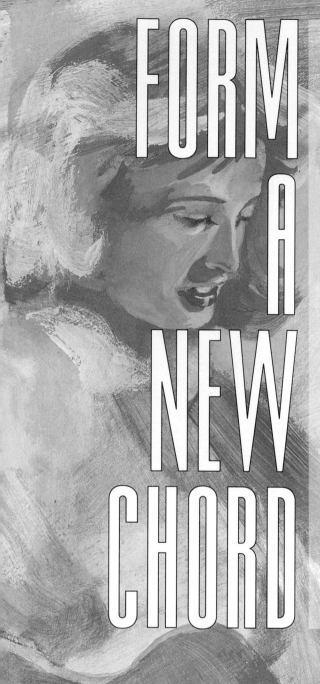

FORM A NEW CHORD

When it comes to accompanying the blues, the guitar player usually plays more chords than melody. The blues harmony is usually built around the I, IV, and V chords. These are the chords built on the first, fourth, and fifth steps of the scale. "Good Mornin', Blues" is in F major, so the I, IV, and V chords are F, B♭, and C. The root of each chord is given below.

IDENTIFY the names of the other pitches in each chord.

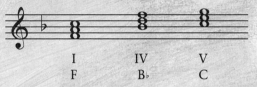

| I | IV | V |
| F | B♭ | C |

Harmony in the blues is usually provided by a specific chord progression called a blues progression. One of the most characteristic blues progressions is twelve measures, or bars, long. That's why it is called the **twelve-bar blues.** On the right is the chord sequence for "Good Mornin', Blues."

SING the chord roots as you listen to the twelve-bar blues
progression of "Good Mornin', Blues."

Good Mornin', Blues

Words and Music
by Huddie Ledbetter

4/4	1 I I I I F Good	morn-in',blues; _____	2 I I I I F Blues, how do you do?	3 I I I I F _____	4 I I I I F Good
	5 IV IV IV IV B♭ morn - in', blues; ____		6 IV IV IV IV B♭ Blues, how do you do?	7 I I I I F _____	8 I I I I F I'm
	9 V V V V C do-ing all right,__good		10 IV IV IV IV B♭ morn - in', how are	11 I I I I F you?_____	12 I I I F

New words and new music arrangement by Huddie Ledbetter. Edited with new additional material by Alan Lomax, T.R.O.
© Copyright 1959 renewed Folkways Music Publisher, Inc., N.Y., Used by permission.

LISTENING

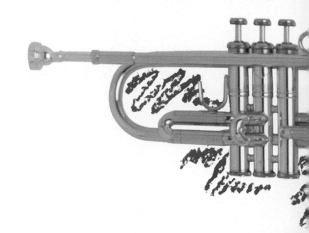

Rondeau

from *Symphonies de Fanfares*, No. 1
by Jean-Joseph Mouret

*In the 1700s, a French composer, Jean-Joseph Mouret, wrote a rondeau, or rondo. It is played by a **brass quintet** like the one below. How is this chamber ensemble different from the wood-wind quintet? Which musical instrument is used in both quintets?*

trumpet   French horn   tuba   trombone   trumpet

COUNT the number of times the A section occurs as you listen to "Rondeau." What instrument plays the theme? Is "Rondeau" a rondo?

288 FORM A NEW CHORD

A RONDO?

Listen again to "Savalivali." Is it in rondo form? Explain why or why not. List the sections.

MOVE to "Savalivali," choosing a different movement for each section.

Start WITH A FEELING

Look at this picture. How do you suppose
he feels? What might have happened? Have
you ever looked this way? Could he be having a
case of "the blues"?

CREATE your own blues lyrics, or words.

The first thing you need is the feeling—something you can "feel
blue" about. How do you choose a topic? What about the time
you had three tests on the same day? What about when your
best friend moved to another city? Or when your dog died?

Now that you have the idea, you need to know about the rhyme
scheme of blues lyrics. Look at the lyrics of "Joe Turner Blues."

Joe Turner Blues

American Blues

1. They tell me___ Joe Turn-er's___ come and gone.___
2. He came here___ with for-ty___ links of chain.___

They tell me___ Joe Turn-er's___ come and gone.___
He came here___ with for-ty___ links of chain.___

He left me___ here to sing___ this___ song.
He left me___ here to sing___ this___ song.

Notice the rhyme scheme of "Joe Turner Blues." Two identical lines are followed by a different line that rhymes. Each line fits into the same number of beats.

Does "Joe Turner Blues" have the same form as "Good Mornin', Blues"?

Use this rhyme scheme as a model to write your own blues lyrics. Then sing the lyrics to the melody of "Good Mornin', Blues." Remember, your new lyrics will need to have about the same number of syllables as "Good Mornin', Blues" to fit the melody.

When you have written your blues lyrics, you're ready to "sing the blues."

ACCOMPANY yourself or a friend with the twelve-bar blues chord progression. Use the F, B♭, and C chords as the I, IV, and V chords.

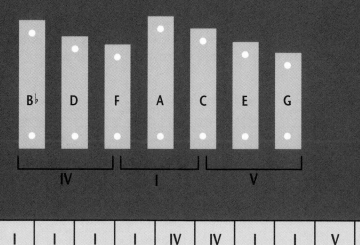

CHOOSE instruments for your blues piece. Use instruments and players that are available. You may want to include a part for someone who plays an instrument such as flute, trumpet, or clarinet.

PAST AND @ PRESENT RHYTHMS

Flamenco dancer from Spain

"Canten, señores cantores" is a song from the northern part of Argentina. Notice the rhythms in the song. The sixteenth-eighth-sixteenth (♫♩♫) rhythm is twice as fast as the ♪♩ ♪ syncopated pattern.

PRACTICE these rhythm patterns. They appear in songs both old and new.

1. 𝄴

2. 𝄴

3. 𝄴

4. 𝄴

Argentine guitarist

294

Canten, señores cantores

Sing, Gentlemen Singers

Argentine Traditional Song
English Words by MMH

Spanish: Can - ten se - ño - res can - to - res lo que ve - ní - an can - tan - do;
Pronunciation: kan ten se nyo ɾes kan to ɾes lo ke βe ni an kan tan do
English: Sing, now, se - ño - res can - to - res, you, who have come to sing your song.

Yo co - mo re - cién lle - ga - do al - zo mi voz con re - ce - lo.
yo ko mo ɾe syɛn ye ga ðo al so mi βos kon ɾe se lo
Though I am hes - i - tant and shy, I raise my voice and sing a - long.

Na - ran - ja - les, du - raz - na - les, que bo - ni - tos car - na - va - les.
na ɾan xa les ðu ɾas na les ke βo ni tos kaɾ na βa les
Or - an - ges sweet, peach - es to eat; beau - ti - ful is car - ni - val time!

What are some contemporary Hispanic groups today? What songs have they made popular in your area?

Gloria Estefan and Miami Sound Machine

295

WRITTEN RHYTHMS, OLD AND NEW

If you compare the score for a song written in the time of Haydn with one written in your lifetime, you'll see that they both communicate the rhythm by note values and rests.

Haydn String Quartet

"Young People of the World"

TWO HORSES

Compare the two sculptures. One was created over 2500 years ago. The other was made recently. How are the sculptures the same? How are they different?

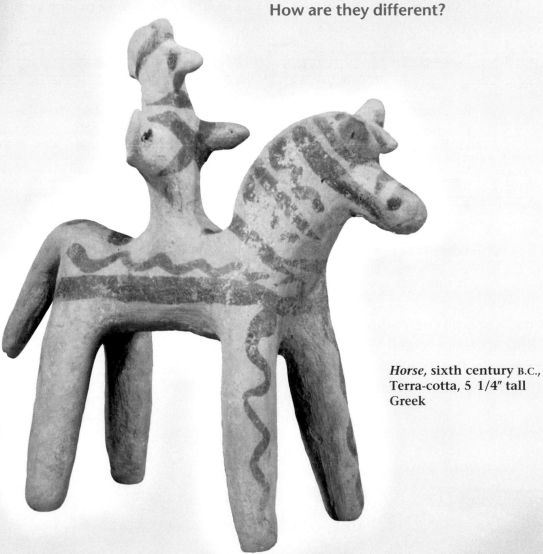

Horse, sixth century B.C., Terra-cotta, 5 1/4" tall Greek

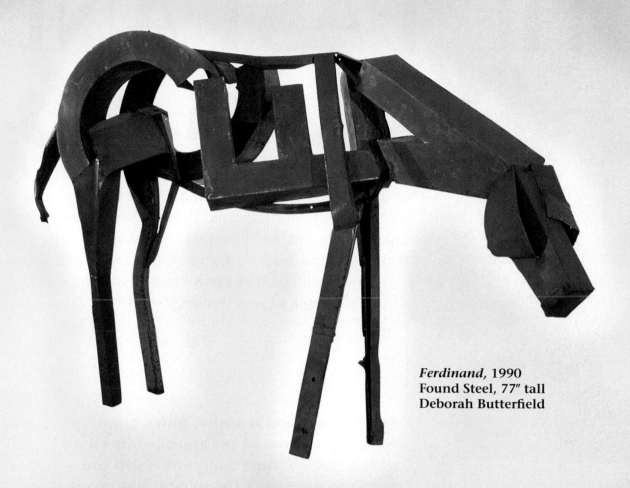

Ferdinand, 1990
Found Steel, 77″ tall
Deborah Butterfield

Music from very different times and places can have the same rhythm patterns.

LOOK at the notation fragments below. Can you tell, just by looking, which comes from an Argentine song or which comes from a Mohawk song? Can you tell which one is Samoan?

CLAP each rhythm and see if you can identify the song.

THE PAST AND *blues*

One of the musical elements that gives the blues its special sound is the bass line. The bass line is often played in such a way that it seems to sing out almost as much as the melody. Often the root of each chord is used as a bass note. What are the roots of the I, IV, and V chords below?

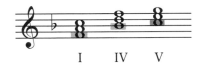

I   IV   V

LISTEN to "Good Mornin', Blues," and point to the root of the appropriate chord as it is played. How many times did you hear the B♭ used as the root? What about the C?

I   I   I   I

IV   IV   I   I

V   IV   I   I

A bass line is often played by a string bass (left) or an electric bass (right).

PRESENT

Musicians have all kinds of tricks to make a bass line come alive. Sometimes the bass line is heard all by itself as a solo, then other instruments join in to make the harmony complete.

Below is a bass line pattern to play with "Good Mornin', Blues" or your own blues. It is based on the same chord progression you learned earlier.

PLAY these *arpeggios,* which are "broken" chords.

You have learned about rondo form and blues harmony. Now combine these two elements to create a new blues rondo.

LEARN this rap as the A section.

A RHYME IN TIME

Words and Music by René Boyer-White

With a Swing

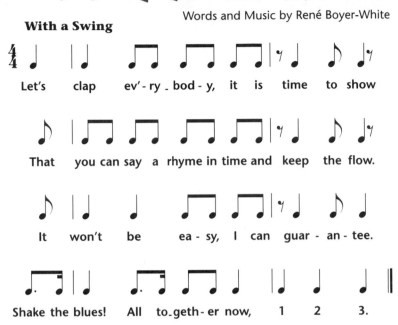

Let's clap ev'-ry - bod - y, it is time to show

That you can say a rhyme in time and keep the flow.

It won't be ea - sy, I can guar - an - tee.

Shake the blues! All to - geth - er now, 1 2 3.

USE the original blues lyrics you created for your B section.

USE an original jazzy body-percussion pattern for your C section, or use a short poem or rhyme.

ACCOMPANY the B section of the rondo with the twelve-bar blues bass line.

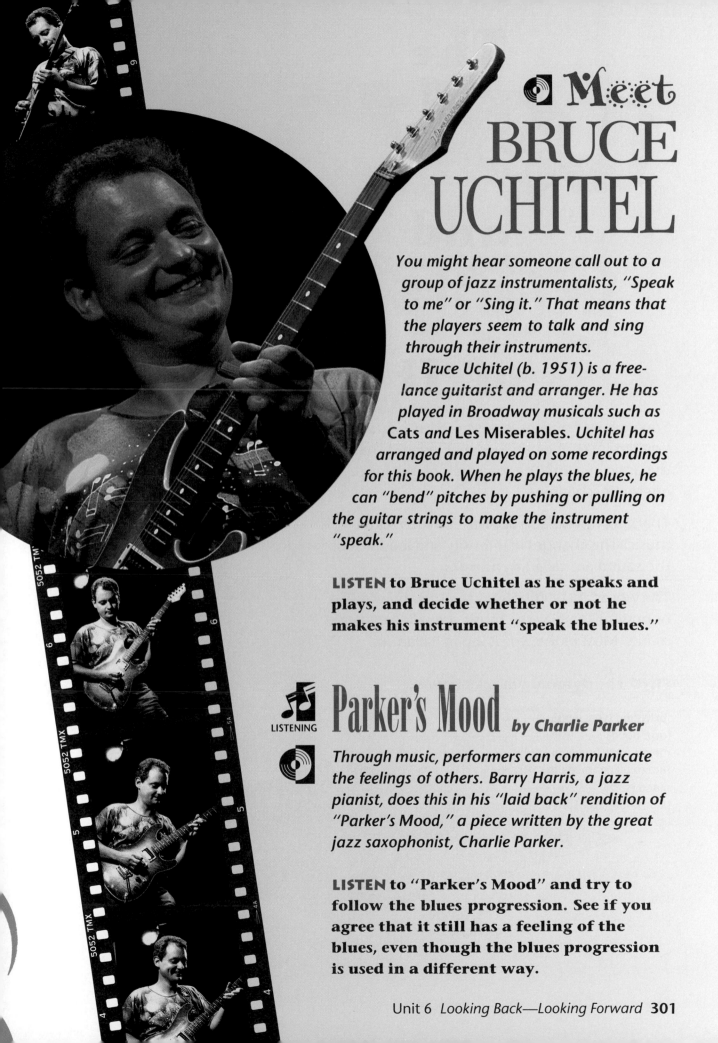

BRUCE UCHITEL

You might hear someone call out to a group of jazz instrumentalists, "Speak to me" or "Sing it." That means that the players seem to talk and sing through their instruments.

Bruce Uchitel (b. 1951) is a free-lance guitarist and arranger. He has played in Broadway musicals such as Cats *and* Les Miserables. *Uchitel has arranged and played on some recordings for this book. When he plays the blues, he can "bend" pitches by pushing or pulling on the guitar strings to make the instrument "speak."*

LISTEN to Bruce Uchitel as he speaks and plays, and decide whether or not he makes his instrument "speak the blues."

♫
LISTENING

Parker's Mood *by Charlie Parker*

Through music, performers can communicate the feelings of others. Barry Harris, a jazz pianist, does this in his "laid back" rendition of "Parker's Mood," a piece written by the great jazz saxophonist, Charlie Parker.

LISTEN to "Parker's Mood" and try to follow the blues progression. See if you agree that it still has a feeling of the blues, even though the blues progression is used in a different way.

The LOUD and SOFT of It

You've heard of people described as being "dynamic," but what does that mean? What is a dynamic person? That person is on the move, energetic, changing.

That description also applies to dynamics in music. The changes in intensity and loudness of the sound are called **dynamics.**

The words and symbols that tell you how loud or how soft to play the music are called dynamic marks. Most of the words are in Italian.

FIND the dynamic marks below.

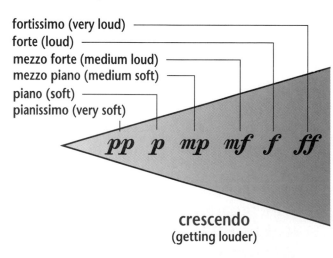

fortissimo (very loud)
forte (loud)
mezzo forte (medium loud)
mezzo piano (medium soft)
piano (soft)
pianissimo (very soft)

pp p mp mf f ff   ff f mf mp p pp

crescendo
(getting louder)

decrescendo
(getting softer)

YOUTH

Even though you may not be aware of it, you use dynamics in your everyday conversation. When you call out a greeting or whisper a secret, you are using extremes of dynamics.

READ the lines from the poem, using dynamic variations. Try some contrasts in dynamics and ask a partner what the effect was.

We have tomorrow
Bright before us
Like a flame.

Yesterday
A night-gone thing,
A sun-down name.

And dawn-today
Broad arch above the road we came.

We march!

—Langston Hughes

Sail into your future with this song.

SING "Sail Away" using different dynamics to make the music expressive.

SAIL AWAY

Finnish Folk Song
New Words Arranged by
Elizabeth Gilpatrick

Verses 1, 3: unison   Verses 2, 4: canon

1. Who can sail a - way with no wind?
2. Who can fly to the top of the hill?
3. I can sail a - way with no wind,
4. I can fly to the top of the hill,

Who can row with - out oars?
Who can reach the sky?
I can reach the sky,
I can reach the sky,

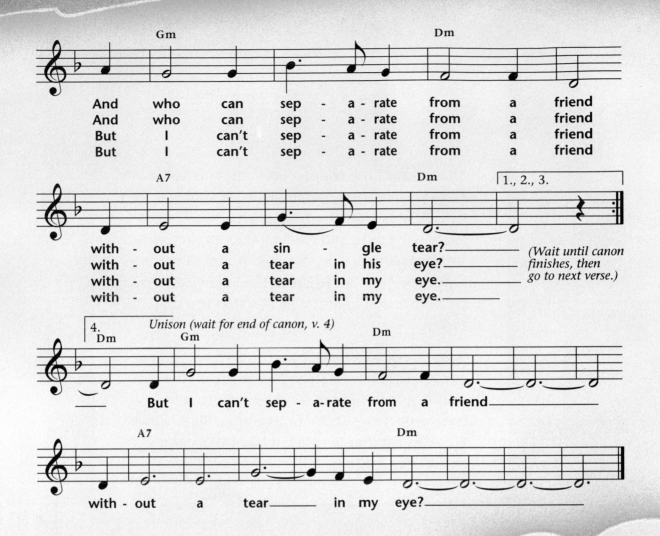

And who can sep - a - rate from a friend
And who can sep - a - rate from a friend
But I can't sep - a - rate from a friend
But I can't sep - a - rate from a friend

with - out a sin - gle tear?_____
with - out a tear in his eye?_____
with - out a tear in my eye._____
with - out a tear in my eye._____

(Wait until canon finishes, then go to next verse.)

4.
Unison (wait for end of canon, v. 4)

_____ But I can't sep - a-rate from a friend_____

with - out a tear_____ in my eye?_____

THINK IT THROUGH

Describe the dynamics, tempo, and style in "Sail Away." Then compare the dynamics, tempo, and style of "Sail Away" with "Good Mornin', Blues" or "Joe Turner Blues."

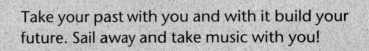

Take your past with you and with it build your future. Sail away and take music with you!

REVIEW

TO THE FUTURE!

The music of the twenty-first century is just around the corner. Without even trying, you are helping it take shape. What each person listens to, understands, and enjoys influences in some small way the development of musical form and style. You have already seen the influence of the past in the sound and style of songs you sing today.

Sing "Good Mornin', Blues," a song whose style continues to have a strong influence on the music of today. Listen for the characteristic twelve-bar blues chord progression. "Joe Turner Blues" is another twelve-bar blues that came out of the same era.

"Jazz Round" uses blue notes, but it is not in the twelve-bar blues form or blues style. Blue notes have been used in the early blues as well as more modern jazz styles. Listen for the blue notes as you sing "Jazz Round" in canon.

Rondo form has been popular for centuries. Listen for the return of the A section in the fourth movement of String Quartet Op. 33, No. 3 by Franz Joseph Haydn.

A blending of the old and new happens in music from all over the world. In the Samoan song "Savalivali," the traditional Samoan language is combined with English, a language newer to these islands.

Looking back, looking forward. Take all you can from the past and the present with you into the future. Let it give you insight, understanding, and vision. Sing "Young People of the World." In what way do you most want to change the world of the future?

CHECK IT OUT

1. Choose the form that you hear.

   a. A B A   **b.** A B A C A   **c.** A B   **d.** A A B A

2. Choose the form that you hear.

   a. A B A C A   **b.** A B   **c.** A B A   **d.** A B C

3. Choose the form that you hear.

   a. A B   **b.** A B A   **c.** A A B A   **d.** A B A C A

4. Which chord progression do you hear?

   a. I IV V I   **b.** I V IV I   **c.** I IV I V   **d.** I I IV V

5. Which chord progression do you hear?

   a. I V IV V   **b.** I IV IV I   **c.** I IV V I   **d.** I V IV I

CREATE

Create and Perform a Rondo

Work in a small group to create a rondo. Choose a short song or part of a longer song for the A section. Use its subject as a theme for your rondo. Let your choices for the other sections be guided by what is appropriate to express your theme.

CREATE music for the B and C sections. You may design a percussion piece with rhythm only, make up a melody to fit the blues chord progression, or use a poem that expresses your theme. The sections should be roughly the same length.

Choose instruments and voices to perform each part. Practice each section with your group.

ORGANIZE the sections into rondo form. Choose one of the following: A B A C A B A, A B A C A, A B A C A D A.

Write

What will the music of the future be like? Imagine that you are a music critic attending a concert sometime after the year 2010. Write a review of the performance, including as many details as possible about the music and musicians.

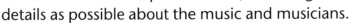

So Long

Words and Music by Woody Guthrie

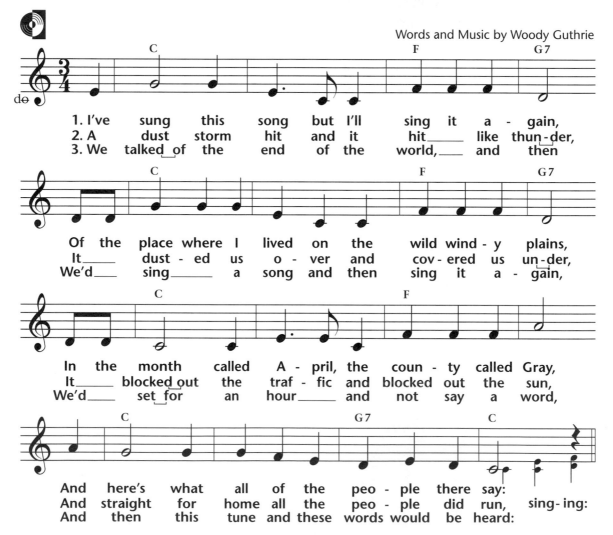

1. I've sung this song but I'll sing it a - gain,
2. A dust storm hit and it hit___ like thun - der,
3. We talked of the end of the world,___ and then

Of the place where I lived on the wild wind - y plains,
It___ dust - ed us o - ver and cov - ered us un - der,
We'd___ sing___ a song and then sing it a - gain,

In the month called A - pril, the coun - ty called Gray,
It___ blocked out the traf - fic and blocked out the sun,
We'd___ set for an hour___ and not say a word,

And here's what all of the peo - ple there say:
And straight for home all the peo - ple did run, sing - ing:
And then this tune and these words would be heard:

Refrain

"So long, it's been good to know you,

So long, it's been good to know you,

So long, it's been good to know you,

This dust-y old dust is a-get-ting my home,

and I've got to be mov-ing a-long."

Encore NEW VOICES:

Musicians in our time often know as much about computers as they do about music. Computers, digital recording, and electronic instruments are changing the way many musicians create sounds.

Pitches, rhythms, dynamics, tempo, and other musical information can now be processed through a computer device called MIDI, or **M**usic **I**nstrument **D**igital **I**nterface. A composer can play music on a keyboard or other MIDI-connected instrument into a computer. The computer remembers what was played and can play it back exactly as it "learned" it. The composer can then play second, third, or more additional parts, and the computer can remember them all. It can then play the music back, becoming an electronic orchestra.

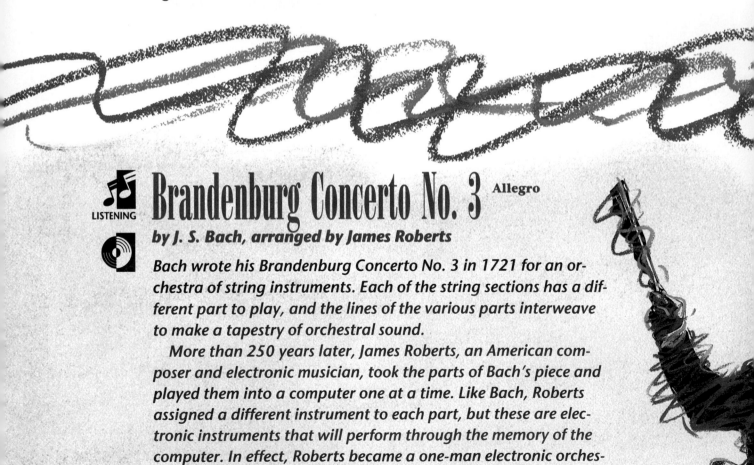

LISTENING

Brandenburg Concerto No. 3 Allegro

by J. S. Bach, arranged by James Roberts

Bach wrote his Brandenburg Concerto No. 3 in 1721 for an orchestra of string instruments. Each of the string sections has a different part to play, and the lines of the various parts interweave to make a tapestry of orchestral sound.

More than 250 years later, James Roberts, an American composer and electronic musician, took the parts of Bach's piece and played them into a computer one at a time. Like Bach, Roberts assigned a different instrument to each part, but these are electronic instruments that will perform through the memory of the computer. In effect, Roberts became a one-man electronic orchestra, creating a new and modern tapestry from a traditional piece of music.

Making Music with Technology

▲ Computer technology has made it possible for composers to hear the sound of their instrumental music and revise it on the spot.

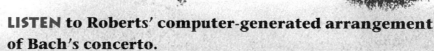

LISTEN to Roberts' computer-generated arrangement of Bach's concerto.

Technology is also being used to change musical performance. Musicians are experimenting with computerized instruments that sound like an entire orchestra. Even the gestures or ways a performer plays an instrument or a conductor moves a baton can be captured and reproduced. Once this information is stored in the computer, it can be used to give recorded music the rich sounds you would hear at a live performance.

▲ Tod Machover, of the M.I.T. Media Lab, enters hand movement information for playing the cello into the computer.

► Max Matthews, of Stanford University, plays an electronic violin.

LISTENING

Cannon River Wave/Forms (excerpt)
by David Means

The development of computer technology has enabled composers to put together sound sources in new and creative ways. Often, composers combine computer-generated sounds with live performances. In an outdoor performance in Northfield, Minnesota, musicians and sound engineers worked together to create a public art event. The natural sounds of the Cannon River were used as a backdrop for a sound event that included computers, electronic and acoustic instruments, live environmental sounds, and voices. In the score, the composer used the symbols on page 283.

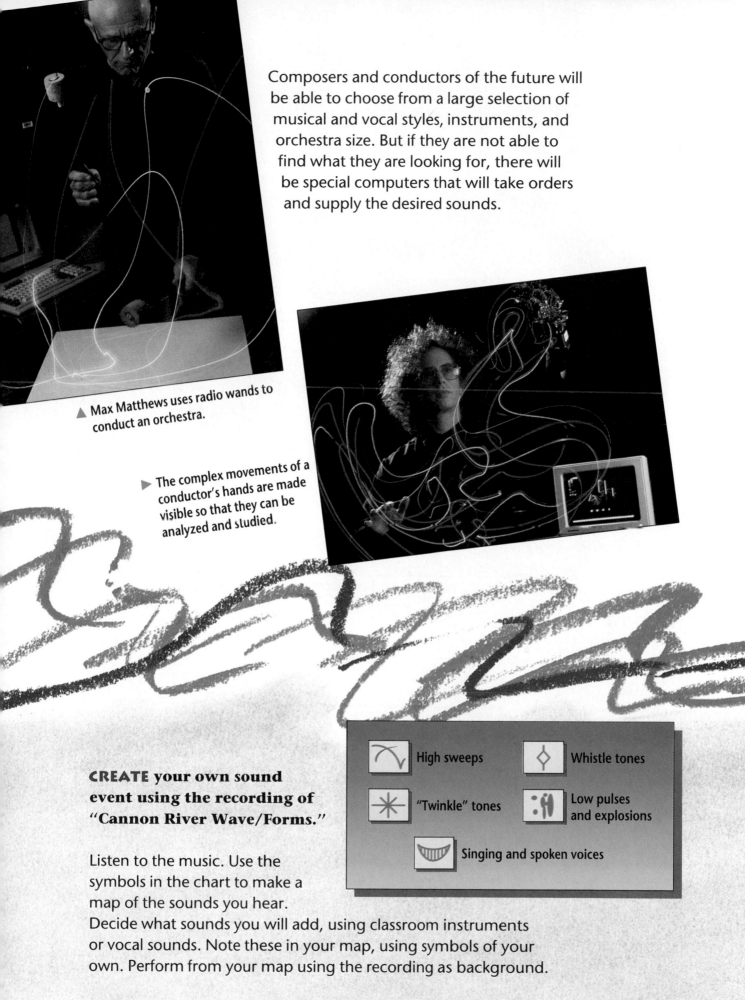

Composers and conductors of the future will be able to choose from a large selection of musical and vocal styles, instruments, and orchestra size. But if they are not able to find what they are looking for, there will be special computers that will take orders and supply the desired sounds.

▲ Max Matthews uses radio wands to conduct an orchestra.

▶ The complex movements of a conductor's hands are made visible so that they can be analyzed and studied.

CREATE your own sound event using the recording of "Cannon River Wave/Forms."

Listen to the music. Use the symbols in the chart to make a map of the sounds you hear.
Decide what sounds you will add, using classroom instruments or vocal sounds. Note these in your map, using symbols of your own. Perform from your map using the recording as background.

⌒	High sweeps
✳	"Twinkle" tones
◇	Whistle tones
:⁞	Low pulses and explosions
⌣	Singing and spoken voices

CELEBRAT

CELEBRATION

I shall dance tonight.
When the dusk comes crawling,
There will be dancing
    and feasting.
I shall dance with the others
     in circles,
      in leaps,
       in stomps.
Laughter and talk will
    weave into the night,
Among the fires
    of my people.
Games will be played
And I shall be
    a part of it.

—Alonzo Lopez

Hooray for the RED, WHITE, AND BLUE

The 50 states that make up the United States are each special in their own way—from Alaska, the northernmost state, to Hawaii, the southernmost. However, one thing that many of the states have in common is a name with Native American origins. The name Alaska, for example, came from *alakshak,* an Inuit word for "peninsula," "great lands," or "land that is not an island."

★★★ FIFTY NIFTY ★★★ UNITED STATES

Words and Music
by Ray Charles

Fif - ty nif - ty U - nit - ed States from thir - teen o - rig - i - nal col - o - nies;

Fif - ty nif - ty stars in the flag that bil - lows so beau - ti - f'ly in— the breeze.

Each in - di - vid - u - al state con - tri - butes a qual - i - ty that is great.

Each in - di - vid - u - al state de - serves a bow, we sa - lute them now.

Fif - ty nif - ty U - ni - ted States from thir - teen o - rig - i - nal col - o - nies,

Shout 'em, scout 'em, Tell all a - bout 'em, One by one till we've

giv - en a day to ev'- ry state in the U. S. A. Al - a -

2nd time as fast as possible

bam - a A - las - ka, Ar - i - zo - na, Ar - kan - sas, Cal - i -

for - nia, Col - o - ra - do, Con - nect - i - cut; Del - a - ware,

Flor - i - da,   Geor - gia,   Ha - wai - i,   I - da - ho,   Il - li - nois,   In - di -

an - a;   I - o - wa,   Kan - sas,   Ken - tuck - y,   Lou - i - si -

an - a,   Maine,   Mar - y - land,   Mas - sa - chu - setts,   Mich - i - gan;

Min - ne - so - ta,   Mis - sis - sip - pi,   Mis - sou - ri,   Mon -

tan - a,   Ne - bras - ka,   Ne - vad - a;   New Hamp - shire,

New Jer - sey,   New Mex - i - co,   New York,   North Car - o - li - na,

North Da - ko - ta,   O - hi - o;   Ok - la - ho - ma,   Or - e - gon,

Penn - syl - va - nia,   Rhode Is - land, South Car - o - li - na,   South Da - ko - ta,

Ten-nes-see, Tex-as; _____ U-tah, Ver-mont, Vir-gin-ia, Wash-ing-ton,

West Vir-gin-ia, Wis-con-sin, Wy-o-ming. Al-a - o - ming.

Tempo I

North, south, east, west, in our calm, ob-jec-tive o-pin-ion, (name of

home state) is the best _____ of the Fif-ty nif-ty

U-nit-ed States from thir-teen o-rig-i-nal col-o-nies,

Shout 'em, scout 'em, Tell all a-bout 'em, One by one till we've

giv-en a day to ev'-ry state in the good old

U. _____ S. _____ A. _____

"The Star-Spangled Banner" was inspired by a battle in the War of 1812. Francis Scott Key, aboard a ship, waited for the outcome of the attack. The "red glare" of artillery fire lit the sky, reassuring him that the American flag still flew. The bombing stopped at dawn. The star-spangled banner still waved. The artist, J. Bower, showed the battle in his etching on page 323.

THE STAR-SPANGLED BANNER

Music Attributed to J. S. Smith
Words by Francis Scott Key

1. Oh, say! can you see, by the dawn's ear - ly light,
2. On the shore, dim - ly seen through the mists of the deep,
3. Oh, thus be it ev - er when free men shall stand

What so proud - ly we hailed at the twi - light's last gleam - ing?
Where the foe's haugh - ty host in dread si - lence re - pos - es,
Be - tween their loved homes and the war's des - o - la - tion!

Whose broad stripes and bright stars, through the per - il - ous fight,
What is that which the breeze, o'er the tow - er - ing steep,
Blest with vic - t'ry and peace, may the heav'n res - cued land

O'er the ram - parts we watched were so gal - lant - ly stream - ing?
As it fit - ful - ly blows, half con - ceals, half dis - clos - es?
Praise the Pow'r that hath made and pre - served us a na - tion.

And the rock - ets' red glare, the bombs burst - ing in air,
Now it catch - es the gleam of the morn - ing's first beam,
Then con - quer we must, for our cause it is just,

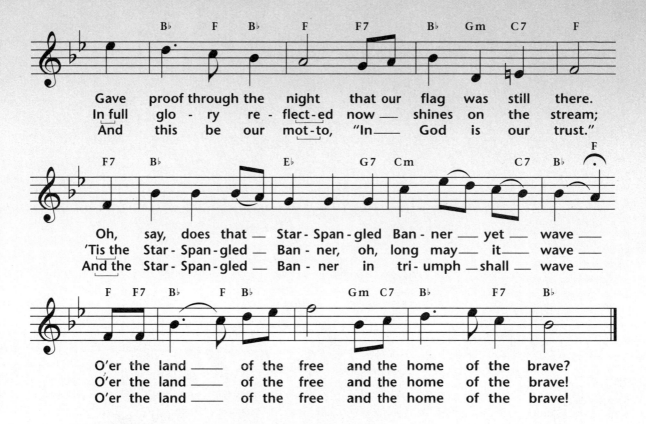

| | B♭ | F | B♭ | F | F7 | B♭ | Gm | C7 | F |

Gave   proof through the   night   that our   flag   was   still   there.
In full   glo - ry   re - flect-ed   now ___   shines   on   the   stream;
And   this   be   our   mot-to,   "In___   God   is   our   trust."

| | F7 | B♭ | | E♭ | G7 Cm | | C7 B♭ | F |

Oh,   say,   does that ___   Star - Span-gled   Ban - ner ___ yet ___ wave
'Tis the   Star - Span-gled ___   Ban - ner,   oh,   long may___ it___ wave
And the   Star - Span-gled ___   Ban - ner   in   tri - umph ___shall ___ wave

| | F F7 | B♭ | F B♭ | | Gm C7 | B♭ | F7 | B♭ |

O'er the land ___   of the   free   and the home   of the   brave?
O'er the land ___   of the   free   and the home   of the   brave!
O'er the land ___   of the   free   and the home   of the   brave!

LISTENING

Washington Post March *by John Philip Sousa*

John Philip Sousa was a famous bandmaster and composer. Because he composed so many marches, he earned the title "The March King." This is one of his most popular marches.

The Bombardment of Fort McHenry, J. Bower, 1814.

The Granger Collection

Halloween's a Scream

LISTENING

Halloween Montage

Do you recognize these tunes? They all have something to do with the Halloween spirit—identify them if you can!

Halloween is a time when "the shivers" can be fun. Watch for a slight case of these as you sing this old English folk song.

Nottamun Town

English Folk Song

1. In Not - ta - mun Town,—— not a soul would look
2. I rode a gray horse—— that was called a gray
3. She stood so still,—— she threw me to the
4. Set down on a hard,—— hot, cold froz - en

up.—— Not a soul would look up,—— not a soul would look
mare,—— With a gray mane and tail,—— green stripe down her
dirt,—— She tore—— my hide—— and bruised—— my
stone.—— Ten thou - sand stood a-round—— me and yet I's a -

down.—— Not a soul would look up,—— not a soul would look
back,—— Gray mane and gray tail,—— green stripe down her
shirt,—— From sad - dle to stir - rup I mount - ed a -
lone;—— Took my hat in my hands—— for to keep my head

down—— to show me the way to fair Not - ta - mun Town.
back,—— There wa'nt a hair on her be - what was coal black.
gain—— And on my ten toes I rode o - ver the plain.
warm;— Ten thou - sand got drownd - ed that nev - er were born.

from # The Headless Horseman

The headless horseman rides tonight
through stark and starless skies.
Shattering the silence
with his otherworldly cries,
he races through the darkness
on his alabaster steed.
The headless horseman rides tonight
wherever the fates would lead.

And he rides upon the wind tonight,
he rides upon the wind,
galloping, galloping, galloping on
out of the great oblivion,
galloping till the night is gone,
he rides upon the wind tonight,
he rides upon the wind.

—Jack Prelutsky

Think about the poem "The Headless Horseman" as you sing this song. How does the horseman in this song compare with the one in the poem?

The Horseman

Music by Marilyn Davidson
Words by Walter de la Mare

1 *p*
I heard a horse-man Ride o-ver the hill;

2 *mp*
The moon shone clear, The night was still;

3 *f*
His helm was sil-ver, and pale was

4 *p*
he; And the horse he rode was of i-vor-y.

Gathering FOR Thanksgiving

The early settlers of New England came together to give thanks for a successful corn harvest. We remember this first Pilgrim harvest as we celebrate Thanksgiving today.

Come, Ye Thankful People, Come

Music by Sir George Job Elvey
Words by Henry Alford

1. Come, ye thank-ful peo-ple, come, Raise the song of har-vest home;
2. All the world is God's own field, Fruit un-to his praise to yield;

All is safe-ly gath-ered in Ere the win-ter storms be-gin;
Wheat and tares to-geth-er sown, Un-to joy or sor-row grown;

God, our Mak-er, doth pro-vide For our wants to be sup-plied;
First the blade, and then the ear, Then the full corn shall ap-pear;

Come to God's own tem-ple, come, Raise the song of har-vest home.
Lord of har-vest, grant that we Whole-some grain and pure may be.

For Thy Gracious Blessings

Traditional Melody
Arranged
by Marilyn C. Davidson
Words by Lester S. Bucher

Descant

For Thy gra - cious bless - ings,

Melody

For Thy gra - cious bless - ings,

For Thy won - drous Word,

For Thy won - drous Word,

For Thy lov - ing kind - ness,

For Thy lov - ing kind - ness,

We give thanks, Oh Lord.

We give thanks, Oh Lord.

Celebrate the Moon

The people of China, Vietnam, and Thailand, as well as other Southeast Asian countries, celebrate the beauty of the full moon with festivals. Asian American communities in the United States celebrate these holidays with special music, food, and traditions.

The Vietnamese Children's Festival is part of their Mid-Autumn Festival. Dancing and singing children fill the streets, carrying lighted lanterns.

This Vietnamese song honors the full moon.

Tết Trung
Children's Festival

Vietnamese Song
Collected and Transcribed by
Kathy B. Sorensen
English Words by MMH

Vietnamese: Tết trung thu rước đèn đi chơi. Em rước đèn đi khắp phố phường.
Pronunciation: tɛt trung tu rʊk dɛn di choi em rʊk dɛn di kap fo fʊng
English:
1. At Mid-au-tumn Fes-ti-val, Walk a-round with lan-terns lit.
2. Beau-ti-ful and full the moon, At Mid-au-tumn Fes-ti-val.

Long vui sướng với đèn trong tay Em múa ca trong ánh trăng rằm.
lʌng vui sʊng voi dɛn trʌng tai em muə ka trʌng ʌn trʌng ram
Take them all a - cross the town, Sing-ing— to the au-tumn moon.
Wait-ing for the— moon to rise, I can— hear the sound of drums,

Đèn ông sao với đèn cá chám. Đèn thiên nga với đen bướm bướm,
dɛn ʌng sau voi dɛn ka cham dɛn tiɛn nga voi dɛn bʊm bʊm
Lan-terns all in dif-fer-ent shapes, Lan-tern an-gel, lan-tern dream,
Tung yin yin kak tung yin yin, Tung yin yin kak tung yin yin.

em rước đèn này đến cung trăng. Đèn xanh lơ với đèn tím tím.
em rʊk dɛn nai dɛn kung trʌng dɛn sʌn lə voi dɛn tim tim
Lan-tern fish, or lan-tern star, Lan-tern swan or but-ter-fly.
I can hear the sound of drums, Tung yin yin kak tung yin yin,

Đèn xanh lam với đèn trắng trắng, trong ánh đèn rực rỡ muốn màu.
dɛn sʌn lam voi dɛn trʌng trʌng trʌng ʌn dɛn rʊk rʊ mun mau
Take my lan-tern to the sky; Take my lan-tern to the moon.
Tung yin yin kak tung yin yin. Wel-come, la-dy in the moon!

Loy Kratong is an autumn ceremony in Thailand. It is a time to forget, or float away, the bad experiences of the year that is ending and hope that the new year will be happy. "Pung Noy Loy Kratong" is often sung at Loy Kratong ceremonies.

Pung Noy Loy Kratong

Full Moon Float

Thai Folk Song
Collected and Transcribed by
Kathy B. Sorensen
English Words by MMH

Thai: ผึ้ง น้อย ลอย กระ ทง รำ วง กัน แบบ ไทย ไทย
Pronunciation: pʊng nɔi lɔi kra tong ram wong kan bæb tai tai
English: Cel- e- brate Loy Kra- tong, Oh, do the float— dance.

เดือน และ ดาว ลอย เด่น เห็น จันทร์ เพ็ญ แล้ว ชื่น ใจ ลำ
dʊan læ dau lɔi den hen jan pen læu chʊn jai lam
When the ca- nals are full, moon and stars are float - ing. The

คลอง น้ำ นอง เต็ม เปี่ยม เอ๋ย เรียม จะ ช้า อยู่ ใย น้อง
klɔng nam nɔng tem piem əi riem ja cha yu yai nɔng
full moon— makes us dance, oi!— Broth- er, why so slow? Broth- er,

เอ๋ย พี่ เอ๋ย น้อง เอ๋ย พี่ เอ๋ย มา รำ วง
əi pi əi nɔng əi pi əi ma ram wong
oi!— Sis- ter, oi! Come,— oi!— Let's dance and cel- e -

กัน วัน ลอย กระ ทง มา รำ วง กัน วัน ลอย กระ ทง
kan wan lɔi kra tong ma ram wong kan wan lɔi kra tong
brate the Loy Kra- tong, Oh, dance on full moon Loy Kra- tong.

LISTENING

The Moon on High (excerpts)
Chinese Folk Music

Images of the moon are often suggested by music and visual art forms. Musicians play "The Moon on High" on traditional Chinese instruments. You will hear bowed and plucked strings, wind, and percussion instruments.

LISTEN to this traditional Chinese music. Describe how you think the moon portrayed by the music looks.

LISTENING

Celestial Guests (excerpt)
Chinese Folk Melody

Bill Douglass, an American musician, plays this traditional melody on a Chinese flute. The word celestial *describes the sun, the moon, the stars and anything else related to the sky. Celestial also describes anything related to China or the Chinese. Why do you think this music is called "Celestial Guests?"*

Celebrating
Loy Kratong
in Thailand.

Loy Kratong is celebrated when the moon is full, and the water is high in the rivers or canals. People make floats out of flowers and send them down the water.

Winter

SNOW

As though pretending to be blooms
The snowflakes scatter in the winter sky.
—Sei Shonāgon

The beauty of winter can be enchanting despite the harsh effects of a cold climate. What sights and sounds come to your mind when you think of winter? Imagine the winter scene described in this song.

WINTER WONDERLAND

Music by Felix Bernard
Arranged by Marilyn Davidson
Words by Dick Smith

Sleigh bells ring, are you lis-t'nin'? In the lane snow is
way is the blue-bird, Here to stay is a

glis-t'nin' A beau-ti-ful sight,— We're hap-py to-night—
new bird, He sings a love song,— As we go a-long—

Walk-in' in a win-ter won-der-land! Gone a- land!

Enchantment

In the mead - ow we can build a snow - man; (And we'll)

Then pre - tend that he is Par - son Brown.

He'll say, "Are you mar - ried?" We'll say, "No, man!_____ But

you can do the job when you're in town."_____ Lat - er

on we'll con - spire_____ As we dream by the fire_____ To

face un - a - fraid_____ the plans that we made_____

Walk - in' in a win - ter won - der - land._____

"Mark my footsteps, my good page, . . .", illustrated by Jessie Marion King, 1919

This song tells the story of King Wenceslas and his page going
out to help a poor man on a cold winter night.

**LISTEN to the dialogue between the king and his page.
Are their voices changed or unchanged?**

GOOD KING *Wenceslas*

Spring Carol
from *Piae Cantiones* 1582
Words by
Rev. John Mason Neale

1. Good King Wen - ces - las look'd out   On the feast of Ste - phen,
2. "Hith - er, page, and stand by me,   If thou know'st it, tell - ing,
3. "Bring me food and drink so fine,   Bring me pine logs hith - er;
4. "Sire, the night is dark - er now,   And the wind blows strong - er;
5. In his mast - er's steps he trod,   Where the snow lay dint - ed;

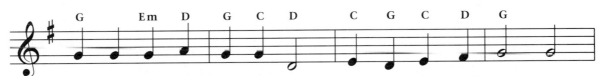

When the snow lay round a - bout,   Deep and crisp and e - ven;
Yon - der peas - ant, who is he?   Where and what his dwell - ing?"
Thou and I shall see him dine   When we bear them thith - er."
Fails my heart, I know not how,   I can go no long - er."
Heat was in the ver - y sod   Which the saint had print - ed;

Bright - ly shone the moon that night,   Though the frost was cru - el,
"Sire, he lives a good league hence,   Un - der-neath the moun - tain;
Page and mon - arch forth they went,   Forth they went to - geth - er,
"Mark my foot-steps, my good page,   Tread thou in them bold - ly;
There-fore, ev' - ry - one, be sure,   Wealth or rank pos - sess - ing,

When a poor man came in sight,   Gath-'ring win - ter fu - el.
Right a - gainst the for - est fence,   By Saint Ag - nes' foun - tain."
Through the rude wind's wild la - ment   And the bit - ter weath - er.
Thou shalt find the win - ter's rage   Freeze thy blood less cold - ly."
Ye who now will bless the poor,   Shall your-selves find bless - ing.

THE Festival OF LIGHTS

The ceremony of lighting candles is often part of celebrations. Hanukkah is sometimes called the Festival of Lights.

Hanukkah celebrates an event that took place over 2,000 years ago. After a long fight for freedom, Judah Maccabee led the Jews to victory. Judah and his people found that their city of Jerusalem, including the holy temple, had been treated disrespectfully. The people wanted to relight the holy lamps in the temple since they were supposed to burn at all times. They found only enough oil for one day. Amazingly the oil lasted for eight days.

The word *Hanukkah* means "rededication" in Hebrew. The holy lamps were lit to rededicate the temple.

Families celebrate Hanukkah by gathering to light candles. Each night of the holiday they light one more candle and observe traditions of the holiday.

WHO CAN RETELL?

Music by M. Ravino
Arranged by
Harry Coopersmith
Translation by B.M. Edidin

Hebrew: מִי יְמַלֵל גְבוּרוֹת יִשְׂרָאֵל אוֹתָן מִי יִמְנֶה?

Pronunciation: mi yə ma lel gvu rot yis ra el o tan mi yim nɛ

English: Who can re-tell the things that be-fell us? Who can count them?

Fine

עָם הָ אֵל גוֹ בּוֹר גָה הַ קוּם יַ דוֹר כָל בְ הֵן!

hɛn bə xɔl dor ya kum ha gi bor go el ha am

In ev'-ry age a he-ro or sage came to our aid!

זֶה הַ מָן בַ הֵם הָ מִים יָ בַ שְׁמַע!

shma ba ya mim ha hem baz man ha zɛ

Hark! At this time of year in days of yore,

דֶה פוֹ וּ עַ שִׁי מוֹ בִּי כַ מַ.

ma ka bi mo shi a u fo dɛ

Mac-ca-bees the tem-ple did re-store,

אֵל רָ יִשְׂ עַם כָל נוּ מֵי יָ בְ וּ.

uv ya me nu kɔl am yis ra el

and to-day our peo-ple as we dreamed,

D.C. al Fine

אֵל גָ וְיִ וּ קוּם יָ חֵד אַ יִת.

yit a xed ya kum və yi ga el

Will a-rise, u-nite and be re-deemed.

EIGHT
Are the
LIGHTS

Eight are the lights
    of Hanukkah
We light for a week
    And a day.
We kindle the lights,
    And bless the Lord,
And sing a song,
    And pray.

Eight are the lights
    of Hanukkah
For justice and mercy
    and love,
For charity, courage
    and honor and peace,
And faith in Heaven
    above.

Eight are the lights
    of Hanukkah
To keep ever bright
    Memories
Of the valiant soul
    And the fighting heart
And the hope of the
    Maccabees!

—Ilo Orleans

In Hebrew songs of praise, there is a tradition of substituting syllables or short words for part of the text. This helps to create a strong rhythmic quality in the songs.

Hanerot Halalu

Words and Music by
Baruch J. Cohon
Arranged by Blanche Chass

ha ne rot ha la lu ha ne rot ha la lu ko desh hem

ba ya ha ne rot ha la lu ha ne rot ha la lu ko desh hem

35 Part 2 Begin very slowly; increase tempo to end; clap on beat.

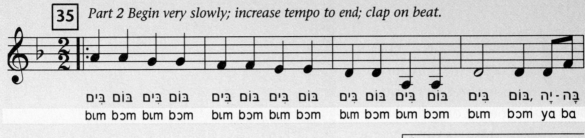

bim bom bim bom bim bom bim bom bim bom bim bom bim bom ya ba

1.

bim bom bim bom bim bom bim bom bim bom bim bom

Parts 1 & 2   2.

bim bom ya ba bim bom bim bom bim hei

Besides singing songs and lighting the menorah, Hanukkah festivities include playing a dreidel game and exchanging gifts and gelt. Gelt can be real money or chocolate in the shape of gold coins.

THE SCANDINAVIAN CHRISTMAS

Scandinavia is a region of Europe that includes Sweden, Norway, and Denmark. These countries share many Christmas customs. Many Scandinavian traditions are practiced in parts of the United States where Scandinavian immigrants settled.

CHRISTMAS AT SANBORN

Carl Larsson painted this Christmas scene in 1907 at his Swedish home. Two other paintings, or panels, fit with this one to create one large picture called a *triptych*. The other panels show more Christmas festivities.

Helsingborg Museum/photo by Sven-Olof Larsen

GOD JUL ※ ※ GLEDELIG JUL ※

SEASON

SWEDEN

The holiday season begins long before Christmas in Swedish communities. Santa Lucia Day is celebrated on December 13. Santa Lucia was an Italian saint from the early Christian era. During the Middle Ages, a Swedish peasant thought he saw her walking on a lake. She was dressed in white, wore a crown of lights, and carried gifts of food.

To honor Santa Lucia, the oldest girl in each family rises before dawn. She dresses in white and puts on a crown of evergreens and lights. After waking her family by singing "Santa Lucia," she serves coffee and freshly baked rolls.

LISTENING

Sankta Lucia *Italian Folk Song*

"Sankta Lucia" was originally an Italian song. It traveled to Sweden with the legend of Santa Lucia. Listen to the song in Swedish.

❋ GLAEDELIG JUL ❋

The Swedish holiday season continues into the new year, including much feasting and fun on Christmas Eve and Christmas.

On Knut's Day, January 13, the Swedes clean up after celebrating the holidays, and Christmas is "swept out" for another year.

Nu är det Jul igen
Yuletide Is Here Again

Swedish Dance Carol

Swedish: Nu är det Jul i - gen, och nu är det Jul i - gen, Och
Pronunciation: nu æɾ dɛt yu li yɛn ɔk nu æɾ dɛt yu li yɛn ɔk
English: Yule - tide is here a - gain, Oh, Yule - tide is here a - gain, The

Ju - len va - ra ska' till Pas - ka.
yu lɛn va ɾa ska tɪl pɔ ska
hol - i - days will last 'til Eas - ter.

Sa är det Pask i - gen, och so är det Pask i - gen, Och
sɔ æɾ dɛt pɔ ski yɛn ɔk sɔ æɾ dɛt pɔ ski yɛn ɔk
Then it is Eas - ter time, Oh, then it is Eas - ter time, and

Pask - en va - ra ska' till Ju - la.
pɔ skɛn va ɾa skɔ tɪl yu la
Eas - ter time will last 'til Yule - tide.

NORWAY

"Ringing in Christmas" is a Norwegian tradition—at 5:00 P.M. on Christmas Eve, church bells ring. That night, many Scandinavian children believe that an elf brings gifts from Santa. In Norway this elf is called *Julenissen.*

Jeg er så glad hver Julekveld
I Am So Glad on Christmas Eve

Norwegian Carol
English Words by MMH

Norwegian: Jeg er så glad hver ju - le - kveld For
Pronunciation: yɛy ær so glɑ vær yu lə kvɛl foɾ
English: I am so glad on Christ - mas Eve, The

da blev Je - sus fodt, Da lys - te stjer - nen
da blɛ ye sus föt da lüs tɛ styæɾ nɛn
night when Christ was born. That night the an - gels came

som en sol, Og en - gle sang så sodt.
som ɪn sul o ɛn glɛ sang so söt
from on high, And sang their won - der - ful song.

Celebrations *Christmas* **347**

CHRISTMAS JOY

One of the joys of the Christmas season is the sound of bells. From sleigh bells to church bells, their music is heard. Many words describe the tone color of bells. *Silver* can mean "a soft, resonant sound." Do you think silver describes ringing bells?

Silver Bells

Words and Music by
Jay Livingston and Ray Evans

1. Cit - y side - walks, bus - y side - walks dressed in hol - i - day style
2. Strings of street lights, ev - en stop - lights blink a bright red and green,

In the air there's a feel - ing of Christ - mas.
As the shop - pers rush home with their trea - sures.

Chil - dren laugh - ing, peo - ple pass - ing, meet - ing smile af - ter smile,
Hear the snow crunch, see the kids bunch, this is San - ta's big scene,

And on ev' - ry street cor - ner you hear:
And a - bove all this bus - tle you hear:

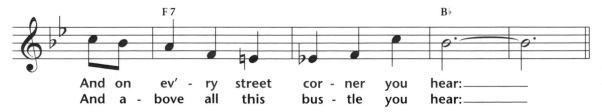

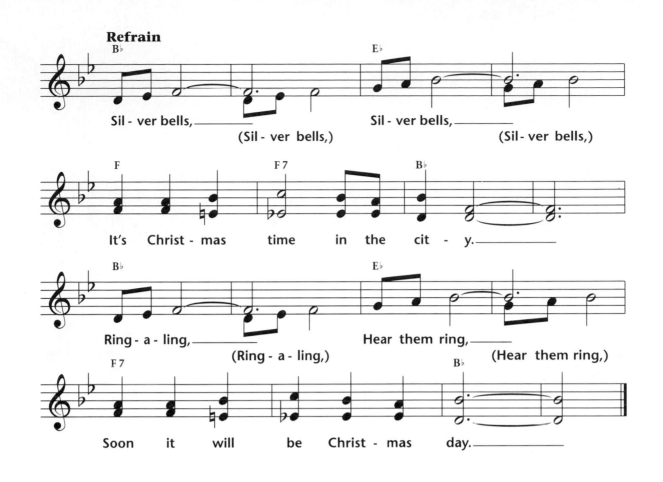

Refrain

Sil - ver bells, _____ (Sil - ver bells,)   Sil - ver bells, _____ (Sil - ver bells,)

It's Christ - mas time in the cit - y. _____

Ring - a - ling, _____ (Ring - a - ling,)   Hear them ring, _____ (Hear them ring,)

Soon it will be Christ - mas day. _____

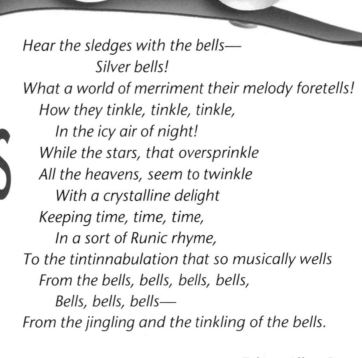

from
The Bells

Hear the sledges with the bells—
*   Silver bells!*
What a world of merriment their melody foretells!
*   How they tinkle, tinkle, tinkle,*
*   In the icy air of night!*
*   While the stars, that oversprinkle*
*   All the heavens, seem to twinkle*
*   With a crystalline delight*
*   Keeping time, time, time,*
*   In a sort of Runic rhyme,*
To the tintinnabulation that so musically wells
*   From the bells, bells, bells, bells,*
*   Bells, bells, bells—*
From the jingling and the tinkling of the bells.

—Edgar Allan Poe

The Christmas season brings thoughts of peace and good will. The words to this carol, written by a famous American poet, honor that tradition.

I Heard the Bells on Christmas Day

Music by Jean Baptiste Calkin
Words by Henry Wadsworth Longfellow

I heard the bells on Christ - mas day

Their old fa - mil - iar car - ols play,

And wild and sweet the words re - peat

Of peace on earth, good will to men.

In this carol from Catalonia, a region in the northeast of Spain, the words *fum, fum, fum* imitate the rhythmic strumming of a guitar.

Fum, Fum, Fum

Catalonian Carol

Spanish: **En** di - ciem - bre vien - ti - cin - co, fum, fum, fum;
Pronunciation: ɛn di syem bɾe βen ti sing ko fum fum fum
English: **On** De - cem - ber five and twen - ty, fum, fum, fum;

En di - ciem - bre vein - ti - cin - co, fum, fum, fum.
en di syem bɾe βen ti sin ko fum fum fum
On De - cem - ber five and twen - ty, fum, fum, fum;

Ha na - ci - do un ni - ñi - to, ro - sa - di - to
a na si ðo un nin yi to ro sa ði to
Oh, a child was born this night, a child so fair, so

y blan - qui - to, Hi - jo de la Vir - gen pu - ra,
i blang ki to i xo ðe la βiɾ xen pu ɾa
ros - y bright,_____ Son of Mar - y, mai - den ho - ly,

Que ha na - ci - do en un es - ta - blo, fum, fum, fum.
kea na si ðowen un es ta blo fum fum fum
in a sta - ble small and low - ly, fum, fum, fum.

Most musical traditions on the island of Puerto Rico are Spanish in origin. José Feliciano, who composed "Feliz Navidad," was born in Puerto Rico. He uses both English and Spanish words for Christmas wishes in this song.

Feliz Navidad

Words and Music
by José Feliciano

Spanish: Fe - liz Na - vi - dad._____ Fe - liz Na - vi -
Pronunciation: fe lis nɑ βi ðɑð fe lis nɑ βi

dad._____ Fe - liz Na - vi -
ðɑð fe lis nɑ βi

dad, Pros - pe - ro a - ño y fe - li - ci - dad.___
ðɑð prɔs pe ɾo a nyo i fe li si ðɑð

I want to wish you a Mer - ry Christ - mas

With lots of pres - ents to make you hap - py.

José Feliciano has won numerous Grammy Awards. He continues to compose and record while performing all over the world.

I want to wish you a Mer - ry Christ - mas from the

bot - tom of my heart.

I want to wish you a Mer - ry Christ - mas with mis - tle - toe and

lots of cheer. With lots of laugh - ter through-

out the years from the bot - tom of my heart.

The words of this Puerto Rican Christmas song describe Mary and Joseph's trip to Bethlehem.

ALEGRÍA, ALEGRÍA
Joy, Joy

Puerto Rican Folk Song
English Version by MMH

Spanish: Ha - cia Be - lén se en - ca - mi - na Ma - ria
Pronunciation: a sya βe len seng ka mi na ma rya
English: On to Be - lén goes Ma - ri - a, lov - ing

con su a - man - te es - po - so lle - van - do en su com - pa
kon swa man tes po so ye βan doen su kam pa
hus - band close be - side her. God is with them, a com-

ñi - a a to - do un Dios po - de - ro - so. A - le -
nyi a a to doun dyos po de ro so a le
pan - ion, to pro - tect them on their jour - ney. A - le -

grí - a A - le - grí - a A - le - grí - a, A - le - grí - a A - le - grí - a y pla-
gri a le gri a le gri a a le gri a le gri ai pla
grí - a A - le - grí - a A - le - grí - a, A - le - gría, joy and pleas - ure to-

cer que la Vir - gen va de pa - so con su es-
ser ke la βir xen ba ðe pa so kon swes
day. On to Be - lén, they will jour - ney, they will

1. po - so ha - cia Be - lén. A - le -
po soa sya βe len a le
pass us on their way. A - le -

2. po - so ha - cia Be - lén.
po soa sya βe len
pass us on their way.

This song, with its calypso style, expresses the excitement of preparing for Christmas.

MAMA, BAKE THE JOHNNYCAKE, CHRISTMAS COMIN'

Words and Music by
Blake Alphonso Higgs

Celebrate KWANZAA

Kwanzaa is a holiday observed by many African Americans. Dr. Maulana Karenga created it in 1966. He based Kwanzaa on African harvest celebrations. Families and communities choose their favorite African or African American music to help celebrate. This song, often called the African American National Anthem, is frequently sung during Kwanzaa.

Lift Every Voice and Sing

Music by Rosamond Johnson
Words by James Weldon Johnson

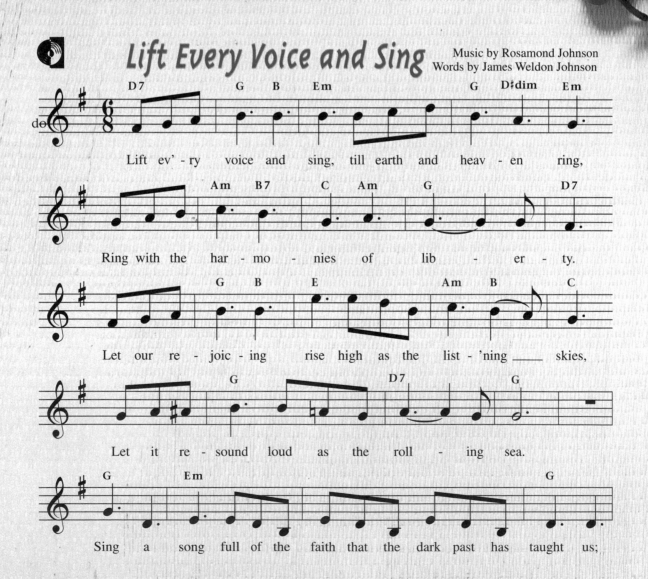

Lift ev'-ry voice and sing, till earth and heav-en ring,

Ring with the har-mo-nies of lib-er-ty.

Let our re-joic-ing rise high as the list-'ning ____ skies,

Let it re-sound loud as the roll-ing sea.

Sing a song full of the faith that the dark past has taught us;

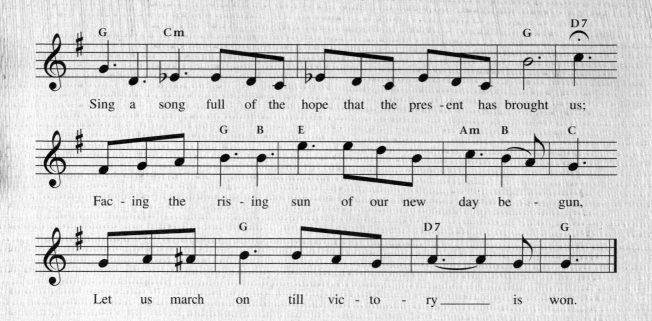

Sing a song full of the hope that the pres-ent has brought us;

Fac - ing the ris - ing sun of our new day be - gun,

Let us march on till vic - to - ry _____ is won.

Kwanza means "first" in Swahili, a language used in parts of Africa. The holiday name is spelled with an extra *a* to give it seven letters. The number *seven* holds special meaning because of the seven principles of Kwanzaa. The celebration lasts seven days from December 26 to January 1.

Each evening, families light a candle in a candleholder called the *kinara* and discuss one of the seven principles. On the last day of the holiday, the community gathers for a feast with music and dancing called the *karamu*.

  LISTENING **Ajaja** *by Babatunde Olatunji*

Kwanzaa is a time for all music of African origins. "Ajaja," a modern work, is based on traditional west African music. You will hear many percussion instruments, including several types of drums, agogo bells, and beaded gourds called shekeres.

GREETING THE NEW YEAR

An unknown poet wrote the words to "A New Year Carol." The phrase *levy dew* may come from Welsh words. In modern language, *levy* refers to drawing up water, as in pulling water from a well. *Dew* means "moisture," like the drops of water found on grass in the morning. There was an early British belief that drops of dew gathered on Christmas or May Day had special qualities.

A New Year Carol

Music by Benjamin Britten
Words Anonymous

1. Here we bring new wa - ter from the well so clear,
2. Sing reign of Fair Maid, with gold up - on her toe,
3. Sing reign of Fair Maid, with gold up - on her chin,

For to wor - ship God with this hap - py New Year.
O - pen you the West Door and turn the Old Year go.
O - pen you the East Door and let the New Year in.

358

1., 2.
mf   *cresc.*

Sing le-vy dew, sing le-vy dew, the wa-ter and the wine;

The sev-en bright gold wires and the bu-gles that do shine.

3.
pp

Sing le-vy dew, sing le-vy dew, the wa-ter and the wine;

dim. *pp*

The sev-en bright gold wires and the bu-gles that do shine.

Spotlight on

BENJAMIN BRITTEN

Benjamin Britten (1913–1976) was a famous British composer. Growing up, he frustrated his brother and sisters because he monopolized the piano when they wanted to play. Besides writing songs, operas, and symphonies, he also wrote background music for movies. He is well known for his music for children, including **The Young Person's Guide** *to the Orchestra, which he composed in 1945.*

Let FREEDOM Ring

Dr. Martin Luther King, Jr., devoted his life to achieving freedom and justice for African Americans and people everywhere. The words of this song tell of Dr. King's life and the ideals for which he worked.

The Dream of Martin Luther King

Words and Music by
Merle Gartrell and
Students of Cummings
Elementary School

Allegro

1. Once there was a gen-tle-man_____ who talked a-bout a prom-ised land.
2. In his dream he saw the peo-ple of this land__ walk-ing side by side.

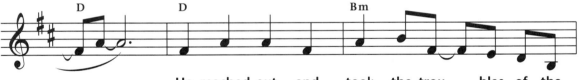

_____ He reached out and took the trou-bles of the
_____ White man, black man, red man, yel-low man_____

peo-ple in his strong__ black hands._____ He had a dream that
lov-ing one an-oth-er with pride._____ Now he's__ gone a-

ev'-ry-bod-y ought to hear the bells of free-dom ring._____
way be-fore__ the day his dream be-came a real__ thing._____

Now the peo-ple shout and sing a-bout the dream of Mar-tin Lu-ther King.
But he'll hear the an-gels sing a-bout the dream of Mar-tin Lu-ther King.

The term *civil rights* describes the right of all people to fair treatment. In the 1960s, many people felt it was time to stand up for the civil rights of African Americans.

LISTENING

I Have a Dream (excerpts)
by Dr. Martin Luther King, Jr.

You will hear parts of Dr. King's speech twice—once as delivered by Dr. King, and once read by someone else. Dr. King was a powerful speaker. He spoke to further the cause of civil rights for African Americans, and for all people unfairly treated.

COMPARE the two versions of Dr. King's speech. How are they different?

The words *free at last* have special meaning for African American people. Dr. King used these words in his "I Have a Dream" speech. They have come to represent the hope of all Americans for freedom from the effects of prejudice.

FREE AT LAST

African American Spiritual

Free at last, free at last,

Thank God a'-might-y I'm free at last.

1. Sure-ly been 'buked, and sure-ly been scorned,
2. If you don't know that I been re-deemed,

Thank God a'-might-y I'm free at last.

But still my soul is a-heav-en born,
Just fol-low me down to Jor-dan's stream,

Thank God a'-might-y I'm free at last.

The Luck of the Irish

"Harrigan" was first performed as part of a play in 1908. George M. Cohan wrote the song during a time in history when great numbers of immigrants were arriving in the United States. Many of these immigrants were Irish.

HARRIGAN

Words and Music by
George M. Cohan

1. Who is the man who will spend or will e-ven lend? Har-ri-gan, that's me! Who is your friend, when you find that you need a friend? Har-ri-gan, that's me!— For I'm just as proud of my name, you see, As an Em-per-or, Czar, or a King could be. Who is the man helps a man ev'-ry-time he can?

2. Who is the man nev-er stood for a 'gad-a-bout'? Har-ri-gan, that's me! Who is the man that the town's simp-ly mad a-bout? Har-ri-gan, that's me!— Thy la-dies and ba-bies are fond of me, I'm— fond of them, too, in re-turn, you see. Who is the gent that's de-serv-ing a mon-u-ment?

Har - ri - gan,   that's   me!
Har - ri - gan,   that's   me!

Refrain

H - A - dou-ble-R - I - G - A - N spells Har - ri - gan.

Proud   of   all   the   I - rish blood that's   in   me.
                                                                     (him).

Nev - er a man can say a word a - gin' me.   H - A -
                                                   (him).

dou-ble-R - I - G - A - N, you   see,——   Is   a name that a shame ne - ver

has   been con - nect - ed with,   Har - ri - gan,   that's   me!

HELP THIS
PLANET EARTH

This photograph by Ansel Adams is a vivid reminder of the beauty of our environment. Such fragile beauty deserves our attention and respect. Imagine this same photograph filled with garbage and covered by a haze of air pollution. These are just two of the problems that confront us and require each of us to take action.

Earth Day is more than 20 years old. Concerns about protecting the planet and preserving natural resources increase daily. Many people celebrate Earth Day by singing songs about the beautiful, but fragile, environment.

DISCUSS how you can help inform people by singing songs about our environment.

The earth revolves on its axis once every 24 hours. The continuous melody of a round is like the continuous motion of our spinning planet.

ROUND THE EARTH TURNS

Music by Mary Goetze
Words by Doug Goodkin

1. Round the earth turns from morn - ing to night.

2. Turn - ing a - gain from dark to the light.

3. Turn - ing and turn - ing for all our de - light.

Meet Raffi

Do you remember Raffi's songs from when you were younger? For many years, Raffi has been a well-loved composer and performer of music for children. More recently, Raffi has turned his attention toward helping to save the environment. Many of his songs celebrate the beauty and wonder of our planet.

LISTEN as Raffi tells about songwriting and how to help save our planet.

Raffi used this photo on his 1990 recording "Evergreen, Everblue."

Evergreen, Everblue

Words and Music by Raffi

Ev-er-green,___ ev-er-blue, As it was in the be-gin-ning,___ we've got to see it through.___ Ev-er-green,___ ev-er-blue, At this point in time, it's up to me, it's up to you.___

1., 2. *First and second time to verse.*
3. *Third time to Interlude.*
4. *Fine*

The rhythms and rhymes of rap music express feelings about life today.

EARTH DAY RAP

Words and Music by
Doug Goodkin

The sky is high—— and the o-cean is deep, But

we can't treat the plan-et like a gar-bage heap.—— Don't

wreck it, pro-tect it, keep part of it wild,—— And

think a-bout the fu-ture of your great-grand-child. Re-

cy-cle, bi-cy-cle, don't you drive by your-self,—— Don't

buy those plas-tic pro-ducts on the su-per-mar-ket shelf.

Boy-cott, pe-ti-tion, let the big bus-'ness know,—— That if we

mess it up here, there's no-where else we can go.

Don't shrug your shoul - ders, say, "What can I do?" On - ly

one per - son can do it and that per - son is you!

LISTENING

Lullaby from the Great Mother Whale to the Baby Seal Pups *by Paul Winter*

Paul Winter's music combines instrumental jazz with recordings of animal voices. He is strongly committed to saving the environment. The out-of-doors inspires much of his music.

Several years ago, Winter had a unique experience. A baby sea lion came ashore and spent the night near his campfire. This piece honors the sea lion pup he and his friends called Silkie.

More Songs to Read

Quarter Notes, Quarter Rests, Eighth Notes

You can show sounds and silences with notation.

A common symbol for one sound to a beat is
a quarter note: ♩ or ♪

One beat of silence is often shown with a
quarter rest: 𝄽

Two equal sounds to a beat can be shown with
two eighth notes: ♫ or ♫

Eighth notes can also be written separately: ♪♪ or ♪♪

**ECHO the pattern your teacher claps with "Get Up!" on
pages 12 and 13. Decide which of the following patterns
you clapped.**

Pattern A:

Pattern B:

Which beats in each pattern have quarter notes? Quarter rests?
Two eighth notes?

Conducting patterns help musical
groups stay together by showing
each beat in a measure.

**DETERMINE how many beats
are in each measure of "Get Up!"**

**PRACTICE conducting the beat
for ²⁄₄ during the middle section
of "Get Up!"**

1   2

Read *Do Re Mi*

Using hand signs for pitches is a way to help you to remember the sound of each pitch.

SING *do re mi* as you show the hand sign for each pitch.

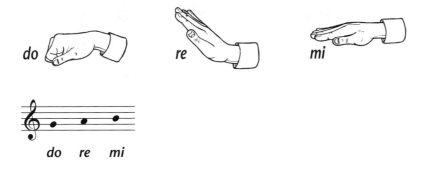

SING the melody below with pitch syllables. Then sing it with letter names.

SING the melody as a two-part canon.

CLAP this ostinato with the melody.

More with *Do Re Mi*

LISTEN to "Good News" and discuss its meaning.

African American Spiritual

Good news! Char - i - ot's a - com - in',

Good news! Char - i - ot's a - com - in',

Good news! Char - i - ot's a - com - in',

and I don't want it to leave me be - hind.

Just singing the right pitches does not mean that your performance of a song will communicate its meaning to listeners. You also need to sing with expression.

In music, expression marks can help you make all the difference! Two of these expressive elements are *accent* and *crescendo*.

An **accent** (>) in music puts more emphasis on a note. A crescendo (⎯⎯ or *cresc.*) in music builds excitement by gradually getting louder.

FIND the accents and the crescendo in "Good News."

FOLLOW these signs to help you sing the song more expressively.

374

Roll de Ole Chariot Along

African American Spiritual
Adapted by René Boyer-White

Refrain

Roll de ole char-i-ot a-long,— Roll de ole char-i-ot a-long,—

Roll de ole char-i-ot a-long,— Ef yo' don't hang on be-hin'. hin'.

Verse

1. We are trav-el-in' from man-sions, man-sions, man-sions;
2. Ef yo' mud-der want to go, she shall wear a star-ry crown; Ef yo'

Trav-el-in' from man-sions, man-sions, man-sions;
mud-der want to go, she shall wear a star-ry crown; Ef yo'

Trav-el-in' from man-sions, man-sions, man-sions, You
mud-der want to go, she shall wear a star-ry crown, And she

must hang on be-hin'.
must hang on be-hin'.

Practice with a New Rhythm

LEARN a drum part for "Funga Alafia," page 69.

SAY and pat this ostinato rhythm with "Funga Alafia."

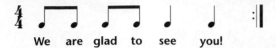

We are glad to see you!

COMPARE the ostinato rhythm with the first measure of the song. Which beats are different?

This ostinato rhythm can also be written with the eighth notes separated.

We are glad to see you!

By using a tie ⌢, you can change the ostinato to match the rhythm of the song's first measure. A tie joins two notes into a single sound equal to their total length.

NAME a note that can replace the two tied eighths.

The pattern now looks like this.

CLAP this syncopated pattern with "Funga Alafia."

How can you change the words to fit this rhythm?

PLAY the syncopated ostinato on drums with "Funga Alafia."

Practice with the Pentatonic Scale

FIND new pitches and rhythms to read in this syncopated song.

A pentatonic (five-tone) scale is made up of five pitches. In this song, these pitches are: *do re mi so la*. A pentatonic scale may also include higher or lower pitches with the same syllable name. How many different pitch syllables do you find in this song?

do re mi so la do'
C D E G A C

Reading Rhythms with Ties and Slurs in Pentatonic

Curved lines connecting notes of different pitches are called **slurs** (‿).

They are used when more than one pitch is sung on a single syllable.

Curved lines connecting notes on the same pitch are called **ties**.

FIND and observe the ties and slurs in "Trampin'."

African American Spiritual
Adapted by René Boyer-White

Refrain

I'm tramp-in',— tramp-in',— Tryin' to make Heav-en my home,

I'm tramp-in',— tramp-in',— Tryin' to make Heav-en my home.

Verse

I've nev-er been to Heav-en but I've been told,

Tryin' to make Heav-en my home, The streets up there are

paved with gold, Tryin' to make Heav-en my home.

Sounds of Syncopation and Dotted Quarter Notes

Rainbow Sister

Chinese Folk Song
Collected and Transcribed by Kathy B. Sorensen
English Words by MMH

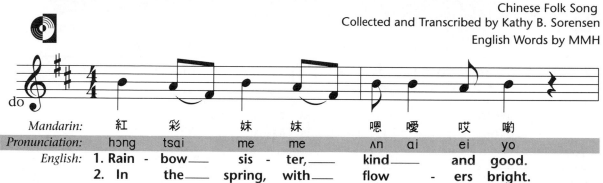

Mandarin: 紅　彩　妹　妹　嗯　嗳　哎　喲
Pronunciation: hɔng　tsai　me　me　ʌn　ai　ei　yo
English: 1. Rain - bow___ sis - ter,___ kind___ and good.
2. In the___ spring, with___ flow - ers bright.

長　得　那　麼　嗯　嗳　哎　喲
jang　də　na　mɔ　ʌn　ai　ei　yo
I would___ see her___ if___ I could.
I met___ sis - ter there___ one night.

櫻　桃　小　嘴　嗯　哎　呦　喲
ing　tau　shiau　jwe　ʌn　ai　ei　yo
I can't for - get___ her,___ I don't know why,___
In the___ fall,___ when___ flow - ers die,

一　點　點　那　麼　嗯　哎　呦　喲
i　dien　dien　na　mɔ　ʌn　ai　ei　yo
Think - ing of her,___ I al - ways cry.
Rain - bow sis - ter___ said___ good - bye.

Play this ostinato with the song.

Add a Descant

All Through the Night

Welsh Folk Song

1. Sleep, my child, and peace at-tend thee,
2. While the moon her watch is keep-ing, } All through the night.

Guard - ian an - gels God will send thee,
While the wea - ry world is sleep-ing, } All through the night.

Soft the drow-sy hours are creep-ing, Hill and vale in slum-ber steep-ing,
O'er thy spir - it gen-tly steal-ing, Vi-sion of de-light re-veal-ing,

I, my lov-ing vig - il keep-ing,
Breathes a pure and ho - ly feel-ing, } All through the night.

Descant *Sing descant with lines 1, 2, and 4*

Sleep, my child,_____ All through the night.

Sing a Song with Sixteenth Notes

Four sixteenth notes equal one quarter note. (♬♬ = ♩)

Beats can be divided into equal and unequal sounds.

Two ways that beats can be divided unequally are:

♩. ♪ and ♫

FIND both of these rhythm patterns in "Cindy."

Cindy

Appalachian Folk Song

1. I wish I was an ap-ple a-hang-ing on a tree,
2. She told me that she loved me, She called me "su-gar plum,"
3. I wish I had a nee-dle as fine as I could sew,

and ev-'ry time my Cin-dy passed, she'd take a bite of me!
She threw her arms a-round me, and I thought my time had come.
I'd sew that gal to my coat-tail, and down the road I'd go.

Refrain *Descants*

Get a-long home! Get a-long home!

Refrain *Melody*

Get a-long home, Cin-dy, Cin-dy, get a-long home, Cin-dy, Cin-dy,

Get-a-long home! I'll mar-ry you some-day.

get a-long home, Cin-dy, Cin-dy, I'll mar-ry you— some-day.

Another New Pitch

FIND the new pitch in this song.

American Folk Song

1. I'm rid-in' on that new riv-er train,_____ I'm
2. Dar-ling, you can't love_____ two,_____
3. Dar-ling, you can't love_____ three,_____
4. Dar-ling, you can't love_____ four,_____
5. Dar-ling, you can't love_____ five,_____

rid-in' on that new riv-er train;_____ The
Dar-ling, you can't love_____ two,_____ You
Dar-ling, you can't love_____ three,_____ You
Dar-ling, you can't love_____ four,_____ You
Dar-ling, you can't love_____ five,_____ You

same old train that brought me here's gon-na
can't love two, and still to me be true,
can't love three, and still be true to me,
can't love four, and love me an-y - more,
can't love five, and have my love sur - vive,

car - ry me home a - gain._____
Dar - ling, you can't love two._____
Dar - ling, you can't love three._____
Dar - ling, you can't love four._____
Dar - ling, you can't love five._____

6. Darling, you can't love six, (twice)
   You can't love six, and do those tricks, . . .

7. Darling, you can't love seven, (twice)
   You can't love seven, and ever get to heaven, . . .

8. Darling, you can't love eight, (twice)
   You can't love eight, and pass the Pearly Gate, . . .

382

Still Another New Pitch!

SING the melody below using pitch syllables. Hum the pitches that are not named. Identify the tune.

do do re mi do mi re so, do do re mi do ? so,

do do re mi fa mi re do ? so, la, ? do do

The new pitch is *ti*.

FIND *fa* and *ti* in the following song.

ti

Wachet auf
Waken Now

Words and Music by
Johann Jakob Wachsmann
English Words by MMH

German: Wach - et auf, Wach-et auf es kräh - te der Hahn,
Pronunciation: va xət ɑʊf va xət ɑʊf ɛs kɾe tə der han
English: Wak - en now, Wak-en now, proud chan - ti - cleer cries,

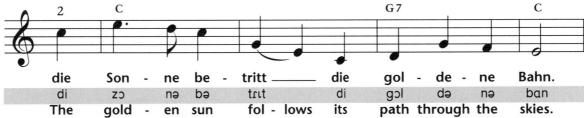

die Son - ne be - tritt ——— die gol - de - ne Bahn.
di zɔ nə bə tɾɪt di gɔl də nə ban
The gold - en sun fol - lows its path through the skies.

Ostinato

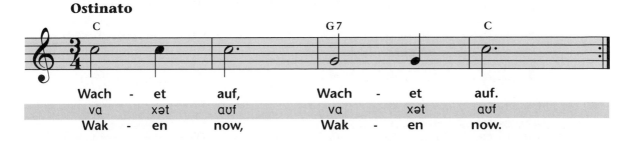

Wach - et auf, Wach - et auf.
va xət ɑʊf va xət ɑʊf
Wak - en now, Wak - en now.

A Round in Major

Mi gallo
My Rooster

Three-part round
English Words by MMH

1

Spanish: Mi ga - llo se mu - rió a - yer,
Pronunciation: mi ga yo se mu ɾyo a yeɾ
English: My roost - er just died yes - ter - day,

Mi ga - llo se mu - rió a - yer.
mi ga yo se mu ɾyo a yeɾ
My roost - er just died yes - ter - day.

2

Ya no can - ta - rá co - co - rí, co - co - rá,
ya no can ta ɾa ko ko ɾi ko ko ɾa
He will nev - er sing co - co - rí, co - co - rá,

Ya no can - ta - rá co - co - rí, co - co - rá.
ya no can ta ɾa ko ko ɾi ko ko ɾa
He will nev - er sing co - co - rí, co - co - rá.

3

Co - co - rí, co - rí, co - rá,____
ko ko ɾi ko ɾi ko ɾa
Co - co - rí, co - rí, co - rá,____

Co - co - rí, co - rí, co - rá.____
ko ko ɾi ko ɾi ko ɾa
Co - co - rí, co - rí, co - rá.____

384

A Song in Minor

Music by Shalom Altman
Hebrew words from Isaiah 2:4
English Version by Leah Jaffa and Fran Minkoff
based on Micah 4:3–4

La is the tonal center in minor. In minor, *so* is often raised a half step, as it is in "Vine and Fig Tree." The pitch syllable then changes from *so* to *si*.

si

COMPARE pitches and tonal centers in "Mi gallo" and "Vine and Fig Tree."

Reading a Mixolydian Song in $\frac{2}{4}$ Meter

Going to Boston

American Play-Party Song

1. Good - bye, girls, I'm goin' to Bos - ton, Good - bye, girls, I'm
2. Clear the way, you'll get run o - ver, Clear the way, you'll
3. Sad - dle up, girls, and we'll go with them, Sad - dle up, girls, and

goin' to Bos - ton, Good - bye, girls, I'm goin' to Bos - ton,
get run o - ver, Clear the way, you'll get run o - ver,
we'll go with them, Sad - dle up, girls, and we'll go with them,

Ear - ly in the morn - ing.

Refrain

Won't we look pret - ty in the ball - room? Won't we look pret - ty in the ball - room?

Won't we look pret - ty in the ball - room? Ear - ly in the morn - ing.

In the mixolydian mode, the pitch *ti* is lowered one half step and is called *ta*.

ta

LEARN the hand sign for *ta*.

386

Reading ²⁄₂ and Upbeats

Deep in the Heart of Texas

Music by Don Swander
Words by June Hershey

The stars at night are big and bright,

Deep in the heart of Tex - as!

The prai - rie sky is wide and high,

Deep in the heart of Tex - as!

The sage in bloom is like per - fume,

Deep in the heart of Tex - as!

Re - minds me of the one I love,

Deep in the heart of Tex - as!

Using the Major Scale

Moderately Bright

Words and Music by Charles R. Grean

C

do

1. While I was walk - ing down the beach one
2. I picked it up and ran to town as
3. I turned a - round and got right out a -
4. I wan - dered all a - round the town un -
5. I wan - dered on for man - y years, a

F   C   G7   C

bright and sun - ny day,_____ I saw a great big
hap - py as a king._____ I took it to a
run - nin' for my life,_____ And then I took it
til I chanced to meet_____ a ho - bo who was
vic - tim of my fate._____ Un - til one day I

C   D7

wood - en box a - float - in' in the
guy I know who'd buy most an - y -
home with me to give it to my
look - ing for a hand - out on the
came up - on Saint Pe - ter at the

G7   C

bay._____ I pulled it in and
thing._____ But this is what he
wife._____ But this is what she
street._____ He said he'd take most
gate._____ And when I tried to

6. The moral of the story is if you're out on the beach
   And you should see a great big box and it's within your reach,
   Don't ever stop and open it up, that's my advice to you,
   'cause you'll never get rid of the xxx, no matter what you do.
   Oh, you'll never get rid of the xxx, no matter what you do.

Major and Minor Scales

PLAY these scales as you say the pitch syllables. Then play them as you say the letter names.

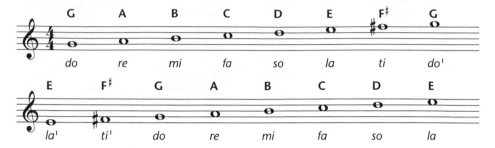

Why do these scales sound different even though they both use the same pitches?

Bohemian Folk Song

1. Where are the clouds that were here last night?
2. How far a - way is the dis - tant sky?

Why does the moon give a sil - v'ry light?
How do we know which is you or I?

Who can tell? Who can say?
Who can tell? Who can say?

When will to - mor - row be yes - ter day?
How man - y miles would be far a - way?

390

Chords and Chord Roots

The words to this Hawaiian song say that the hala trees are beautiful as they sway by the sea. The breezes blow in Naue.

SING "Nani Wale Na Hala" with pitch syllables and words.

An eighth rest 𝄾 has the same value as an eighth note. In $\frac{2}{4}$ meter, the eighth rest gets half a beat of silence.

Hawaiian Folk Song

Hawaiian: Na - ni wa - le na ha - la, E - a, e - a.
Pronunciation: na ni va le na ha la e a e a

O Na - u - e i - ke ka - i, E - a, e - a.
o na u e i ke ka i e a e a

C and G7 are the chords for this song.

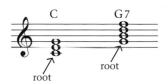

CREATE harmony. One group sings the melody while another group sings the chord roots. A third group sings the other pitches of the chords.

More Practice with Sixteenth Notes

FIND the measures in this song that have the same rhythm patterns.

LISTEN to the song and decide if it is in major or minor.

Czechoslovakian Canon

An - nie, An - nie   was a mill - er's daugh - ter,   Far she wan - dered

by the sing - ing wa - ter.   I - dle, i - dle,   An - nie went a - may - ing,

Up - hill, down - hill,   went her flock a - stray - ing.   Hear them, hear them

call - ing as they roam,   "An - nie, An - nie,   bring your white sheep home."

Using What You Know

READ this cowboy song. Use what you have learned about pitch, meter, and rhythm.

Streets of Laredo

Cowboy Song

1. As I_____ walked out in the streets of La - re - do,
2. "I see by your out - fit that you are a cow - boy,"
3. "Now once in the sad - dle I used to ride hand - some,
4. "Get six jol - ly cow - boys to car - ry my cof - fin,
5. We'll beat the drum slow - ly and play the fife low - ly,
6. We swung our ropes slow - ly and rat - tled our spurs low - ly,

As I_____ walked out in La - re - do one day,
These words he did say as I bold - ly walked by;
'A hand - some young cow - boy' is what they would say.
Get six pret - ty maid - ens to sing me a song;
We'll play the dead march as we bear him a - long.
And gave a wild whoop as we bore him a - long,

I spied a young cow - boy all wrapped in white lin - en,
"Come, sit down be - side me and hear my sad sto - ry,
I'd ride in - to town and go down to the card - house,
Take me to the val - ley and throw the clods o'er me,
We'll go to the val - ley and throw the clods o'er him;
For we all loved our com - rade, so brave, young, and hand - some.

All wrapped in white lin - en and cold as the clay.
I'm shot in the chest and I know I must die."
But I'm shot in the chest and I'm dy - ing to - day."
For I'm a young cow - boy and know I've done wrong."
He was a young cow - boy, but he had done wrong.
We all loved our com - rade, al - though he'd done wrong.

More with Chords and Chord Roots

There are only two chords in this round.

LISTEN for the chord changes.

German Round
English Words by MMH

German: Es tö - nen die Lie - der, der Früh - ling kehrt wie - der,
Pronunciation: ɛs tö nən di li dəɾ dɛɾ fɾü lɪŋ keɾt vi dəɾ
English: The glad songs are ring - ing, for spring is re - turn - ing,

Es spie - let — der — Hir - te auf sei - ner — Schal - mei.
ɛs shpi lət dɛɾ hiɾ tə ɑʊf sɑɪ nəɾ shal mɑɪ
The shep-herd — is — play - ing up - on his — schal - mei.

La la - la la - la la - la la, la, la, la - la la - la la - la la!

394

A Different Sixteenth-Note Pattern

FIND the sixteenth notes in this song.

J'entends le moulin
I HEAR THE MILL WHEEL

French Canadian Folk Song

French: J'en - tends le mou - lin, ti - que ti - que ta - que,
Pronunciation: ʒɑ̃ tɑ̃ lə mu lɛ̃ ti kə ti kə tɑ kə
English: I hear the mill wheel, tick - a tick - a tack - a,

J'en - tends le mou - lin, ta - que.
ʒɑ̃ tɑ̃ lə mu lɛ̃ tɑ kə
I hear the mill wheel, tack - a.

Mon père a fait bâ - tir mai - son,
mɔ̃ pɛʁ ɑ fɛ bɑ tiʁ mɛ zɔ̃
My fa - ther built a house so strong,

ti - que ta - que, ti - que ta - que,
ti kə tɑ kə ti kə tɑ kə
tick - a tack - a, tick - a tack - a,

J'en - tends le mou - lin, ti - que ti - que ta - que,
ʒɑ̃ tɑ̃ lə mu lɛ̃ ti kə ti kə tɑ kə
I hear the mill wheel, tick - a tick - a tack - a,

J'en - tends le mou - lin, ta - que.
ʒɑ̃ tɑ̃ lɛ mu lɛ̃ tɑ kə
I hear the mill wheel, tack - a.

More Dotted Rhythms

PLAY and sing the rhythm patterns in this round.

Tzena, Tzena

Music by Issachar Miron and Julius Grossman
Words by Mitchell Parish

Hebrew/English: Tze-na, tze-na, tze-na, tze-na, Hear the hap-py sounds of dan-cing,
Pronunciation: tsɛ na tsɛ na tsɛ na tsɛ na
Tze-na, tze-na, tze-na, tze-na, Ev'-ry-one can sing a-long, so

come____ and dance a-long.   La la la la,
join____ us in our   song.

la la la la la la,   Join us as we dance to-geth-er, sing-ing.

La la la la,   la la la la la la,   Join us in our hap-py

song.   Clap your hands and   *(clap)* raise your voic-es high-er,

Make a cir-cle   while we dance a-round the fire.____ Dance the ho-ra

(clap) to your heart's de-sire.__ All the world sings Tze-na, tze-na, tze-na.

396

Singing the Blues

The CITY BLUES

American Folk Blues

1. Cloud - y in the west, Looks like rain;— I spent all my mon - ey on the sub - way train— In New York Cit - y,——— In New York Cit - y,——— In New York Cit - y, you real - ly got to know your way.—

2. Went to Detroit, it was fine,
   I watched the cars movin' off th' assembly line,
   In Detroit City, In Detroit City,
   In Detroit City, you really got to know your way.

3. I looped the loop, I rocked and reeled,
   I thought the Cubs played ball in Marshall Field,
   In the Windy City, In the Windy City,
   In the Windy City, you really got to know your way.

Choral Anthology

Imagine gazing up at the sky at nightfall. First you see one star sparkling, then suddenly another, and then another. Use your voice to sparkle each time you begin "Star Canon."

Star Canon

Music by Mary Goetze
Words from *Firefly* by Li Po

I think,—— if you flew up to the sky be-

side— the— moon,— you would spar-kle like a star,—— Oh,

Sometimes the sounds in music are used to paint a picture. "Autumn Canon" traces the path of a leaf as it leaves the branch and falls slowly to the ground.

Autumn Canon

Words and Music by Lajos Bárdos
Translated by Sean Deibler

1. Fly, fly, fly,———————— the
2. Cry, cry, cry,———————— the

leaf takes leave of the branch, breez - es are
tears come soft - ly be - hind, turn - ing to

strong, win - ter is com - ing.
frost, touch - ing my heart.———

398

THE ASH GROVE

Welsh Folk Song

1. Down yon-der green_ val - ley where stream-lets_ me - an - der,
   Or at the bright_ noon-tide in sol - i - tude_ wan - der

2. The ash-grove, how_ grace - ful, how plain - ly _'tis_ speak-ing,
   When-ev - er the_ light through its branch - es_ is_ break-ing,

When twi - light_ is_ fad - ing I pen - sive - ly rove,
A - mid the_ dark_ shades of the lone - ly ash grove.
The harp through_ it_ play - ing has lan - guage for me;
A host of_ kind_ fac - es is gaz - ing on me;

'Tis_ there where_ the_ black - bird is cheer - ful - ly_ sing - ing,
The_ friends of_ my_ child - hood a - gain are_ be - fore me,

Each war - bler_ en - chants with his note from the tree.
Each step wakes_ a_ mem - 'ry as free - ly I roam;

Ah, then lit - tle_ think I of sor - row_ or_ sad - ness;
With soft whis - pers_ la - den, its leaves rus - tle_ o'er me,

The ash grove_ en - chant - ing spells beau - ty for me.
The ash grove,_ the_ ash grove a - lone is my home.

Where'er You Walk

Music by George Frideric Handel
Words by William Congreve

Where'-er you_ walk, cool gales shall fan the glade; Trees, where you_ sit, shall

crowd in-to a shade, Trees, where you_ sit, shall crowd in - to_ a shade;

Where'-er you walk, cool gales shall fan the_ glade; Trees, where you sit, shall

crowd in-to a_ shade, _____ Trees, where_ you_ sit,

shall crowd___ in - to___ a shade. Where'-er you_ tread, the

blush-ing flow'rs shall rise, And all things flour - ish, and

all things flour - ish Where' - er you turn your eyes, Where'-

er you turn your eyes, Where'-er you turn your eyes.

The **art song** was popular in the 1800s. When creating an art song, composers would select the finest poetry. Then they would set the words to music. **Strophic** songs have more than one verse, each of which uses the same music. In a **through-composed song**, a composer would use new music as each idea of the poem unfolds. Which form of composition did Hugo Wolf use for "Fussreise"?

Fussreise
Tramping

Words by Eduard Mörike
Music by Hugo Wolf
English Version by Charles Fonteyn Manney

German: Am frisch - ge - schnitt - en ____ Wan - der - stab,
Pronunciation: am frɪsh gə shnɪ tən van dər shtap
English: With fresh - cut staff at ____ break of day

wenn ich in der Frü - he so durch____
vɛn ɪç ɪn der frü ə zo dʊrç
To the road I'm tak - ing, Thro' the ____

Wäl - der sie - he, ____ Hü - gel ____ auf und ab:
vɛl dər zi ə hü gəl aʊf ʊnt ap
woods a - wak - ing, ____ O'er the ____ hills a - way.

Dann, — wie's Vög-lein im Lau-be sin-get und sich
dan vis fög laın ım lau bə zıng ət ont zıç
Like — a bird sing-ing glad - ly Where green leaves en -

rührt, — o - der wie die gold' - ne Trau-be
rürt o dər vi di gold nə trau bə
fold, — Or the rap - ture cours - ing mad - ly

Won - ne - gei - ster spürt — in der er - sten Mor - gen
von nə gaı stər shpürt ın der er stən ıɔr gən
Thro' the grapes of gold — When the sun ap - pears at

son - ne: so fühlt auch mein — al - ter, lie - ber
zɔ nə so fült aux maın al tər li bər
dawn - ing: Thus old A - dam — in me mov - ing

A - dam Herbst und — Früh - lings - fie - ber gott - be - herz - te,
a dəm herpst ont frü lings fi bər gɔt bə herts tə
Stirs me, spring and — fall to — rov - ing, Heav'n de - scend - ed,

nie ver - scherz - te Erst - lings Pa - ra - di - ses - won -
ni fer sherts tə erst lıngs pa ra di zəs vɔ
Nev - er - end - ed Joy of Par - a - dise' — first morn -

ne. Al - so bist du — nicht so schlimm, o
nə al zo bıst du nıçt zo shlım o
ing. Thou de - serv - est — not so much dis -

402

al - ter A - dam, wie die stren-gen Leh - rer sa-gen;
al tər a dəm vi di shtrɛŋ ən le rər sa gən
fa - vor, A - dam, as stern teach-ers oft‿have stat-ed;

liebst und lobst du im - mer doch, singst und prei-sest im - mer noch,
lipst ʊnt lopst du ɪm mər dɔx zɪŋst ʊnt pɾaɪ zəst ɪm mər nɔx
Thou to-day, in love and praise, Still a joy-ous hymn dost raise

Wie an e - wig neu - en Schö-pfungs - ta - gen,
vi ɑn e vɪç nɔɪ ən shœp fʊŋs ta gən
as on that first day of things cre - at - ed

dei - nen lie - ben Schö - pfer und ‿ Er -
daɪ nən li bən shœp fər ʊnt er
To thy great Cre - a - tor and ‿ Pre -

hal - ter. Möcht' es die - ser ‿ ge - ben und mein
hal tər mœç tɛs di zər ge bən ʊnt maɪn
serv - er. Naught I'd need of ‿ heav - en Could this

gan - zes Le - ben wär' im ‿ leich - ten Wan - der-schwei-sse
gan tsəs le bən ver ɪm laɪç tən van dər shvaɪ sə
boon be giv - en: All my ‿ life en - tranced to wan - der

ei - ne sol - che Mor - gen - rei - se!
aɪ nə sɔl çə mɔɾ gən ɾaɪ zə
While earth smiles in morn - ing splen - dor!

"The Kettle Valley Line" is about a now-abandoned railroad in British Columbia, Canada. Imagine riding on the old Kettle Valley railroad. As you travel, you feel and hear the strong and steady clicking created as the wheels move on the rails. Place the sound and feel of this rhythm in your voice as you sing. Create the clicking sound by pronouncing consonant sounds quickly and with rhythmic accuracy, especially at the ends of words. Make the vowel sounds as focused and short as you can.

FIND the repeated melodic and rhythmic patterns.

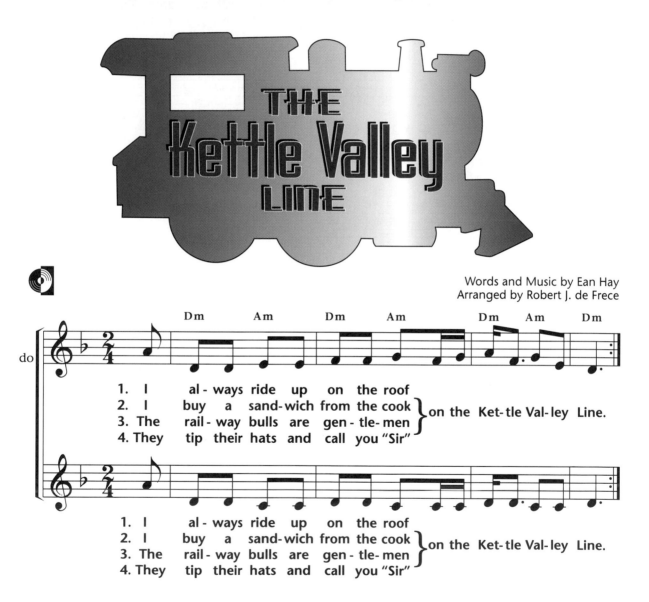

Words and Music by Ean Hay
Arranged by Robert J. de Frece

1. I always ride up on the roof
2. I buy a sand-wich from the cook } on the Ket-tle Val-ley Line.
3. The rail-way bulls are gen-tle-men
4. They tip their hats and call you "Sir"

1. I always ride up on the roof
2. I buy a sand-wich from the cook } on the Ket-tle Val-ley Line.
3. The rail-way bulls are gen-tle-men
4. They tip their hats and call you "Sir"

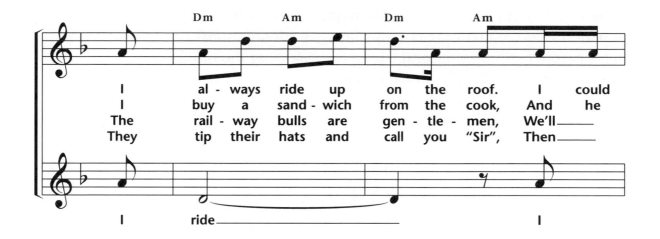

Robert Starer, the composer of "Midnight," wrote words for this song that contain many unusual images. Identify some of these before learning the song. Listen for ways that the music emphasizes some of the unusual images. As you sing, use breathing, diction, and dynamics to bring out the contrasting images. Doing this will help you to perform musically.

Words and Music by Robert Starer

Gently moving

It is mid-night; it is mid-night. The sun is shin-ing bright-ly, and a car is rac-ing slow-ly down the ri-ver.

It is sum-mer; it is sum-mer. Snow is fall-ing light-ly. It is warm and yet I

shiv-er.   I saw a rock-et walk.— I heard a tur-tle talk.— I saw a

dog with three legs. I saw four square eggs. Do you know, do you know why I

Part 1

shiv-er? It is mid-night;   it is mid-night.   The sun is shin-ing

Part 2

shiv-er?   It is sum-mer;   it is sum-mer.   Snow is

bright-ly,   and a car   is rac-ing   slow-ly down the riv-er. It is

fall-ing light-ly.   It is warm   and yet   I   shiv-er. It is

Unison

hot, ver-y hot.   It is ver-y, ver-y hot and yet I   shiv-er.

"Éinīnī" is a Gaelic lullaby. Gaelic is one of the languages spoken in Scotland and Ireland. The words mean: Little birdies sleep, sleep beside the fence over there. The lullaby should have a peaceful, rocking feel to it. Let the rise and fall of the pitches guide your dynamics. Get a bit louder as the pitches rise and a bit softer as the pitches fall.

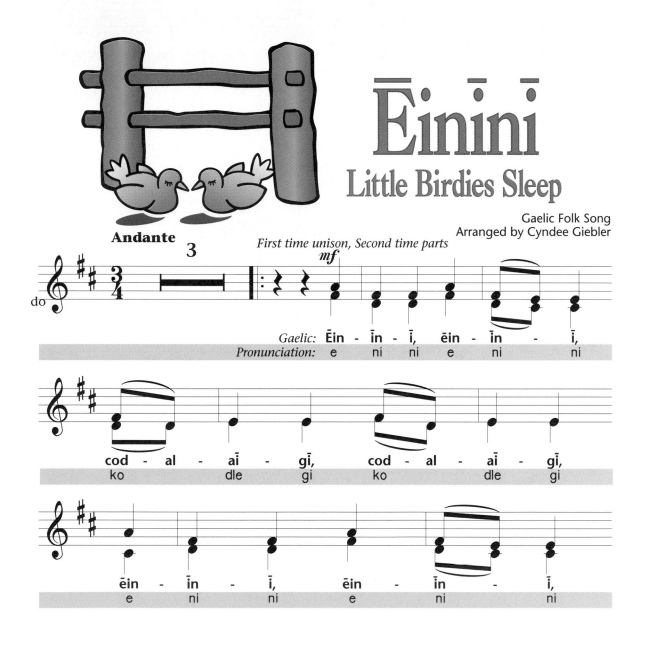

Éinīnī
Little Birdies Sleep

Gaelic Folk Song
Arranged by Cyndee Giebler

Andante

First time unison, Second time parts

Gaelic: Éin - īn - ī, éin - īn - ī,
Pronunciation: e ni ni e ni ni

cod - al - aī - gī, cod - al - aī - gī,
ko dle gi ko dle gi

éin - īn - ī, éin - īn - ī,
e ni ni e ni ni

To Music

16th-Century German Chorale Melody
Words and Arrangement by Betty Bertaux
Arrangement Adapted by Judy Bond

1. To sing-ing and to mu-sic, to joy-ful friend-ship true;
2. Lift ev'-ry voice to mu-sic, to love's ex-pres-sion sing;
3. For through this gift to hu-man-kind, we each to all be-long;

To mo-ments filled with hap-pi-ness, re-fresh-ing each day a-new.
Let mu-sic live in mind and heart, let joy and laugh-ter ring!
It's mu-sic that has joined us in life's sweet mas-ter song.

From val-leys and from hill-tops, from sea to shin-ing sea,
From val-leys and from hill-tops, from sea to shin-ing sea,
From the val-leys and from hill-tops, from sea to shin-ing sea,

Let earth re-sound with mu-sic, and life the rich-er be.

Add harmony on Verse 3

From the val-leys and from hill-tops, from sea to shin-ing sea,

Let earth re-sound with mu-sic, and life the rich-er be.

Legato means to perform in a smooth, connected manner.
Sing "A Gentle River Runs" in a legato manner.

A Gentle River Runs

Words and Music by Andrea Klouse
Adapted

glad   praise   yields   a   song._____   From

place   where   hearts   are   free._____   Where the
oth - er   hand   in   need._____   Where____
love   has   con - quered greed._____   And____

each   song   of   peace,   a   path   to

ten - der   hopes   a - rise_____   with the
cour - age   leads   the   heart_____   and____
with   you   by   my   side_____   we will

fol - low_____   will   lead   your

warm - ing   winds   of   spring,_____   near the
no - ble   dreams   are   dreamed,_____   near the
join   the   winds   of   spring,_____   near the

dim.

heart where its gen - tle riv - er goes.____ *to verse 2*

place where a gen - tle riv - er runs.____ *to refrain*
place where a gen - tle riv - er runs.____ *to verse 3 with descant*
place where a

gen - tle riv - er goes.____

gen - tle riv - er runs.____

Coda

In the where a
place In the place

gen - tle riv - er runs, a gen - tle riv - er runs.

YOU'RE INVITED
Chamber Music Concert

Chamber music is written for a small group of instruments. Only one performer plays on each part. Originally, this music was often played in a chamber, or room, instead of a concert hall, church, or theater. Today, chamber music can be heard on recordings, on the radio or television, or in concert halls. Many instrumentalists enjoy playing chamber music in their homes.

woodwind quintet

brass quintet

When the musicians enter for a concert, clap to greet them. As they perform, listen to the complete piece, then show your appreciation by clapping. If the piece has several movements, clap only at the end of the piece rather than at the end of each movement.

You may notice the musicians nodding or swaying as they play. Since chamber music is played without a conductor, the musicians use these movements to communicate with each other about starting, stopping, or staying together.

LISTENING

Chamber Music Concert

Presented by Smalltown Chamber Players

"RONDEAU" FROM SYMPHONIES DE FANFARES, No. 1 .... Jean-Joseph Mouret

Smalltown Brass Quintet

SUITE FOR WIND QUINTET, FIRST MOVEMENT .... Ruth Crawford-Seeger

Smalltown Woodwind Quintet

Intermission

STRING QUARTET IN B MINOR, FOURTH MOVEMENT .... Teresa Carreño

STRING QUARTET OP. 33, No. 3, ... Franz Joseph Haydn FOURTH MOVEMENT

Smalltown String Quartet

string quartet

PLAN your own chamber music concert. Choose recordings or put together a program that those in your school can play. Prepare the program and present it.

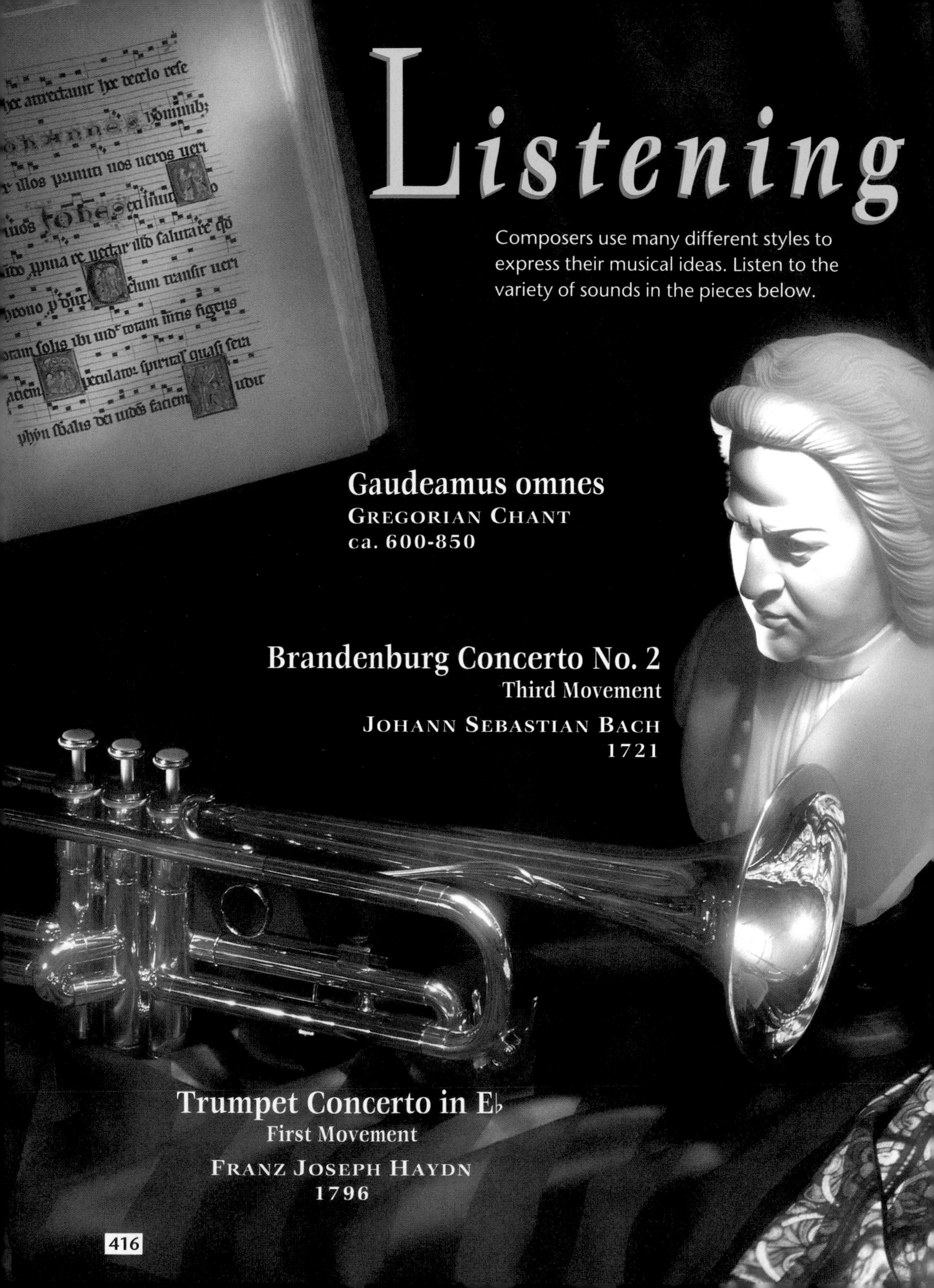

Listening

Composers use many different styles to express their musical ideas. Listen to the variety of sounds in the pieces below.

Gaudeamus omnes
GREGORIAN CHANT
ca. 600-850

Brandenburg Concerto No. 2
Third Movement

JOHANN SEBASTIAN BACH
1721

Trumpet Concerto in E♭
First Movement

FRANZ JOSEPH HAYDN
1796

Discoveries

Polonaise in A Major Op. 40, No. 1
(Military Polonaise)
FRÉDÉRIC FRANÇOIS CHOPIN
1841

Sanctus
from *Requiem*
GABRIEL URBAIN FAURÉ
1887

String Quartet in B Minor
Fourth Movement
TERESA CARREÑO
1896

Possibilities

Words and Music by Teresa Jennings

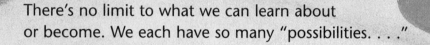

There's no limit to what we can learn about
or become. We each have so many "possibilities. . . ."

Possibilities

Words and Music by Teresa Jennings

Energetically

*First time in unison;
on D.S. sing in two-part canon*

So

man - y pos - si - bil - i - ties._____ So man - y ways to go._____ So

man-y things to choose from._____ All the things that I could know. { I can / I will

Part 1   first time in unison

learn, and I can grow. I can do, and I can know. I can
work, and I will do. I will al - ways make it through. I will

Part 2   on D.S. only

Work   and   do.   Make   it   through.

* Part 2 of canon stops here

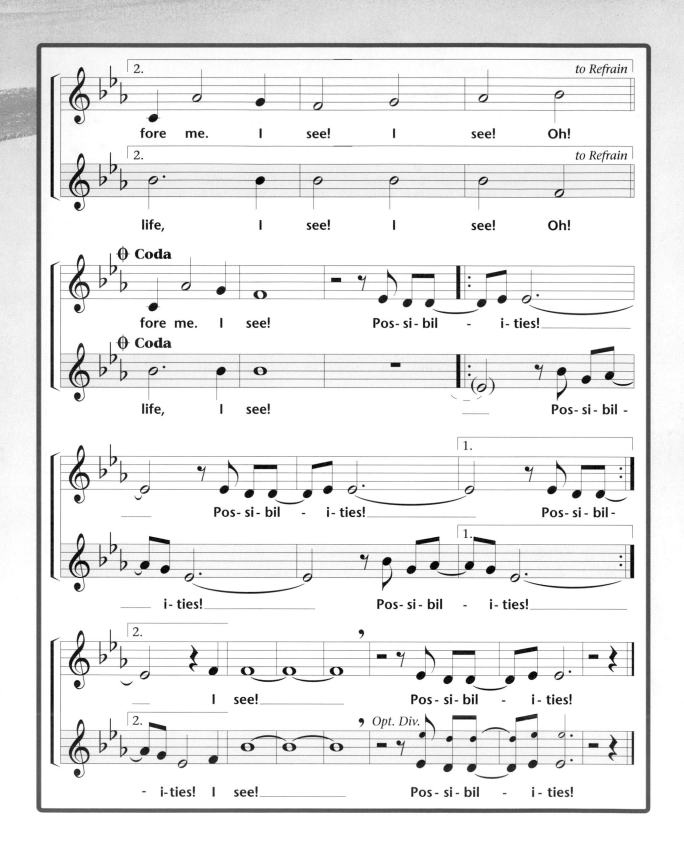

The toughest part of having so many possibilities is deciding which ones to pursue. Possibilities come from inside us. Soon after we are born, we start reaching out to make choices for ourselves. All of us have dreams—big dreams!

We all have big dreams in common. When we think of possibilities as careers, jobs, or occupations, the sky is the limit. If I'm good at science, I might think about becoming a scientist or doctor. If I like to read or write, maybe I will become an author. If my computer is my favorite thing, maybe I will write programs or invent my own computer software. But for now, it's fun to think about anything and everything!

I'm Gonna Be

Techno Rock
7 measures introduction

Words and Music by Teresa Jennings

1. I'm gon - na be an act - or or a sur - geon.
2. I'm gon - na be a writ - er or a sol - dier.

I'm gon - na be in ar - chae - ol - o - gy. I'm gon - na be a
I'm gon - na be in so - ci - ol - o - gy. I'm gon - na be a

teach - er or a pi - lot. I'm gon - na start my own com - pa - ny. I'm gon - na
fire - man or a plumb - er. I'm gon - na build my own fac - to - ry. I'm gon - na

℅ **Refrain**

be. I'm gon - na be. An - y - thing, an - y - where is a
be. I'm gon - na be. An - y - thing, an - y - where is an

1., 3., 5.
pos - si - bil - i - ty. I'm gon - na

2., 4.
Opt. Div.
op - tion I can see! I'm gon - na

2nd ending to D.C.
4th ending to Bridge
be!

6.
Fine
op - tion I can see! I'm gon - na be!

Did you know that everything we do in life is a choice? We can't choose the way other people act or the way things happen. But, we can choose the way *we* will be. We have the possibility to choose whether to let things bother us or not. It isn't always easy to let things roll off of you, especially things that hurt. The point is, your choices are yours. Choose to believe in yourself, and don't ever give up!

Don't Ever Give Up

Words and Music by Teresa Jennings

Gospel Swing

1. All of your life, you will have man-y choic-es:
2. Some-times it's tough, and you have man-y prob-lems.

how you will be, and what you will do.
How you will cope is all up to you.

That's just the point. It's your life, your choice.
Look deep in-side. It's your life, your choice.

Trust in your-self and your faith will show through!
You can be-lieve and your light will shine through!

Refrain

Don't ev-er give up. Don't ev-er lose the
Don't ev-er lose heart. Know who you are.

dreams that you dream ev'-ry day. life your way, your way.
Live your own

Life is a journey, so enjoy the journey exploring all the possibilities before you. It's a great adventure!

It's My Journey!

Words and Music by Teresa Jennings

With Great Energy!

Unison, verses 1–2; opt. divisi verses 3–4
Sing verses 3–4 on D.S.

1. I am on my way!___ Ev' - ry
2. Ev' - ry path I take,___ ev' - ry
3. Ev' - ry sin - gle day___ is a
4. Pos - si - bil - i - ties___ come a -

bend in the road__ and cor - ner shows me one__ more day!___
moun - tain and ev' - ry riv - er, leads me on__ my way!___
part of the road__ I trav - el. When and where__ it goes
long ev' - ry time__ I won - der. I'm the one__ who knows__

1.
___ And it's my day!___
___ And it's

2.
my way!___
___ you will find me!___
___ what I can be!___

divisi on D.S. only

Min - utes and hours___ are fly - ing by,

nev - er to come__ back a - gain.___ Each one is pre - cious, and that__

___ is why each one is al - so my friend! Oh!

Playing the RECORDER

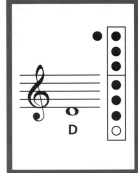

C

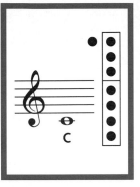

D

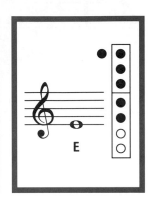

E

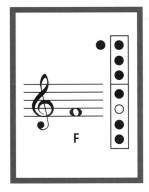

F

F#

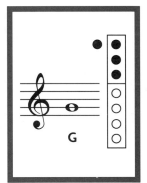

G

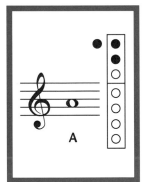

A

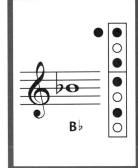

B♭

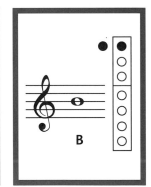

B

C'

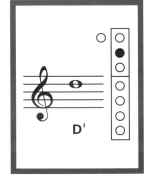

D'

Glossary

A

a cappella without instrumental accompaniment, **136**

accent (>) a sign that puts more emphasis on a note, **374**

accidental a sharp (♯), flat (♭), or natural (♮) placed before a note, used to alter the note within a measure, **179**

accompaniment a musical background to a melody, **49**

alto the second highest of the adult vocal ranges, **122**

andante at a moderate tempo, **284**

arpeggio a broken chord, **299**

arranger a person who makes decisions about how style, instrumentation, tempo, harmony, and dynamics can be changed in a piece of music, **242**

art song a type of song popular in the 1800s which uses the finest poetry, **401**

B

bar line (|) a line separating sets of beats into measures, **35**

bass the lowest adult vocal range, **122**

bass clef (𝄢) a clef used to show low pitches, often used by tenors and basses, **122**

bass line the lowest musical part, often played by low-pitched instruments, **133**

beat a steady silent pulse that underlies most music, **14**

blue notes notes that are lowered or "bent" in the blues, **278**

blues a style of music characterized by blue notes that grew out of the sorrow and troubled feelings of Africans who were enslaved and brought to this country, **276**

brass quintet an ensemble usually including two trumpets, French horn, trombone, and tuba, **288**

C

call and response a song form in which a phrase sung by a solo leader is followed by a phrase sung by a group; the response is usually a repeated phrase or pattern, **184**

calypso a folk style originating in the Caribbean islands, **234**

canon a musical form in which a melody is imitated in one or more parts, similar to a round, **53**

chamber music music usually played by a small ensemble, **280**

changed voice an adult singing voice, usually categorized as soprano, alto, tenor, or bass, **122**

chord three or more pitches sounded together, **227**

chord progression a series of chords used to harmonize a song, **239**

common tone a pitch found in two different chords, **238**

countermelody a contrasting melody written to go with a song, **88**

crescendo (⟨) gradually louder, **302**

cut time (¢ or $\frac{2}{2}$) a meter signature in which there are two beats in a measure and the half note gets one beat, **201**

D

decrescendo (⟩) gradually softer, **302**

diatonic scale a scale that includes *do re mi fa so la ti do'*, **140**

Dixieland jazz a style of music in the early 1900s characterized by improvisation using trumpet, clarinet, banjo, trombone, tuba, drums, **126**

dotted eighth note (♪.) equal in length to one eighth note plus one sixteenth note, **275**

dotted quarter note (♩.) equal in length to one quarter note plus one eighth note, **87**

double bar (‖) a thin and a thick line that show the end of the piece, **35**

downbeat the strong beat, **173**

duration length, **84**

dynamics changes in intensity and loudness of sound, **302**

E

eighth note (♪) two eighth notes equal two sounds to a beat (♫) when the quarter note gets one beat, **34**

eighth rest (𝄾) a silence for the length of an eighth note, **244**

ensemble a musical group, **37**

F

fanfare a short showy tune for trumpets or brass, played to honor important people or to announce an important event, **135**

fermata (𝄐) symbol that means that the note or rest under it should be held longer than its normal value, **176**

flat (♭) lowers a pitch a half step, **179**

folk song a song passed on from one person to another for such a long time that no one knows who composed it, **226**

form the order of phrases or sections in music, **272**

forte (*f*) loud, **302**

fortissimo (*ff*) very loud, **302**

G

G clef or treble clef () tells that a note placed on the second line of the staff is G, **21**

H

half note (♩) a sound that lasts for two beats in meters where the quarter note gets one beat, **43**

half rest (▬) a silence that lasts for two beats in meters where the quarter note gets one beat, **43**

half step the smallest distance between pitches in most western music; the distance between a pitch and the next closest pitch on the keyboard, **179**

harmony two or more pitches sounding at the same time, **31**

heavier register a vocal quality that is heavy, usually produced in the lower range, **22**

I

improvise to make up music while performing it, **36**

J

jazz a type of popular American music created by African Americans in the South, often using syncopation, improvisation, and strong rhythms, **78**

K

kettledrums two or more large tunable drums in the shape of a kettle, played with mallets; also known as timpani, **133**

key signature sharps or flats placed at the beginning of each staff, **179**

kulinatang a musical ensemble from Mindanao using gongs and drums; the lead instrument for that group, **36**

L

legato in a smooth, connected manner, **411**

lighter register a vocal quality that is light, usually produced in the higher range, **22**

lyrics the words of a song, **123**

M

major scale a diatonic scale with *do* as the tonal center, using pitches *do re mi fa so la ti do'*, **140**

measure a group of beats, set off by bar lines, **35**

melodic direction the way that a melody moves: upward, downward, staying the same, **19**

melody a pattern of pitches that moves upward, downward, or stays the same, **19**

meter the organization of beats and accents in recurring sets, **35**

meter signature tells the number of beats in a measure and what rhythm value equals one beat, **35**

mezzo forte (*mf*) medium loud, **302**

mezzo piano (*mp*) medium soft, **302**

430

minor scale a diatonic scale with *la* as its tonal center, using pitches *la, ti, do re mi fa so la*, **143**

motive a small building block of melody or rhythm, **101**

musical a musical form featuring a story told with singing, drama, and dancing, **76**

N

natural (♮) used to cancel a sharp or flat, **181**

notation written symbols showing how to perform music, **34**

O

ornament to decorate a melody, **249**

ostinato a short repeated pattern, **37**

P

partner songs separate songs that sound good when sung at the same time, **88**

pentatonic scale a scale of five pitches, usually *do re mi so la*, **73**

percussion instruments played by striking, scraping, or shaking, **36**

percussion ensemble a group playing only percussion instruments, **43**

phrase a short segment of music that is one complete thought or idea, **44**

pianissimo (*pp*) very soft, **302**

piano (*p*) soft, **302**

pitch the highness or lowness of a sound, **19**

processional music for a procession or parade, **14**

program music story-telling or image-making music, **200**

Q

quarter note (♩) one sound to a beat, **34**

quarter rest (𝄽) a beat with no sound, **34**

R

range the distance from the highest to the lowest pitch that can be sung or played by a performer, **22**

rhythm combinations of longer and shorter sounds and silences, **14**

ritardando (*rit.*) a gradual slowing down, **284**

rondo a form based on repetition and contrast, often organized as A B A C A, A B A C A B A, or A B A C A D A, **274**

root the pitch on which a chord is built, **227**

S

scale an ordered series of pitches, **73**

scat syllables nonsense syllables, popular with jazz singers, **279**

score written music, often showing all the parts to be performed together, **20**

section a group of related phrases that form a larger unit, **46**

sharp (♯) raises a pitch a half step, **181**

sixteenth note (♪) four sixteenth notes equal one beat (♬) in meters where the quarter note gets one beat, **95**

sixteenth rest (𝄿) a silence that equals the length of a sixteenth note, **244**

slurs (⌒) curved lines connecting notes of different pitches, **378**

soprano the highest of the adult vocal ranges, **122**

staff the five lines and four intervening spaces on which musical notes are written, **20**

steel drums pitched percussion instruments made from oil drums, **70**

string quartet an ensemble made up of two violins, viola, and cello, **274**

strophic song a type of song that uses the same music for each verse, **401**

style the distinct way that people use the elements of music to express themselves, **222**

symphony a musical work usually composed for instruments, consisting of several movements, **131**

syncopation a type of rhythm in which stressed sounds occur between beats instead of on beats, **71**

system staffs connected by a vertical line that are performed at the same time, **32**

T

tag extra measures of ending, **78**

tempo the speed of the beat, **14**

tenor the second lowest adult vocal range, **122**

texture the sound created by different pitches, rhythms, and tone colors played or sung together, **48**

through-composed song a type of song that uses new music for each new poetic idea, **401**

tie () a sign that joins two notes of the same pitch into a single sound equal to their total duration, **84**

timpani two or more large tunable kettle-shaped drums played with mallets; also known as kettledrums, **133**

tonal center a pitched resting place in music, the focus or home tone of a scale, **73**

tone color the special sound of each instrument or voice, **22**

tone poem a work for orchestra that tells a story through music, **150**

twelve-bar blues a blues chord progression of 12 measures, usually following a set pattern, **286**

U

unchanged voice a young person's voice that has not changed to an adult voice, **122**

unison all perform the same part, **31**

upbeat a weak beat before the downbeat, also called an anacrusis, **173**

V

variation a changed version of a theme or melody, **100**

verse-refrain a form of a song in which the words of the verse change following each repetition of the refrain; the verse and refrain usually have different melodies, **184**

W

whole step twice the distance of a half step, **182**

woodwind quintet a musical ensemble usually consisting of flute, oboe, clarinet, French horn, and bassoon, **280**

Z

zydeco a style of music from Louisiana using a mixture of jazz and blues with Creole music, style, and language, **186**

ACKNOWLEDGMENTS *continued*

Glen Everhart for *Young People of the World* by Glen Everhart © 1991, 1222 Westminster Street, #203, St. Paul, MN 55101.

Exley Publications Ltd. for *Chorus of the World* from DEAR WORLD by Richard and Helen Exley, reprinted by permission of Exley Publications Ltd., Watford, UK.

Faber Music Ltd. For *Chan mali chan*, transcribed by Peter Gritton, from FOLKSONGS FROM THE FAR EAST by Peter Gritton. © 1991 by Faber Music Ltd. Reproduced by permission of Faber Music Ltd., London. All rights reserved.

Folkways Music Publishers, Inc. for *So Long* by Woody Guthrie. Copyright © 1950 by Folkways Music Publishers, Inc., New York, NY. Used by permission.

Mark Foster Music Company for *Hanerot Halalu* by Baruch J. Cohon. © 1974 Fostco Music Press. Sole selling agent: Mark Foster Music Company, Champaign, IL. Used by permission.

Fulcrum Publishing for *How the Fawn Got Its Spots* from KEEPERS OF THE ANIMALS: NATIVE AMERICAN STORIES AND WILDLIFE ACTIVITIES FOR CHILDREN by Michael Caduto and Joseph Bruchac. © Fulcrum Publishing, 350 Indiana St. #350, Golden, CO 80401.

Genesis III Music Corp. for *Music! Music!* By Frederick Silver. Copyright © 1976 by Frederick Silver, Genesis III Music Corp.

Geordie Music Publishing Co. for *Peace Round*, lyrics by Jean Ritchie. © 1964 Jean Ritchie, Geordie Music Publishing Co. For *Going to Boston* by Jean Ritchie. © 1952 Jean Ritchie, Geordie Music Music Publishing, Inc. Used by permission.

Elizabeth Gilpatrick for *Sail Away*, words for the second verse and arrangement contained herein, Reprinted from MUSIC FOR THE MIDDLE by Elizabeth Gilpatrick.

Mary Goetze for *Star Canon* by Mary Goetze, text by Li Po. © Mary Goetze.

HarperCollins Publishers Inc. for Quote from preface page 7, *What we call world music really*, from PLANET DRUM: A CELEBRATION OF PERCUSSIONS AND RHYTHM by Mickey Hart. Copyright © 1991 by Mickey Hart. Reprinted by permission of HarperCollins Publisher Inc. See pg. 256.

Mary E. Hay for *The Kettle Valley Line* by Ean Hay. Orff arrangement by Bob deFrece. Used by permission.

D.C. Heath & Company for *Campanas vespertinas* by Julio Z. Guerra and Juana Guglielmi from MASTERING MUSIC, 6th GRADE. By permission of D.C. Heath & Company.

Homeland Publishing for *Evergreen, Everblue*. Words and Music by Raffi. © 1990 Homeland Publishing, a Division of Troubadour Records Ltd. All rights reserved. Used by permission.

Jim Jacobs & Warren Casey for *We Go Together* from GREASE. Words and Music by Jim Jacobs and Warren Casey. © 1971, 1972 by Warren Casey and Jim Jacobs. All rights throughout the world controlled by Edwin H. Morris & Company, a division of MPL Communications, Inc. International copyright secured. All rights reserved. Used by permission.

Jenson Publications, Inc. for *We Want to Sing* by Roger Emerson and the Shasta Music Camp Staff. Copyright © 1977 Jenson Publications, inc. International copyright secured. Made in U.S.A. All rights reserved.

Jobete Music for *Reach Out and Touch Somebody's Hand* by Nickolas Ashford and Valerie Simpson. Copyright © 1970 by Jobete Music Corporation, Inc., 25457 Woodward Ave., Detroit, MI. Used by permission.

Neil A. Kjos Music Company for *By the Singing Water*. © 1952 Neil A. Kjos Music Company, Publisher. Reprinted with permission 1992.

Alfred A. Knopf, Inc. for *African Dance* (excerpt) from SELECTED POEMS OF LANGSTON HUGHES by Langston Hughes. Copyright 1926 by Alfred A. Knopf, Inc. Copyright renewed 1954 by Langston Hughes. Reprinted by permission of Alfred A. Knopf, Inc. For *Youth* from THE DREAM KEEPER AND OTHER POEMS by Langston Hughes. Copyright 1932 by Alfred A. Knopf, Inc. and renewed 1960 by Langston Hughes. Reprinted by permission of the publisher.

Larrabee Publications for The *Yellow Rose of Texas*. © Copyright 1962 LARABEE PUBLICATIONS, 263 Veterans Boulevard, Carlstadt, NJ 07072. International Copyright Secured. Made in U.S.A..

Hal Leonard Publishing Corporation for *A Gentle River Runs* by Andrea Klouse. Copyright © 1993 by Hal Leonard Publishing Corp. International Copyright Secured. All rights reserved.

Lorenz Publishing Co. for *Song of Peace*. Words by Leland Isaac. (Copyright for Music by Jean Sibelius by Breitkopf and Hartel, Wiesbaden, Germany).

Melody Lane Publications for *Deep in the Heart of Texas*. Words by Don Swander. Words by June Hershey. Copyright © 1941 by Melody Lane Publications, Inc. Used by permission.

Memphis Musicraft Publications for *The Dream of Martin Luther King* by Merle Gartrell and Students of Cummings Elementary School, from HOLIDAYS, 21 FESTIVE ARRANGEMENTS, © 1980 Memphis Musicraft Publications, 3149 Southern Ave., Memphis, TN 38111.

William Morrow & Company, Inc. for *The Headless Horseman* from THE HEADLESS HORSEMAN RIDES TONIGHT by Jack Prelutsky. Copyright © 1980 by Jack Prelutsky. By permission of Greenwillow Books, a division of William Morrow & Company, Inc.

Music Corporation of America, Inc. (MCA Music Publishing) and Songs of Polygram International, Inc. for *God Bless the U.S.A.* by Lee Greenwood. © Copyright 1984 by Music Corporation of America, Inc. and Hall-Clement Publications (c/o The Welk Music Group). International copyright secured. Made in U.S.A. All rights reserved. Exclusively distributed by Hal Leonard Publishing Corporation.

Music Sales Corporation for *Harriet Tubman* by Walter Robinson. Copyright © 1980 Shawnee Press, Inc. International Copyright Secured. All Rights Reserved. Used by Permission.

New Directions Publishing Company for *As I row over the plain* from ONE HUNDRED POEMS FROM THE JAPANESE by Kenneth Rexroth. All rights reserved.

Northern Songs Ltd. for *Yesterday* by John Lennon and Paul McCartney. © 1965 Northern Songs Ltd. Copyright renewed. All rights controlled and administered by EMI Blackwood Music, Inc. under license from SONY/ATV SONGS LLC. All rights reserved. International copyright secured. Used by permission.

Oxford University Press for *Jazz Round* by John Coates from SING FOR PLEASURE (Book 10); copyright Oxford University Press. By permission.

Plank Road Publishing for *Get Up!* by Teresa Jennings. © 1991, Plank Road Publishing. All Rights Reserved. For "Possibilities" by Teresa Jennings © 1996, 1997 Plank Road Publishing, Inc. International copyright secured. All rights reserved.

Plymouth Music Co. for *All Join In* by Aden G. Lewis. Copyright © 1965 by Plymouth Music Co., Inc., 1841 Broadway, NY. International Copyright Secured. Printed in the U.S.A. All Rights Reserved.

Random House, Inc. for *Equality* (excerpt) from I SHALL NOT BE MOVED by Maya Angelou. Copyright © 1990 by Maya Angelou. Reprinted by permission of Random House, Inc.

Marian Reiner for *Music* from WHAT IS THAT SOUND! By Mary O'Neill. Copyright © 1966 Mary L. O'Neill. Reprinted by permission of Marian Reiner. For *Sidewalk Racer* from THE SIDEWALK RACER AND OTHER POEMS OF SPORTS AND MOTION by Lillian Morrison. Copyright © 1965, 1967, 1968, 1977 by Lillian Morrison. Reprinted by permission of Marian Reiner for the author.

Ricordi Americana S.A.E.C. for *Canten, señores cantores* from 150 MELODIAS DEL CANCIONERO TRADICIONAL, Vol. 2, by Violeta H. de Gainza and Guillermo Graetzer. Copyright © 1963 by Ricordi Americana S. A. E. C., Buenos Aires, Argentina.

Robbins Music Corporation for *Sing, Sing, Sing* by Louis Prima. Copyright © 1936 (renewed 1964) Robbins Music Corporation. All rights of Robbins Music Corporation assigned to EMI Catalogue Partnership. All rights controlled and administered by EMI Robbins Catalog Inc. International Copyright Secured. Made in U.S.A. All Rights Reserved.

Roncom Music Company for *Nifty Fifty United States* by Ray Charles. Copyright © Roncom Music Company, 305 Northern Blvd., Great Neck, NY 11021.

Shapiro, Bernstein & Co., Inc. for *Side by Side* by Harry Woods. © 1927 Shapiro, Bernstein & Co., Inc., New York. Copyright Renewed. Used by Permission.

Shawnee Press, Inc. for *Simple Gifts*. © Copyright 1976 Shawnee Press, Inc. Delaware Water Gap, PA 18327. All rights reserved. Used by permission.

Jerry Silverman for *The City Blues* from FOLK BLUES by Jerry Silverman. Copyright © 1983 by Saw Mill Music Corporation., 160 High Street, Hastings-on-Hudson, NY. International copyright secured. Made in U.S.A. All rights reserved.

The Society of Authors for *The Horseman*. Words by The Literary Trustees of Walter de la Mare and The Society of Authors as their representative. Music by permission of Marilyn C. Davidson. © 1987.

James E. Solomon for *Mango Walk*.

Songs of Polygram International, Inc. and Music Corporation of America, Inc. (MCA Music Publishing) for *God Bless the U.S.A.* by Lee Greenwood. © Copyright 1984 by Music Corporation of America, Inc. and Hall-Clement Publications (c/o The Welk Music Group). International copyright secured. Made in U.S.A. All rights reserved. Exclusively distributed by Hal Leonard Publishing Corporation.

Kathy B. Sorensen for *Hong Tsai Me Me; Pung Noy Loy Kratong; Savalivali;* and Tết Trung; collected and transcribed by Kathy B. Sorensen. © 1991 Kathy B. Sorensen.

Southern Music Publishing Co., Inc. for *Good Mornin' Blues* by Huddie Ledbetter. © Copyright 1970 by Southern Music Publishing Co., Inc. Used by permission.

Robert Starer for *Midnight* by Robert Starer. © Copyright 1966 by Robert Starer.

Sunstone Press for *Song of the Skyloom* from SONGS OF THE TEWA by Herbert Joseph Spinder. This material courtesy of Sunstone Press (Box 2321, Santa Fe, NM 87504).

Threesome Music for Yellow Bird, music by Norman Luboff, lyrics by Marilyn Keith and Alan Bergman. Copyright © 1957 by Walton Music Corporation and Threesome Music, Renewed.

TRO for *Follow the Drinkin' Gourd* adapted by Paul Campbell. Copyright © 1950 (renewed) Folkways Music Publishers, Inc., New York, NY Used by permission. For *Mama, Bake the Johnnycake* by Blake Alphonso Higgs. © Copyright 1963 TRO (renewed) Hollis Music, Inc., New York, NY. Used by permission. For *Something to Sing About* by Oscar Brand. © Copyright 1963 (renewed) and 1964 (renewed) Hollis Music, Inc., New York, NY. Used by permission. For *The Thing* by Charles R. Grean. © Copyright 1950 (renewed) Hollis Music, Inc., New York, NY. Used by permission, © Grean Music Co. *For This Land Is Your Land* by Woody Guthrie. © Copyright 1956 (renewed), 1958 (renewed) and 1970 Ludlow Music, Inc., New York, NY. Used by permission.

Union of American Hebrew Congregations for *Eight Are the Lights* by Ilo Orleans.

The United Synagogue of America Commission on Jewish Education for *Who Can Retell?* Music by M. Ravino; Arranged by Harry Coopersmith; Translation by B.M. Edidin. From THE SONGS WE SING, selected & edited by Harry Coopersmith. Copyright 1950 by The United Synagogue of America. Utilized with permission of the publisher, The United Synagogue Commission on Jewish Education.

University of New Mexico Press for *The Way to Rainy Mountain* (excerpt) by N. Scott Momaday. First published in THE REPORTER, 26 January 1967. Reprinted from THE WAY TO RAINY MOUNTAIN © 1969, The University of New Mexico Press.

Van Ness Press, Inc. for *Music Brings Us Together!* By Garry Smith. © Copyright 1990 Van Ness Press, Inc. All rights reserved. Used by permission.

Walton Music Corporation for *Yellow Bird*, music by Norman Luboff, lyrics by Marilyn Keith and Alan Bergman. Copyright © 1957 by Walton Music Corporation and Threesome Music, Renewed.

Warner Bros. Publications Inc. for *Everybody Rejoice* by Luther Vandross. © 1975 WB MUSIC CORP. All Rights Reserved. Used by Permission. For *I Got Rhythm*, words by Ira Gershwin, music by George Gershwin. © 1930 (Renewed) WB MUSIC CORP. All Rights Reserved. Used by Permission. For *On the Road Again* by Willie Nelson. Copyright © 1979 FULL NELSON MUSIC, Inc. All rights administered by WINDSWEPT PACIFIC ENTERTAINMENT CO. d/b/a LONGITUDE MUSIC CO. International Copyright Secured. Made in U.S.A. All Rights Reserved. Used by Permission. For *The Rhythm of Life* from SWEET CHARITY, Warner/Chappell, music by Cy Coleman, lyrics by Dorothy Fields. © 1965 NOTABLE MUSIC CO., INC. and LIDA ENTERPRISES, Inc. All Rights Reserved. Used by Permission. For *Winter Wonderland*. Words and Music by Dick Smith. Music by Felix Bernard © 1934 WB Music Corp. All rights reserved. Used by permission.

Arliene Nofchissey Williams for *Go, My Son* by Arliene Nofchissey Williams and Carnes D. Burson, arrangement copyright © 1993 Carnes Burson. All rights reserved.

Acknowledgments for Hal Leonard Showstoppers are on page HL18.

Art & Photo Credits

COVER DESIGN: Robert Brook Allen, A Boy and His Dog

COVER PHOTOGRAPHY: All photographs are by the McGraw-Hill School Division.

ILLUSTRATION

Zita Asbaghi, 272-273, 370-371; George Baquero, 222-225, 306-309; Shonto Begay, 283-285; Doron Ben-Ami, 290-291; Steven Bennett (calligrapher), 65, 116-117, 127-129, 142, 172, 180, 186-187, 196, 232, 250, 254, 318, 334-335, 337, 338, 340, 348; Jeanne Berg, 276-277, Linda Bleck, 78-79, 302-303, 366-367; Yvonne Buchanan, 46-47; Thomas Buchs, 418–419, 420–421, 422–423, 424–425, 426–427; Brian Callanan, 240-241; Jane Caminos, 34-35; Lydia Chang, 74-75; Tony Chen, 246-247; Mark Chickinelli, 102-105; Steve Cieslawski, 218-219; Eulala Conners, 135, 152-153; Marie Corfield, 176-177; David Csicsko, 122-123; Margaret Cusak, 214-215, 232-233, 344-345; Stephan Daigle, 268-269; David Diaz, 92-93; Patricia Doktor, 120-121; Julie Ecklund, 50-53; Rick Faist, 60-63; Clifford Faust, 234-237; Nancy Freeman, 182-183; Brad Gaber, 244-245, 274-275, 414-415; Jack Graham, 174-175; Rob Gregoretti, 352-353; Randy Hamblin, 70-71; Pete Harritos, 72-73; Ed Heins, 280-281; Terry Herman, 213; Oscar Hernandez 126-127, 292-293; Catherine Huerta, 316-317; Susan Johnston, 42-43; Lars Justinen, 94-95, Mark Kaplan, 14-15, 40-41, 172-173, 232-233, 348-349, Lingta Kung, 106-109; Michele Laporte, 84-85; Tom Leonardo, 156-157; Lori Lohstoeter, 206-207, 228-229, 282-283; Lisa Maharian, 48-49; Ginidir Marshall, 28-29; Coco Masuda, 140-141, Richard & Marci McNeel, 86-87; Frank McShane, 192-193, Frank Mendeola, 76; Marilyn Montgomery, 136, 137; Bill Morse, 238-239; David Myers, 98-101, 136, 137; Tom Nachreiner, 10–11, 59, 66–67, 118–119, 311; Joel Nakamura, 188-189; Vince Natale, 324-327; Susan Nees, 97; Nancy Nimoy, 112-115, Eve Olitsky, 164-167; Jose Ortega, 294-295; Lori Osiecki, 96-97; Jim Owens, 16-17; Edward Parker, 216-217; John Pirman, 82-83; Rodica Prato, 336-337; Nikolai Punin, 278-279; Bonnie Rasmussen, 190-191; Barbara Rhodes, 180-181; Robert Roper, 258-261; Robert Sabuda, 44-45; Paul Salmon, 286-287; Robert Sauber, 252-253; Phil Scheuer, 202; John Schilling, 358-359; Bob Shein, 36-37; Bill Scott, 2–3, 4, 263; Michael Shumate, 80-81; Jack Slattery, 88-89; Susan Spellman, 97; Heidi Stevens, 318-319; John Stevens, 414, 415; Joyce Stiglich, 350–351; Maria Stroster, 54-57; James Swanson, 312-315; Leslie Szabo, 134-135, 368-369; Julia Talcott, 8-9; TCA Graphics, 24, 43, 152-153, 179, 181, 182-183, 193, 202, 204, 205, 227, 238, 248, 292, 299, 302; Kat Thacker, 152-153; Russell Thurston, 158-161, 230-231; Winson Trang, 194-199; Jean & Mou Sein Tseng, 97; Cornelius van Wright, 20-21; Dale Versaal, 24-25, 30-31, 304-305; Sharon Watts, 90-91; Meg White, 248-249; Kris Wiltse, 184-185; David & Donna Wisniewski, 334-335.

Tech Art by TCA Graphics, Inc.

PHOTOGRAPHY

All photographs are by the McGraw-Hill School Division (MHSD) except as noted below.

i: r. © Artville. iv: l. © Artville; m. © Artville.v: l. © Artville. vi: l. © Artville; m. © Artville; r. © Artville. vii: l. © Artville. **Unit 1** 6: Superstock. 14: b. John Lewis Stage/The Image Bank; t. Alvin Upitis/The Image Bank. 15: b.r. Blair Seitz; b.r. Scala/Art Resource; m.l. Mark Gibson; m.r. Jack Hoehn, Jr./Profiles West; t.l. Anja Sebunya, Ghana; t.r. Joe Viesti/Viesti Associates. 18: b.l. Woody Guthrie Publications; m.l. Charles Beneo/FPG; r., m.r. Comstock; r.m.r. Ron Thomas/FPG; t.l. Michael Howell/International Stock. 18-19: b.l. Larry Lefever/Grant Heilman. 19: b.m.l. Patricia Fisher; b.m.r. Travel Pix/FPG; b.r. Dimaggio/Kalish/The Stock Market. 22-23: Jeff Sedlik/Outline. 23: b. Jeff Sedlik/Outline. 27: t. Hirshhorn Museum And Sculpture Garden, Smithsonian Institution, gift of Joseph H. Hirshhorn, 1966. Painting by Horace Pippin, 8/9/45. 28: b., t. Jack Vartoogian; m. Joe Compton. 28-29: Bill Waltzer for MHSD. 36, 37: Brian Leng for MHSD. 38: © M.C. Escher/Cordon Art-Baam-Holland Collection Haags Germeentemuseum, the Hague. 40: r., b.m. Joseph Sachs for MHSD. 31: b.l. David Young-Wolff/ PhotoEdit; t.l. Norman Owen Tomalin/Bruce Coleman. 42-43: b. Brian Leng for MHSD. 48: b. Winter Road by Georgia O'Keefe, © Georgia O'Keefe Foundation/ ARS Inc./Photo by Malcolm Varon, NYC, 1987; t. Lee Krasner, Abstract No. 2, 1946-1948/Robert Miller Gallery, NY. 50: b.l., b.r. David Young-Wolff/Photo Edit; b.m.r. Jeffrey W. Meyers/Uniphoto; t.m.l. Sah Zarehber/The Image Bank; t.m.r. Mireille Vautier/Woodfin Camp. 60: b.l. Courtesy of Museum of New Mexico; b.r. © Jerry Jacka, 1984, courtesy of the Heard Museum. 60-61: © Edward S. Curtis/Courtesy of Museum of New Mexico. 61: l., r. © Gail Russell. **Unit 2** 52: l. Vidoc, Dept. of Visual Documentation, Royal Tropical Institute, Amsterdam. 64-65: Photo by Eliot Elisofon, 1971/National Museum of African Art. 68: b.l. Stanley Rowin/The Picture Cube; t.l. Lissa Wales; t.m. Jack Vartoogian; t.r.Babajide Adeniyi-Jones. 69: Scott Harvey for MHSD. 71: b. Scott Harvey for MHSD. 74-75: t. Shanghai Museum, detail, Viewing Mountains by Shih-Tao. 78: t.r. Culver Pictures; b.l. Archive Photos. 79: t. Miriam Schapiro, Pas de Deux, 1986. Acrylic & fabric on canvas, 90 x 96. Collection of Dr. and Mrs. Acinapura; courtesy of Bernice Steinbaum Gallery, NYC. 84, 85: Scott Harvey for MHSD. 93: Jim Powell Studio for MHSD; t.m.r. Yamaha Corporation of America. 96: Scott Harvey for MHSD. 101: Culver Pictures, Inc. 102-104: Scott Harvey for MHSD. 112: Michael Oletta for MHSD **Unit 3** 120 Martha Swope. 122: b.l. Tom Martin Aspen/The Stock Market; b.r. Myrleen Ferguson/Photo Edit; m.l. Frank Siteman/Stock Boston, t.l. Bob Daemmrich/Stock Boston; t.r. Herb Snitzer/Stock Boston. 123: b. Clay Tomas for MHSD. 128: Scott Harvey for MHSD. 130: l. by Josef Karl Stieler, 1781-1853/ Superstock; l. (frame) Scott Harvey for MHSD. 130-131: bkgnd. Mitchell Confer; m. Steve J. Sherman. 131: b.r., m.r., t.r. Steve J. Sherman. 132: Marilyn Root/Light Sources Stock. 133: Jim Powell Studio for MHSD. 134: Raoul Dufy/Galerie Louis Carre et Cie, Paris. 142: b. M. Angelo/Westlight. 142-143: t. Moati/Gontier/The Image Works. 143: t. M. Angelou/Westlight. 144: The Granger Collection. 149: b. GRP Records. 149-150: Superstock. 150: l. The Bettmann Archive. 150-151: b. Garry Gay/The Image Bank. 151: frame, Scott Harvey for MHSD. 154-155: A.C. Levenger/Westlight. 155: b. Wolfgang Kaehler; t. L. Hughes/The Image Bank. 158: The Granger Collection. 159: Ken Karp for MHSD. 160: l. GRP Records; r. The Bettmann Archive. 161: r. Josef Karl Stieler, 1781-1853/Superstock. 165: Virginia Opera Company. 166: Virginia Opera Company. 166-167: b. Virginia Opera Company. 167: t. Jack Mitchell. **Unit 4** 168-169: Imtek Imaging-1/Masterfile. 171: Charles Gupton/The Stock Market. 172: Randy Wells/Allstock; T.J. Florian/ Photo Network; William Stanton/International Stock. 173: Fred Dole/FPG; Ray Atkeson/Photri. 176: The Bettmann Archive. 177: Courtesy of the New-York Historical Society. 178: Culver Pictures. 181: Ken Nahoum/Sygma. 186: Sydney Byrd/Mark Maclarin, Inc. 190: Andrew Russell/Culver Pictures; t. Bill Waltzer for MHSD. 191: t. Bill Waltzer for MHSD. 195: Superstock. 196: l. Ann Lee Walter, courtesy of Chronicle Books; r. Chandler Pohrt Collection/Detroit Institute of Arts, Cat. 122. 197: b. Museum of the American Indian; t. National Museum of Art #1985,66.346/Art Resource. 199: b. Cheyenne Winter Games by Dick West/Philbrook Museum of Art; l., m. Anna Lee Walter, courtesy of Chronicle Books. 200-201: Bill Ross/Woodfin Camp & Assoc. 203: Scott Harvey for MHSD. 204: t.r. Mark Segal/Panoramic Stock Images; t.l. Superstock. 205: Mark E. Gibson/The Stock Market. 210: inset l. Bill Waltzer for MHSD; inset m. Fridmar Damm/Leo De Wys, Inc.; inset r. Kenneth & Talita Paolini/Profiles West. 210-211: bkgnd. Gary Cralle/The Image Bank. 211: inset b.l. Steve Vidler/Leo De Wys; inset b.r., inset t.l. Bill Waltzer for MHSD; m.r. Kasz Maciag/The Stock Market; t.r. Wenzel Fisher/FPG International. 214: l. Sam Abell/Woodfin Camp. 215-216: b.m., t.m. Paul Rocheleau/Collection of Hancock Shaker Village/Pittsfield, MA. **Unit 5** 221: W. Krutein/Liason. 222: b.l. Ken Karp for MHSD; b.r. Harry Partch Foundation; t.r. Carol Simowitz for MHSD. 223: t.r. Bill Waltzer for MHSD; t.l. Chun Hyong-Kuk/Korean Cultural Services Library. 226-227: Ken Karp for MHSD. 231: b. Culver Pictures. 232: Steve Lynch/The Image Bank. 233: m. Karen Meyers for MHSD. 237: l. Hilde Zehmann; r. Peter Reimer/Interfoto-Pressebild-Agentur. 238: b., t. Ken Karp for MHSD. 238-239: bkgnd. Courtesy of Carvin Corporation. 239: b. t. Ken Karp for MHSD. 242-243: b. Tuskegee Institute Archives. 243: t. The New York Public Library. 244: Doug David for MHSD. 245: b. Doug David for MHSD; t.r. Mike Hodges; t.l. © 1993 The Art Institute of Chicago; b. m. David G. Klein; t.m. Sam Viviano. 247: Ken Karp for MHSD. 249: G. Zawadzki/Explorer. 250: l. Anna Summa. 251: l., m., r. The British Museum. 253: Archiv/Photo Researchers, Inc. 254: l. Bruce Robison, photo/Tammy Tarbell, artist; r. Steve Wall, photo © 1986/Julius Cook, Artist. 255: t. National Museum of the American Indian. 256: b. Jay Blakesburg; t. Neal Preston/Outline Press. 257: b.l. Robert Frerck/Woodfin Camp & Assoc; b.r. Gregory Shaw; m. John Elk III/Stock Boston, m.l. Kay Chernush/The Image Bank; m.r. Joseph Nettis/Photo Researchers, Inc.; t. Glen Allison/Tony Stone Images. 258: l. Elizabeth Crews/Stock Boston. 259: l. Clay Tomas for MHSD; r. Jay W. Sharp/D. Donne Bryant Stock Photo. 260, 261: Ken Karp for MHSD. **Unit 6** 270: Archive Photos/Papperfoto. 271: Corbis/Bettman. 274: The Granger Collection. 276: Frank Driggs Collection. 279: John Bellisimo/ LGI. 280-281: Karen Meyers for MHSD. 281: Performing Arts Research Center, N.Y. Public Library at Lincoln Center, NYC. 283: Mark A. Philbrick for MHSD. 284: l. John for MHSD. 288: m. Karen Meyers for MHSD; t. Jim Powell Studio for MHSD. 289: Jim Powell Studio for MHSD. 293: Ken Karp for MHSD. 294: b. Superstock; t. Eduardo Fuss. 295: b. Brian Smith/LGI. 296: Royal Athena Gallery, NYC. 297: Edward Thorp Gallery. 298: Lisa Seifert. 299: Yamaha Corporation of America. 300: Ken Karp for MHSD. 301: Larry Busacca/Retna Ltd. 306: b. Bill Waltzer for MHSD; t.l. David Hiser/Tony Stone Images; t.r. The Granger Collection. 307: b.l. Bill Waltzer for MHSD; t.l. Culver Pictures; t.r. Michael Ochs Archives. 308, 309: Bill Waltzer for MHSD. 313: t. Peter D. Figin. 314: Peter Menzel. 315: t.l. Peter Menzel; t.r. Peter Peterel. **Celebrations** 323: The Granger Collection. 328-329: Ken Karp for MHSD. 330: APA Photo Agency-Singapore. 333: b. Paul Chesley; t. APA Photo Agency–Singapore. 336: Illus. Jessie Marion King 1919/E.T. Archive (London). 345: t. Richard Rowan/Photo Researchers, Inc. 353: t. LA Clip Productions/Capitol-EMI Records. 357: b. Ken Karp for MHSD. 359: Hulton-Deustch Collection. 360: UPI/Bettman Newsphotos. 362: b. Steve Schapiro/Black Star; m. Declan Haun/Black Star; t. Rafael Macia/Photo Researchers, Inc. 363: Bob Adelman/Magnum Photos. 364: David Pollack/The Stock Market. 364-365: The Bettman Archive. 365: r. Bernice Abbott/Commerce Graphics Ltd. 366: Ansel Adams Publishing Rights Trust. 368: MCA. **Music Library** 414-415: Karen Meyers for MHSD. 416: t. Library of Congress; b. Courtesy Sam Ash Music. 417: t.r. Polish American Museum; b.l. From The Beauty of Stained Glass, Patrick Reyntiens; b.r. Frame, PHP Collection; photo Culver Pictures. 428: t. The Bettman Archive; m. Herb Snitzer Photography; b. Ken Karp for MHSD.

McGraw-Hill School Division thanks the Selmer Company, Inc., and its Ludwig/Musser Industries and Glaesel String Instrument Company subsidaries for providing all instruments used in MHSD photographs in this music textbook series, with exceptions as follows. MHSD thanks Yamaha Corporation of America for French horn, euphonium, acoustic and electric guitars, soprano, alto, and bass recorders, piano, and vibraphone; MMB Music Inc., St. Louis, MO, for Studio 49 instruments; Rhythm Band Instruments, Fort Worth, TX, for resonator bells; Courtly Instruments, NY for soprano and tenor recorder; Elderly Instruments, Lansing, MI for autoharp, dulcimer, hammered dulcimer, mandolin, Celtic harp, whistles, and Andean flute.

Classified Index

MUSICAL

NON-ENGLISH MUSIC

INDEX OF LITERATURE

POETRY

STORIES

INDEX OF LISTENING SELECTIONS

INTERVIEWS

INDEX OF SONGS AND SPEECH PIECES

SHOWSTOPPERS

HAL•LEONARD®

Forever Rock and Roll
American Pop Music

Arranged by Mark Brymer
Script and Choreography by John Jacobson

Surfin' U.S.A.

Music by Chuck Berry
Words by Brian Wilson

If ev-'ry-bod-y had an o - cean ___ a-cross the U. S. A. ___

___ Then ev-'ry-bod-y'd be surf - in' ___ like Cal -i-for-ni-a. ___

___ You'd see them wear-in' their bag - gies,

huar - a - chi san-dals too. ___ A bush-y bush-y blonde

hair - do, ___ surf-in' U. S. A. ___ You'll catch 'em surf-in' at

Grandpa: Yes sir! Those were the days.
Sand, sun, surfin', and fun!

Kid 1: Oh, Grandpa! You never went
surfing . . .did you?

Grandpa: Why, of course I did! There wasn't
a dude on the beach that could "Hang 10"
better than me!

Kid 2: Oh sure, Grandpa! We don't believe you
for a minute!

Grandpa: (*with a chuckle*) Hey kids, don't talk back!

Yakety Yak

Words and Music by Jerry Leiber
and Mike Stoller

1. Take out the pa - pers and the trash,
2. Just fin - ish clean - ing up your room.
3. You just put on your coat and hat.
4. Don't you give me no dirt - y looks.

or you don't get no spend - ing cash.
Let's see that dust fly with that broom.
And walk your - self to the laun - dry mat.
Your fa - ther's hip; he knows what cooks.

If you don't scrub that kitch - en floor,
Get all that gar - bage out of sight,
And when you fin - ish do - ing that,
Just tell your hood - lum friend out - side,

Kid 3: Okay! Okay! We believe you Grandpa.

Grandpa: Well, you should. (*remembering*) I remember after a day at the beach, Annette and I would take a long, leisurely stroll back to the snack bar and enjoy the breeze of those warm southern nights.

American Pop Music

Southern Nights

Words and Music by
Allen Toussaint

South - ern_ nights,_ have you ev - er felt a south - ern_ night?_ Free as a breeze,_ not to men-tion the trees,_ whis-tling tunes that you know_ and love so._____ South-ern_ nights,_ just as good_ e-ven when closed your_ eyes,_ I a-pol-o-gize_____ to an-y- one who can tru-ly say that he has found a bet-ter way.___

2

C   A7

Feel so___ good,_   feel so good,_ it's fright-'ning.

D7

Wish I___ could_   stop this world_ from fight - ing.

Fmaj7

La da da da___ da da la da da da___ da da

Em7   F/G   C

da da da da da___ da da da___ da da da.   Mys - ter - ries_

A7   D7

like this and man - y oth - ers in the_ trees,_

Fmaj7   F/G   C

blow in the night___ in the south - ern skies.___

(Grandma enters)

Grandpa: Speaking of a day at the beach, here Annette comes now!

Grandma: *(fussing)* Oh Grandpa, what have you been telling these young people?

Kid 4: He's been telling us what a great surfer he was in the old days . . .

Kid 5: And how you used to think he was the greatest man that walked the sand.

Grandma: *(warmly)* Well, I don't know about that surfer part. But Grandpa has always been a hero, especially to me!

Hero

Words and Music by Mariah Carey and Walter Afanasieff

Kid 6: I think it's great that Grandma sees Grandpa as her hero.

Kid 7: And Grandpa thinks the same about her.

Grandpa: Well kids, a hero doesn't have to be someone famous.

Grandma: A hero is somebody who takes a look at the world and tries to make it a better place.

Change the World

Words and Music by Gordon Kennedy, Tommy Sims and Wayne Kirkpatrick

If I could reach the stars,— I'd pull one down for you,—

shine it on my heart—

so you could see the truth,— that this love in - side—

is ev - 'ry-thing it seems.—

But for now I find— it's on - ly in my dreams.

Kid 8: What's the best way to change the world, Grandma?

Grandma: Well, I don't have all of the answers,
but in my opinion it all starts with kindness and love.

Kids: *(surprised)* Love?!

Grandpa: Grandma's right. If you want to
make the world better, love your neighbor . . .

Grandma: And your family . . .

Kid 9: Your pets!

Kid 10: Your country!

Kid 11: Your world!

Up Where We Belong

Music by Buffy Sainte-Marie
and Jack Nitzsche
Words by Will Jennings

Who knows what to-mor-row brings; ___ in a
Some hang on to "used to be," ___ live their

world, few hearts sur-vive? All I know is the
lives look-ing be-hind. All we have is ___

way I feel; ___ when it's real, I keep it a-live. ___
here and now; ___ all our life, ___ out there to find. ___ } The

road is long. There are moun-tains in our way, ___

Kid 12: I get it! I hope some day I can be a hero just like Grandpa!

Grandpa: AND Grandma!

Kid 12: I'm gonna do it!

Grandma and Grandpa: You go!

Theme from
The Greatest American Hero

Music by Mike Post
Words by Stephen Geyer

Look at what's hap - pened to me;

I can't be - lieve it my - self. Sud-den-ly I'm up on

top of the world; it should have been some - bod-y else.

Be - lieve it or not, I'm walk-in' on air, I nev-er

thought I could feel so free. Fly-in' a - way on a wing

and a pray'r who could it be? Be -

Grandpa: You know kids, some things stay with you a long time . . . like the feeling of riding your first big wave.

Grandma: *(dreamingly)* Or holding hands on the beach. *(kids moan)*

Kid 13: Or eating a great big chocolate chip cookie. *(kids cheer)*

Grandpa: Or hearing music you know will last forever like . . .

Kids: *(shouting)* Rock and Roll!

American Pop Music

Rock and Roll Is Here to Stay

Words and Music by
David White

Rock, oh, ba - by rock, oh, ba - by

rock, oh, ba - by rock, oh, ba - by!

1. Rock and roll is here to stay, it will ne - ver die.
2. Rock and roll will al - ways be, I dig it to the end.

It was meant to be that way,
It - 'll go down in his - to - ry,

though I don't know why. I don't care what
just you watch, my friend. Rock and roll will

peo-ple say,＿ rock and roll is here to stay!＿ We don't care what
al-ways be, ＿ it-'ll go down in his-to-ry.＿ Rock and roll will

peo-ple say＿ rock and roll is here to stay.＿
al-ways be, ＿ it-'ll go down in his-to-ry.＿

Ev-'ry-bod-y rock, ＿ ev-'ry-bod-y rock, ＿

ev-'ry-bod-y rock, ＿ ev-'ry-bod-y rock.＿

Come on, ev-'ry-bod-y rock, ＿

Rock, oh, ba-by rock,

oh, ba-by rock, oh, ba-by

(Shout)

rock, Rock and Roll!

ACKNOWLEDGMENTS

Grateful acknowledgment is given to the following authors, composers, and publishers.

Change The World
featured on the Motion Picture Soundtrack PHENOMENON
Words and Music by Wayne Kirkpatrick, Gordon Kennedy and Tommy Sims
Copyright © 1996 by Careers-BMG Music Publishing, Inc., Magic Beans Music, BMG Songs, Inc., Universal - PolyGram International Publishing, Inc. and Universal - MCA Music Publishing, A Division of Universal Studios, Inc.
International Copyright Secured   All Rights Reserved

Theme From "The Greatest American Hero"
Words by Stephen Geyer
Music by Mike Post
© 1981 EMI BLACKWOOD MUSIC INC., DAR-JEN MUSIC, EMI APRIL MUSIC INC., SJC MUSIC and STEPHEN CANNELL MUSIC
All Rights for DAR-JEN MUSIC Controlled and Administered by EMI BLACKWOOD MUSIC INC.
All Rights Reserved   International Copyright Secured   Used by Permission

Hero
Words and Music by Mariah Carey and Walter Afanasieff
Copyright © 1993 Sony/ATV Songs LLC, Rye Songs, WB Music Corp. and Wallyworld Music
All Rights on behalf of Sony/ATV Songs LLC and Rye Songs Administered by Sony/ATV Music Publishing, 8 Music Square West, Nashville, TN 37203
All Rights on behalf of Wallyworld Music Administered by WB Music Corp.
International Copyright Secured   All Rights Reserved

Rock And Roll Is Here To Stay
Words and Music by David White
Copyright © 1957 (Renewed) by Arc Music Corporation (BMI) and Egg Music Inc. (BMI)
International Copyright Secured   All Rights Reserved
Used by Permission

Southern Nights
Words and Music by Allen Toussaint
© 1974 SCREEN GEMS-EMI MUSIC INC. and WARNER-TAMERLANE PUBLISHING CORP.
All Rights Controlled and Administered by SCREEN GEMS-EMI MUSIC INC.
All Rights Reserved   International Copyright Secured   Used by Permission

Surfin' U.S.A.
Words by Brian Wilson
Music by Chuck Berry
Copyright © 1958, 1963 (Renewed) by Arc Music Corporation (BMI) and Isalee Music Inc. (BMI)
International Copyright Secured   All Rights Reserved
Used by Permission

Up Where We Belong from the Paramount Picture AN OFFICER AND A GENTLEMAN
Words by Will Jennings
Music by Buffy Sainte-Marie and Jack Nitzsche
Copyright © 1982 by Famous Music Corporation and Ensign Music Corporation
International Copyright Secured   All Rights Reserved

Yakety Yak
Words and Music by Jerry Leiber and Mike Stoller
© 1958 (Renewed) JERRY LEIBER MUSIC and MIKE STOLLER MUSIC
All Rights Reserved

Illustrations by Thomas Buchs

Pronunciation Key
Simplified International Phonetic Alphabet

VOWELS

ɑ	f<u>a</u>ther	æ	c<u>a</u>t
e	<u>a</u>pe	ɛ	p<u>e</u>t
i	b<u>ee</u>	ι	<u>i</u>t
o	<u>o</u>bey	ɔ	p<u>a</u>w
u	m<u>oo</u>n	ʊ	p<u>u</u>t
ʌ	<u>u</u>p	ə	<u>a</u>go

SPECIAL SOUNDS

β — say *b* without touching lips together; *Spanish* nue<u>v</u>e, ha<u>b</u>a

ç — <u>h</u>ue; *German* i<u>ch</u>

ð — <u>th</u>e, *Spanish* to<u>d</u>o

n̩ — sound <u>n</u> as individual syllable

ö — form [o] with lips and say [e]; *French* ad<u>ieu</u>, *German* sch<u>ö</u>n

œ — form [ɔ] with lips and say [ɛ]; *French* c<u>oeu</u>r, *German* pl<u>ö</u>tzlich

ɾ — flipped r; bu<u>tt</u>er

r̄ — rolled r; *Spanish* pe<u>rr</u>o

ɬ — click tongue on the ridge behind teeth; *Zulu* ng<u>c</u>wele

ü — form [u] with lips and say [i]; *French* t<u>u</u>, *German* gr<u>ü</u>n

ü̇ — form [ʊ] with lips and say [ι]

x — blow strong current of air with back of tongue up; *German* Ba<u>ch</u>, *Hebrew* <u>H</u>anukkah, *Spanish* ba<u>j</u>o

ʒ — plea<u>s</u>ure

ʼ — glottal stop, as in the exclamation "uh oh!" [ˈʌ ˈʼo]

~ — nasalized vowel, such as French b<u>on</u> [bõ]

˥ — end consonants *k*, *p*, and *t* without puff of air, such as s<u>k</u>y (no puff of air after *k*), as opposed to *k*ite (puff of air after *k*)

OTHER CONSONANTS PRONOUNCED SIMILAR TO ENGLISH

ch	<u>ch</u>eese	ny	o<u>ni</u>on, *Spanish* ni<u>ñ</u>o
g	<u>g</u>o	sh	<u>sh</u>ine
ng	si<u>ng</u>	ts	boa<u>ts</u>

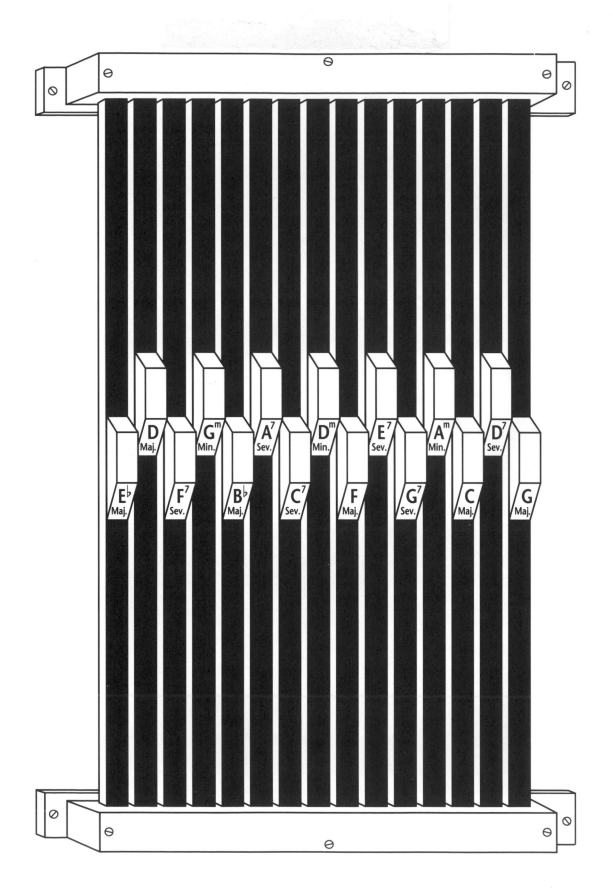